FEMINIST PHOENIX

The Rise and Fall of a Feminist Counterculture

Jerry L. Rodnitzky

Westport, Connecticut
London

Library of Congress Cataloging-in-Publication Data

Rodnitzky, Jerome L., 1936–
    Feminist Phoenix : the rise and fall of a feminist
counterculture / Jerry L. Rodnitzky.
        p.   cm.
    Includes bibliographical references and index.
    ISBN 0–275–96575–9 (alk. paper)
        1. Feminism—United States—History—20th century.   2. Feminism
and the arts—United States—History—20th century.   3. New
Left—United States.   I. Title.
    HQ1421.R64   1999
    305.42 0973—dc21   98–53394

British Library Cataloguing in Publication Data is available.

Copyright © 1999 by Jerry L. Rodnitzky

Library of Congress Catalog Card Number: 98–53394
ISBN: 0–275–96575–9

First published in 1999

Praeger Publishers, 88 Post Road West, Westport, CT 06881
An imprint of Greenwood Publishing Group, Inc.
www.praeger.com

Printed in the United States of America

The paper used in this book complies with the
Permanent Paper Standard issued by the National
Information Standards Organization (Z39.48–1984).

10 9 8 7 6 5 4 3 2 1

For Shirl, my wife and best friend

Contents

Preface

This book grew out of my interest in the 1960s counterculture and my observation of the developing women's liberation movement. As the lone male member of a women's studies committee at The University of Texas at Arlington, I had a unique vantage point. In 1970, we were one of the first such groups in Texas. My 1971 course, History of the American Woman, was perhaps Texas's first women's studies course. I got on well with most of my female colleagues, but was always an interloper in a field dominated by women scholars. I am still somewhat of an interloper. The vast majority of works on recent feminism have been written by women—most of whom are feminist activists or women's studies faculty. I do not sense a conspiracy here. There are logical reasons for female scholars to dominate books on feminism, and some women writers, such as Camille Paglia and Sylvia Hewitt, have been critical of both feminism and feminist scholarship. Yet there has not been much of a gender spectrum in books about feminism. Of course, ideas have no gender, yet gender can sometimes subtly shape point of view. Ironically, that is often a major conclusion of most women who write history.

My earliest writing on countercultural approaches to change dealt with protest songs and protest singers in the 1960s, including some feminist artists. I had been heavily influenced by so-called New Left historians, such as Howard Zinn and Theodore Roszak, while finishing my graduate work. But earlier, while a student at the University of Chicago, I had also been very impressed by two more conservative scholars, economist Milton Friedman and historian Daniel Boorstin. The New Left stress on using the past to exhort contemporary activism captured my imagination, whereas Friedman's arguments about the efficacy and power of free markets and Boorstin's innovative approaches to media influences helped focus me on the free market of popular culture.

My combined interest in activism and popular culture made the counter-culture a logical subject of study. Although many countercultural groups of the 1960s became discouraged and faded in the 1970s, women's liberation continued to woo the next generation with countercultural approaches. Indeed, by 1970 feminists were on the frontier of countercultural change. If the black civil rights movement had been the organizational model for six-ties activism, the women's movement furnished the cultural prototype. The feminist stress on images of women in all media broke new ground, posed new questions, and led to notable reforms. Also the feminist use of topical and personal music flowered, and general protest music languished. And then suddenly in the late-1970s, the feminist counterculture began to un-ravel and decline. Women's liberation increasingly focused on contempo-rary problems as opposed to the next generation of women and men. After some national political defeats, the woman's movement generally retreated to popular limited economic issues, such as equal pay and affirmative action and the multifaceted abortion issue. They wasted energy responding to charges of "political correctness" and hid failures by blaming most feminist problems on "backlash." Feminists traded the future for the present when they replaced long-term countercultural goals with short-term structural is-sues. Feminist activism sometimes dissolved into mere networking—a fe-male version of the good old boy system. It was a long, slippery slope from countercultural visions to pedestrian professional strategies. Legislative and professional gains are essential for women, but subtle, cultural gains are equally important. If contemporary feminists lose the next generation of women while they forge ahead personally, they will have won the battle and lost the war. Something similar occurred in the 1920s, when the suffragists won the right to vote and lost the younger generation.

This book traces the rise and fall of a feminist counterculture from the 1960s to the present. As a prelude, chapter 1 briefly presents my views of relevant countercultural problems and failures affecting women throughout American history. It is necessarily very interpretive and selective for my purposes. It is in no way a brief history of American women or American feminism. The book has three major goals: to describe how the New Left countercultural stress influenced women's liberation; to examine the ways feminists tried to use media such as music, film, television, and advertising as countercultural tools; and finally to analyze the decline of the feminist counterculture under the weight of new problems. The book also provides cultural portraits of Janis Joplin, Joan Baez, and Gloria Steinem. These women seemingly have little in common; however, all three functioned as classic cultural heroines and feminist role models—although only Steinem identified herself as a feminist. Their lives and influence illustrate why cultural change has often been more important than political change for American women.

Talking about the "rise and fall" of a feminist counterculture seems grandiose. Historians have used the term, "rise and fall" to describe developments over centuries. Applying it here to a thirty-year period suggests something about the pace of cultural change in contemporary America. "Rise and fall" is also a depressing metaphor, but I center more on the rise than the fall, for countercultural feminism is indeed a phoenix that will likely rise again from its own ashes in some new future feminist era.

Although this book focuses on the past three decades, it places countercultural feminism in a broad historical perspective. I have the classic historian's faith that one often sees more by looking back than by looking around. People are always tempted to believe that their present experience is more unique than it is. Activists of the 1960s, in particular, were not historically minded, preferring gut feelings to past experience. Characteristically, 1960s feminists seldom felt that they had been there and gone. Thus, the feminist phoenix that arose in the 1960s suffered from a generational and historical amnesia that made the fall of a feminist counterculture more likely. Many contemporary feminists have forgotten that in 1963, the first book to really shape the new feminism—Betty Friedan's *The Feminine Mystique*—had a clear, countercultural focus. Friedan converted many women to feminism because she convincingly showed how the media brainwashed women. However, by 1981 Friedan herself ignored countercultural approaches and wrote about a necessary new "second stage" for feminism to center on specific problems. Like other contemporary feminists, Friedan gave up the countercultural focus that originally made her a feminist leader. She is an ironic symbol of a much broader countercultural failure. Losing the next generation of women can be seen, in Friedan's own idiom, as a new "problem with no name."

I would like to thank the founding members of the Women's Studies Committee of the University of Texas at Arlington, who in the early 1970s helped focus my attention on the cultural aspects of women's liberation. I would especially like to thank Professors Harriet Amster, Jeanne Ford, and

Carolyn Gallerstein who kept women's studies going when there was little financial support. They also helped bring lively, perceptive speakers, such as Germaine Greer, Betty Friedan, Stella Stevens, and Florence Howe, to campus. Women's Studies faculty disagreed with some of my views then and likely would disagree with some of this book. However, past disagreements were friendly and pervaded by the sense that we were all engaged in an important enterprise for future generations. I would hope the same would be true of present differences of opinion.

I would also like to thank my wife, Shirley Reiger Rodnitzky, for her support and encouragement throughout this project and for helping to prepare the final manuscript.

PART I

Historical Origins: The Search for a Feminist Counterculture

1

Countercultural Failure: American Feminism, 1700–1960

Contemporary feminist radicals have difficulty finding their counterparts in American history. Their problem is the traditional American tendency to co-opt its radicals by either making partial concessions to their contemporary demands or by later making radicals historical heroes. This co-optation affects men and women equally. For example, both Roger Williams and Anne Hutchinson, clearly unsuccessful radicals of their different eras, are now enshrined in American textbooks as martyrs for religious freedom and political democracy, respectively. America has a way of neutralizing radical heroes by eventually accepting parts of their programs. But feminist radicals have always had a more basic problem in asserting their radicalism and retaining their radical image over time. Past feminists had to fight for more than their goals; they had to struggle for the right to be radical feminists—the right to argue that they had problems and grievances apart from and as important as those of men.

That struggle for a separate feminist condition and angle of vision was inevitably a countercultural movement. Yet, before the women's liberation movement of the 1960s, countercultural issues were usually lost in the midst of broader campaigns which often won real social, political, and economic gains for American women. Unfortunately, these feminist victories sometimes secured the present by sacrificing the future.

This very interpretive overview centers on examples of past countercultural failure. It is not a short history of American women before 1960, nor even a short history of American feminism. It selectively focuses on instances where feminists lost the countercultural war, even if they won the immediate battle. Centering on failure amidst triumph is an uncommon approach, but if this has been a consistent historical trend, it is important for feminists to confront it, because this trend is clearly not their friend.

Radical American women have usually been co-opted by the general social movements of their eras. They have lost their gender identities in countless campaigns on behalf of black slaves, oppressed male workers, and wronged Native Americans. Their many crusades for America's children and newly arrived immigrants obscured the problems of women in America. Whenever one found abject poverty and general misery affecting whole communities of men and women, gender roles became irrelevant. It is ironic then, that when we think of women radicals, we usually recall 19th-century feminists such as Elizabeth Cady Stanton, Susan Anthony, or, recently, Betty Friedan. These three are part of a radical feminist tradition, but this is not the tradition of Harriet Tubman, Mother Jones, or Joan Baez. The latter three are so submerged in general radical reforms that we do not think of them simply as radical women. Only when women isolate themselves and their reforms from men do we view them as true radicals. Other women radicals are seen as helpmates of radical men or "handmaidens" of reform.[1]

Yet what is more natural than the woman radical. Because American women have always been perceived as more moral than men, their tendency to struggle against social evils should surprise no one. Women were expected to be soft and sympathetic. If they agonized over the horror of war, slavery, and deprivation, who could fault them. In the 1960s, women students, who vigorously protested the Vietnam War early on, were treated much better than their male counterparts. Critics usually perceived the female protester as a misguided, but sincere, pacifist, whereas the draft-burning male was viewed as a cowardly ingrate. Women were more often put down for acting like men than for their beliefs. It was their aggressiveness, not their views, that was unacceptable. Radical women constantly struggled against a false tolerance extended to women, children, and fools.

Because women were often considered notoriously fuzzy thinkers, ruled by runaway emotions, their social critiques need not be taken as seriously. Yet men found that radical women were effective when integrated into radical campaigns. When isolated, women had few victories before 1960. The most notable success was the suffrage movement, culminating in the constitutional amendment granting the right to vote. Even today, the Equal Rights

Amendment (ERA) eludes feminist activists, after seventy years of efforts for passage and seventy-five years after women got the vote.

Contemporary feminist scholars have often been overzealous in searching for past feminist radicals. For example, Eleanor Flexner's history of women's rights in America, *Century of Struggle*, noted that "the question of equal status for women was first raised" when "Anne Hutchinson challenged the Puritan theocracy of Boston." Although the arguments were rather strictly theological, Flexner felt that a major issue was whether a woman could think for herself about God. Because Hutchinson left no letters or other writings, we know her only through the comments of enemies; however, little evidence suggests that she championed women or was radical anywhere outside the theological arena. Indeed, within her theological argument with the Puritan fathers, she appears as narrow-minded and intolerant as they.[2]

However, when Hutchinson is viewed as an example of the Protestant daughter, she does symbolize one of the first of many American women who make their intellectual mark in America from colonial times to the Civil War. These Protestant daughters were invariably the products of homes where fathers brought up their daughters intellectually the same way they brought up their sons. There is little evidence that the considerable number of aggressive and articulate American women in the 17th and 18th centuries were either conscious feminists or even general radical critics. However, these women, from Anne Hutchinson to President John Adams's wife, Abigail Quincy Adams, were clear models for the American feminists who would spring up in the 19th century. From 1600 to the early 1800s, American women were liberated not by feminist principles, but by frontier conditions and necessities. Women accustomed to defending themselves and their families against marauding Indians were hardly loathe to express themselves on current issues. The colonial wife, whose multifaceted economic endeavors made her more valuable to the family than her farmer husband, hardly suffered from an inferiority complex. Without a movement, without a program, and without leaders, American frontier women became feminist models for the world. Their independence, assertiveness, and confidence came directly from their value and cultural role in a frontier society. Wherever the frontier passed, the hardy frontier woman tended to turn into the gentler and more restricted urban lady. However, there was a constantly moving American frontier, throughout the 19th century.

Unfortunately, there was also a constantly encroaching traditional society overtaking the new frontiers. American culture resided in the towns, whereas the most aggressive, independent women often lived and worked in the hinterlands. The cities created the books and magazines, set the fashions, and invented new styles of education. The urban and town culture increasingly affected frontier women, but frontier women did not affect urban culture in general and images of women in particular.

The frontier women of the 18th and 19th century American West came close to a rough equality with men—once married. Even before marriage, the relative scarcity of women on the frontier gave them status and position, which was denied women in the settled East. However, frontier women had limited influence. They presided over a family—not over a culture. They influenced their daughters by example, but they lacked a credo or philosophy to pass on. These women were certainly not part of any defined movement. The unspoken assumption was that like Western frontier conditions, frontier women would soon pass away. At some undetermined time, they could live like "normal" women in a more civilized society.

Men, too, expected to change their ways as the frontier passed. They saw a future of new, more civilized ways. Some men looked forward to the change and others denigrated it, but neither their image nor identity was ever threatened by a passing frontier. Whereas the East created the image of the ideal American women, the West created the ideal American man. Western frontier women had to look and act more Eastern to approximate the ideal and to be more womanly; Eastern men had to become more Western to become more manly.

A Western mystique had made the frontiersman the benchmark of masculine courage, daring, independence, and resourcefulness. Frontiersmen such as Daniel Boone, Andrew Jackson, and Davy Crockett were probably the favorite heros of 19th-century America. Fictional counterparts, such as James Fenimore Cooper's Deerslayer or the later western dime novel heroes, just embellished an established fact.

Men also had to appear more Western to become more American. The West was both America's future hope and national proving ground; it was always the most distinctive part of American culture. Just as European civilization had been carried over and had broken down into American civilization by frontier conditions, the process continued. The new American culture was constantly taken out to new Western frontiers, and there broke down into distinctively new American cultures.

Thus, 19th-century American men tried to talk, dress, and act Western. It was no accident that most of the new idioms and dress styles came from the frontier. The contemporary equivalent of the Western mystique is the youth mystique. Since the 1920s, Americans have tried to look, talk, and dress youthful; just as the West set cultural styles for men in the 19th century, youth sets the cultural pace for both sexes today.

Western women did not benefit much from the Western mystique. Courage, daring, and resourcefulness were not qualities that Eastern women prided themselves on. The 19th-century feminine ideal embodied itself in the concept of the lady. The lady was reticent, refined, and largely removed from the world of men. She was protected from anything that might call for courage or daring. Whether up on a pedestal or trapped in the home, she was a protected species. The Eastern lady had no desire to appear more Western although the Western woman often desired to appear more Eastern and thus more ladylike. To appear more Western was more undesirably masculine; to appear more Eastern was more approvingly feminine. Even today women do not dress in Western-style clothing if they wish to appear more feminine.

The frontier wreaked cultural havoc on women. It made them stronger, more independent, and, important, yet cast doubt on their womanhood. No wonder that wherever the frontier passed, rugged frontier women turned into more passive urban ladies. Lower class women in any region found Western aggressive attributes more helpful for survival, but although these traits preserved their bodies, their unladylike reputation was enhanced. Poor women were caught in the same cultural bind as Western women. Every step forward in function and capability meant a step backward in womanly image. Lower class Eastern women did not suffer as much from cultural insults, because little but disdain from upper class women was expected. But Western women, rich or poor, felt culturally impoverished whenever they read a book or magazine that described a lady.[3]

The Southern mystique similarly hurt Southern women. The Southern gentleman admired courage, daring, and resourcefulness no less than the Westerner. There was no real clash between Southern and Western manhood and, by extension, no clash between Eastern and Southern manhood. There was more talk about gentlemen and honor in the South, but this might be expected in a region with more pronounced, aristocratic class divisions.

The position of Southern women was little affected by region. Southern belles were caught in the cult of the lady, even more surely than their western and northeastern sisters. But the Southern lady was also restricted by Southern chivalry—an important trademark of Southern gentlemen. Yet this chivalry did not apply to lower class or slave women. In theory and practice, this meant that Southern ladies were put on a higher pedestal then Northern ladies and that lower class and slave women had status lower than their Northern counterparts. Thus, a plantation owner who supposedly cherished Southern womanhood might have several slaves or free mistresses without any pangs of conscience. He might even sell his own mulatto children as slaves without acknowledging them.

The double standard which allowed men to marry a lady for her womanly virtues and seek sexual passion from less-ladylike women was also well established in the Northeast. The Southern double standard was, however, particularly pernicious because of racial power positions. Black women were under the thumb of white owners. Southern ladies were told that blacks were inferior and subhuman, yet their husbands often used slaves as sexual partners. Western women did not suffer as much from a double sexual standard because of their scarcity, assertiveness, and importance to their frontier families. Western women were in a much better position to insist on fidelity or to cope with infidelity.

One would have expected feisty Western women to lead the first feminist movement, but they were too busy with survival. The first American feminist movement started in the Northeast and was fueled by status-deprived, middle-class housewives. These ladies were generally well educated and often married to professional men. Perhaps Elizabeth Cady Stanton and Lucy Stone were the two most famous married feminists. Susan Anthony remained single, and although she was less perceptive than Stanton, Anthony was easily the most influential 19th-century feminist leader. Anthony clearly had more time than Stanton, who was weighed down by her duties as a wife and mother. These early feminists had security and comfort but were keenly aware of their lack of status compared with the most ordinary men.

By the 1830s, uneducated male beggars could vote, whereas the college-educated women, who often fed them, could not. Also, certification requirements had driven women out of the legal and medical professions: Physicians had to graduate from a medical school and lawyers were required to study law. Women were not allowed to study either. Indeed, they were barred from almost all serious colleges.

Middle-class feminist housewives clearly saw that the tool for raising their status was higher education and access to the professions. The vote always remained a more distant goal. Many women wanted to vote against slavery and for temperance, but the vote itself remained an abstract lever. Instead, women concentrated on opening the doors to colleges in general and to professions such as law, teaching, and medicine, in particular.[4]

In the period 1830 to 1860, the first women physicians and lawyers appeared. More importantly, the first serious women's colleges opened. Mount Holyoke was the pioneer institution—the forerunner of Vassar, Radcliffe, and Barnard. Also, some small, avant garde frontier colleges, such as Oberlin in Ohio and Knox in Illinois, became coeducational in the 1830s. This set the stage for the many coed state universities founded after the Civil War. The first feminist movement's primary goal was happily its biggest success.

The battle for educational and professional equality has never been completely won. Feminists broke the physical barriers before the Civil War, but some cultural barriers have remained. Families continued to encourage sons to attend college, but often discouraged daughters, or perhaps they would push a son to attend a very rigorous and or expensive school, and tell a daughter to enroll at the local public college. Even the most liberal and aggressive families often practiced this double standard. For example, the Kennedys sent John, Robert, and Ted Kennedy to Harvard; however, their daughters, who were just as talented academically, did not go to Harvard, Barnard, or Radcliffe. They were sent to The Manhattanville College of the Sacred Heart—albeit one of the best Catholic women's colleges, but not in Radcliffe's league. The Kennedy boys were encouraged to compete academically in the rough and tumble outside world; the Kennedy girls were sent to Manhattanville to be safe in the keeping of nuns.

In subtle ways, those women who broke higher education barriers in the 19th century were isolated by new road blocks. At many colleges, women could not attend classes without chaperones and were rigidly segregated from male students. Also, college dress codes hindered women far more than men. Although these restrictions generally died out in the North by 1900, they lingered on in the South. As late as the 1960s, Southern colleges often applied stricter social regulations to women then men.

A more subtle problem was cultural support for women professionals. Long after women could go to medical or law school, many women had trouble seeing themselves as doctors and lawyers. Such professions were deemed socially unnatural for women. If women could not imagine themselves as physicians, lawyers, or business executives, what difference did it make if they actually could become professionals? The few women who did enter the professions in the 19th century became anomalies rather than role models. They were lady doctors or lady lawyers—a quite different kind of professional.

Indeed, the only two professions readily available for 19th-century college women were nursing and teaching. Women had always dominated nursing and did not really need college training to enter the field, but nevertheless some college women entered nursing. Civil War nurses and the exploits of a British nurse, Florence Nightingale, in the Crimean War gave nursing a more glamorous and patriotic image. Feminists such as Julia Ward Howe were instrumental in organizing nurse volunteers for the Union Army in the Civil War. Howe, head of the Union nursing corps, was herself a powerful role model.

Teaching did offer new nontraditional opportunities for women. Before 1860, most public school teachers were male. By 1900, most elementary teachers were women and women also gained share as high school teachers. Two factors account for these numerical gains. Certification reform, pioneered by Horace Mann in Massachusetts before 1860, spread around the country after the Civil War. Certification meant public schools must hire teachers with some college credentials or risk not having their graduates certified by the state. The other factor was cost. Americans have always supported public education, but they always have wanted it at the cheapest price. Women college graduates were willing to work for less. Slowly but surely women edged men out of public school teaching.

Women with high school diplomas also pushed men out of office jobs after 1880. Before then, most business secretaries were males, and that post was a starting point on the executive ladder. Some argued that the typewriter had pushed men out of office work because women had naturally nimbler fingers. But nimble or not, clearly women replaced men in offices because they worked for less.

On paper, the first feminist movement (from 1820 to 1860) had accomplished a lot; in practice, it had changed far less. Women still could not vote, and their inroads into most professions were slight. Even their access to higher education remained painfully slow. The double sexual standard was alive and well, and women were still restricted by traditional clothing and an all encompassing cult of the lady.

Ladylike clothing was particularly pernicious. Traditional dresses covered the ankles and dragged along the ground. Often corsets were used to bring the average woman's waist down to a stylish twenty inches. A lady generally could not move freely unless she used one hand to pull her dress off the ground. Lower class women were excused from these outlandish costumes, but their physical freedom did not find any obvious areas of opportunity.

The feminists themselves fumbled the opportunity for dress reform. Amelia Bloomer had fought for a garment people called bloomers. Although that name later described a lady's undergarment, Amelia had designed billowing loose slacks to replace traditional dress. Chinese and Turkish women had long worn these type of pants. However, Amelia Bloomer's feminist sisters generally refused to wear these pantaloons, often insisting that they were not ladylike, because, among other things, they bared the ankles. Susan Anthony put it succinctly: She could not "earnestly engage a young man in conversation," while he sat staring at her ankles.[5]

The general desire for these feminists to remain ladylike at all costs subtly sapped their various endeavors and the entire movement. Their dress seemed strangely at odds with their goals. Yet they were brave, bright, energetic, and effective—not only in their own movement but in others. Their work in temperance reform and the antislavery crusade were models for effective activism. They had broken the taboo against women public speakers and were now often the most popular reform speakers. Crowds came to hear a feminist speaker the way they went to see exotic animals at the zoo. The audiences were often spellbound, because they had been taught that women could not speak in public. Orators such as Susan B. Anthony and Lucy Stone were, indeed, models for women. They played the same role that Martin Luther King Jr. and Malcolm X played for black Americans a century later. The feminist speakers told women something they never knew about themselves and what they could do.

Feminist bravery had its limits though. Activist women did not mind being attacked as feminists. Before 1860, many Americans thought there were three sexes—men, women, and feminists. Feminists were willing to suffer feminine barbs so that the daughters of "normal" women would have access to professions and higher education. However, they often could not stand being considered unladylike. They were trapped inside the cult of the lady and were their own prison guards. Most were also trapped by domestic life with large families. They often had stormy, marriages, but the children usually kept the marriage together. Susan B. Anthony, who remained single, constantly despaired over her feminist friends who were caught up in domesticity. She warned them not to marry. When they married, she warned them against bearing children. When they bore children, she warned them against having more children. Yet most feminists cherished their family ties and children. It was part and parcel of being ladylike.

Apart from their ideology and reform activities, these first feminists were in many ways more traditional than the average woman. They were more religious than average and more prudish and ignorant about sexual practice than the average woman. Their sexual ignorance was peculiarly class based. In the 19th century, the more educated and sheltered the woman, the more likely she would know relatively little about practical sex. Published sexual advice was notoriously inaccurate and prudish, because middle-class society considered sex both animal and shameful. The lower classes luckily did not read sex manuals and learned by experience; they generally had healthier sexual attitudes, because they did what came naturally.

Nineteenth-century feminists were political and spiritual triumphs and cultural disasters. Their strong religious convictions gave them a secure base for reform activities. Religion encouraged introspection and thinking about the woman's place in society and her responsibilities. It focused people on the way things should be. Middle-class women had gradually taken over the American Protestant religion between 1800 and 1860. Men had given them power by default. Although ministers were male, the real church work was done by cadres of women parishioners. An effective minister had to work with women even though his funding mostly came from their husbands.

There are instructive and interesting parallel differences between 19th- and 20th-century feminist leaders that highlight the peculiar cultural restraints of early feminists. Contemporary feminists such as Gloria Steinem and Betty Friedan, generally have very different cultural profiles than pre–Civil War feminists. Whereas the first feminists were more religious than the average woman, contemporary feminists are less religious than average. Early feminists were much more prudish about sex and ignorant about sexual practice; modern feminists are less prudish about sex and more generally knowledgeable about sexual practice. Although the first feminists were more ladylike than average, their contemporary counterparts are less feminine and ladylike. Early feminists were usually the result of a strong father-daughter bond in which the father brought up the daughter as he would a son. Modern feminists tend to result from a strong mother-daughter relationship, in which the mother passed on feminism as a heritage. The first feminists were generally married and often had many children, whereas modern feminists tend to be more unmarried than average. When married, modern feminists tend to be divorced more often than average and have no children or small families.

Yet, contemporary feminists are often avant-garde models for women. They are more independent of fathers, husbands, boyfriends, and the family claims of children. The first feminists were usually dependent on their husbands' help in carrying on their reform activities. If their spouses were not sympathetic, the women often could not function as feminists. Most early feminists were married to prosperous professionals, farmers, or small businessmen. These men tended to be reform minded themselves, but were usually more enthusiastic about antislavery or pacifism than about feminism.

The earliest feminists, such as Lucretia Mott and Angelina Grimke, had come to feminism after years of devoting themselves to other reforms such as temperance and antislavery. There was a generation gap between these feminists and younger ones. Older feminists were veterans of antislavery and leaders in that struggle; the younger feminists, such as Elizabeth Cady Stanton and Susan B. Anthony, were followers in antislavery, but leaders in feminism. The younger feminists often lived in remote areas such as upstate New York and were cut off from the center of antislavery action, whereas older feminists tended to live in large urban areas such as Boston and Philadelphia.

Feminist historians have had trouble trying to make even the younger, early feminists role models for contemporary women. Their ideology was clear enough: They argued that women should have equality because they were human beings—the same as men. This was really an offshoot of the antislavery arguments that also argued for slaves on the basis of their humanity. Not surprisingly, the feminist movement talked about emancipating women the same way reformers talked about emancipating slaves.

As heroic and important as early feminists were, they just do not usually make suitable modern role models. They were too often middle-class, uptight, privileged housewives whose husbands furnished them with the leisure for introspection and reform. Unable to recognize the cultural restraints that bound them, they were trapped in a world that ostensibly venerated ladies, but relegated them solely to domesticity. They never feared failure, because there was no where to go but up and no obvious penalties. Yet social approbation terrified them. As ladies, they were up on a pedestal where many lower class and frontier women longed to be. They mistakenly thought they could change the economic and political world, while leaving the social and cultural world intact.

In short, the first feminists were not cultural heroines. Their achievements command respect, but their hang-ups discourage hero worship. Their activities are instructive and inspiring, but lack cultural relevance. They are as frozen in time as the clipper ships of their day are now locked in bottles. Their modern relevance is limited.

The most modern of the first-wave feminists was likely Lucy Stone. As the eighth of nine New England children, she became so fed up with woman's lot, she enrolled at newly coed Oberlin College in Ohio. After college, she lectured widely on woman's rights. Stone married Henry Blackwell, brother of America's first woman physician, Elizabeth Blackwell, but only after extracting his promise to let her retain her maiden name. After the Civil War, she became much more conservative and devoted to her large family. Earlier, she showed her cultural radicalism by noting that women were encouraged to marry well to get money that they could not earn. She argued that men suffered by this system, because women might marry men they loathed, just for money. If women had true equality and opportunity, Stone felt they would marry only for affection. Thus, Stone really argued that economic marriage was just a higher form of prostitution. Instead of selling herself to many men, a woman in a loveless, economic marriage sold herself to the highest bidder.[6]

There were certainly cultural heroines all along the 19th-century frontier, but their lives and even identities have largely been lost. While Eastern ladies were fainting at a coarse word, frontier women were shooting rattlesnakes, busting horses, and fighting Indians. They had few doubts about their equality, but little time to think about their condition. They were the real culturally relevant feminist role models, but they left precious little history. They lived an independent proud life that Eastern feminists could not really fathom.

There were glamorous femme fatales on the frontier also. These were often saloon entertainers such as Lola Montez, Carlotta Crabtree, and Baby Doe. Lola Montez was a Bavarian who came to California during the gold rush and captivated miners with her titillating spider dance. Carlotta Crabtree, nicknamed "Lotta the miners darlin'," also worked the California goldfields. Baby Doe (born Elizabeth McCourt) worked in Denver and caught the attention of H.A.W. Tabor, the silver king, in 1880. Tabor left his wife to marry Baby Doe and spent millions pleasing her until his silver empire crumbled. Their story provided the factual background for the opera *The Legend of Baby Doe* and eventually influenced the Broadway musical, *The Unsinkable Molly Brown*.

But these real Western glamor queens were no match for the fictional, idealized women that sprang from the Eastern cult of the lady. These women represented the male ideal as Hollywood movie stars and *Playboy* centerfolds do today. They were modest, chaste, and almost unapproachable. Their beauty was spiritual as well as physical. The women Stephen Foster depicted in his songs are the easiest examples to work with. He wrote of "Jeannie with the Light Brown Hair," "Gentle Annie," "Alice Fair," and "Beautiful Dreamer." These goddesslike Annies, Jeannies, and Alices were what all female dreamers yearned to be. The same virginal, ethereal ladies that Foster sang about appear in that era's romantic poetry. Perhaps Edgar Allan Poe's "Annabel Lee" is the best example. These were women men pined for, but more importantly most women pined to emulate such women.

Cultural instruction for ladies also appeared in early 19th-century romance novels, which were read almost exclusively by upper and middle-class women. Plots generally centered on a triangle consisting of a husband, his chaste wife, and an alluring woman. Invariably, the chaste wife was unassuming and fair haired, and the outside woman was dark haired, exotic, and experienced. The husband is at first drawn to the sensual newcomer, to the wife's despair. However, by novel's end, the husband sees the folly of his wicked ways and begs forgiveness from his faithful wife. These novels convinced wives that it paid to remain chaste and ladylike, thus bolstering the cult of the lady.

Occasionally, women reformers got carried away and overstepped the boundaries of ladylike behavior. For example, women temperance advocates sometimes staged sit-ins at saloons to pray for the sinners inside and to discourage business. In the 1830s, the Moral Reform Society of New York stretched acceptable behavior much further. These women declared war on prostitution and attacked the double standard directly, by placing the moral blame on male customers. They also set up halfway houses to help ex-prostitutes get out of the business and gave advice to parents on proper sexual instruction for children. Properly instructed children supposedly would become neither prostitutes nor customers. Their more controversial activities were staking out known brothels and identifying male customers whose names they then published in their newspaper, *The Moral Advocate*. Befriending prostitutes and descending on brothels did not seem very ladylike, but these actions were easily rationalized. Extreme vice called for extreme actions, but these represented temporary, bold deviations, not new images of womanhood.[7]

After the horrors of the Civil War, romantic idealism of all kinds declined. A crass materialism born in the North merged with the traditional Western pragmatism and played itself out all over America, including the vanquished South. It was an era of ruthless, cutthroat entrepreneurs. This climate offered little opportunity or encouragement to women. Except for those women who moved into office work and the acceptable professions of nursing and teaching, the home was the only respectable place for a real lady. Of course, lower class women might still work in factories, and there were now many more factories—especially in the South.

New myths about women replaced older ones. Before the Civil War, women were denied access to the commercial world because they were too good for the dog-eat-dog business world of men. Men argued that women and religion should operate on a higher plane, above the fray. After 1865, the new myth additionally both glorified and isolated respectable women as mothers. Although women might have a good moral effect on business, they had more important work—bringing up the next generation. Work was now only a last resort, for those women whose defeated husbands could not support them.

Men who could not support their families in style were now demoralized. Especially in the small towns, wives of such men could not work outside the home, and they felt cheated and frustrated by their husband's relative lack of success. They had done a good job with motherhood; the husband had not held up his end. Often these women fastened on their sons and shrewdly managed their futures to give themselves the breadwinner and economic status their own marriage had failed to provide. Thus, sons sometimes became substitutes for an absent or disappointing husband.

Children could now literally be mothered to death by women who thought motherhood was their one vocation. With time on their hands and an inattentive husband always at work, mothers often fastened on sons even if their husbands were economically successful. The American mother who concentrated all her energies on promising sons has often been stereotyped as the Jewish mother. In fact the phrase—my son the doctor or lawyer—is in the hearts of most American mothers. The stereotypical "Jewish" mother has, at least since 1890, been the American middle-class mother.

Despite the real and essential feminist gains in access to education and profession, 19th-century American women had been culturally encapsulated by home and motherhood. The cultural barriers were more effective than laws against social and economic participation. Laws could be changed; cultural perceptions were far more resistant. It would take decades of slow change to alter them, even as laws steadily improved woman's legal position in society.

There were several subtle cultural signs of woman's declining position in 19th-century America. Painted portraits offered some clues. Portraits are a strange blend of what the artist sees and how the subject sees himself or herself. In the 18th century, American men and women tended to have the same expression in their portraits: They looked straight out at the viewer with a stern or serious look. However, early in the 19th century portraits of women began to change. Women subjects began to look demurely off to the side. They were also painted in a softer way, often with softer backgrounds although portraits of men did not change.

These changes are apparent in the paintings of Asher Durand, Samuel Morse, and Winslow Homer before 1860, and even more noticeable in the portraits of Mary Cassat after 1870. She depicted women in a soft impressionist technique and usually painted women tending children. Her impressionism was copied from the French, but her subject matter fit in perfectly with the American cult of motherhood.

Photography, too, featured the new image of women. Late 19th-century photos often pictured women looking shyly to the side and sometimes holding children on their laps. Males in photographs universally looked boldly out at the viewer. Most women no longer wished to be seen as aggressive and direct—it was no longer a suitable image for a lady. Their new, demure expressions told us immediately that women were removed from the brutal male world.

Correspondence between husbands and wives showed similar changes. The Founding Fathers, such as George Washington, John Adams, and Thomas Jefferson, often wrote their wives about politics and current events when they were away. By the Civil War, President Lincoln and his Southern counterpart, Jefferson Davis, no longer wrote their wives about politics. Their letters were overwhelmingly personal. They inquired about children and social events and pointedly ignored economic or political problems.

Nineteenth-century ladies were also in another sphere because of supposed fragile health. Real ladies were considered inherently sickly and unstable because of their delicacy. Thus, they needed constant medical monitoring. Doctors were more than willing to constantly treat rich female patients with chronic complaints. Because there were more physicians and healers per capita in 19th-century America than today, ladies filled a void in medical practice. They were perfect patients. They did not die and they did not get well. Although women were considered too frail to become physicians, they made ideal patients if they were wealthy.

Art supports the image of the debilitated lady. Paintings such as Thomas Eakins's portrait of his wife (*Lady with Setter*) and another of Abigail Van Buren show middle-aged ladies in a veritable state of nervous exhaustion. They look almost unable to move. James Whistler's famous portrait of his mother in a rocker is part of the same genre. These portraits all subtly told women that ladies are too frail to attempt very much.

The same theory that held ladies to be inherently unhealthy, considered lower class women to be naturally healthy. Nothing was further from the truth. Poor women worked long hours in unhealthy factory environments, and the added strain of constant childbearing and housekeeping kept most in very poor health. These women had the highest incidences of contagious diseases, such as tuberculosis, and they had much lower life expectancies than richer men and women. Their poverty, however, made them far from ideal patients for doctors, and their medical care was generally inadequate.

Nineteenth-century Victorian views of sexuality also contributed to the image of the chaste, timid, frail lady. Most printed advice on sexual practice started with the premise that women did not enjoy physical sex. Men, on the other hand, had completely animal approaches to sex. Ladies were brought up to think of sex as something men did to women. The most famous Victorian joke has a newlywed asking her English mother for honeymoon advice. The mother replies: "Lie still dear and think of the British Empire." Sex was something a lady should endure rather than cherish.

From 1820 to 1920, the various feminist movements largely ignored sexual issues. There was a certain logic at work. If women did not like sex and men were animals about it, what could women expect from sexual relations. The one feminist figure who made sex an issue was as Victoria Woodhull. She ran for president in 1872, but her most infamous move was declaring for free love. She defined free love as a concept diametrically opposed to the forced love that was common in arranged marriages. Woodhull's speeches made free reference to sexual organs and orgasms, and she shocked older feminists such as Elizabeth Stanton and Susan B. Anthony as much as the antifeminists.

Elizabeth Cady Stanton eventually accepted Woodhull's help, noting that she would accept anyone's support for feminism—even that of prostitutes. Woodhull eventually recanted her free love doctrine in middle age and married a wealthy Englishman. She later suggested that although free love was exciting when young, it was a nightmare at age fifty.[8]

One cultural area where women made notable strides was the club movement. After 1865, women's clubs became a new base for middle-class women just as religion and reform movements had provided bases before the Civil War. Organized in social clubs, women who could not vote successfully pressured local governments for free kindergartens, public playgrounds, and child labor laws. Although their political achievements were largely limited to children's welfare, their political potential seemed obvious.

Around 1900, the suffrage movement united several long-separated groups of women. After limping along since 1865, suffragists finally convinced some disparate groups that gaining the vote was essential to achieving their various individual goals. For the first time, many women combined across class, regional, religious, ethnic, and party lines. Club women were told they could accomplish more reform with the vote; poor women were told they could do more for their families with the franchise; and upper-class women climbed on board for the increased status of voting.

There were some strange arguments both for and against suffrage. Wealthy white women were urged to support suffrage so that their votes would balance the votes of poor black and immigrant males already voting. Poor women were told that as voters they could support the economic demands of their struggling husbands. Antisuffrage advocates pointed out that poor male workers had not used politics successfully, but had relied on strikes and other economic pressures to improve their economic position.

Some argued that women voters would make the world more peaceful. Opponents contended that history showed a number of bloodthirsty female rulers. Ironically some antisuffragist women apologized for their unladylike political behavior in organizing opposition to suffrage. Upper class opponents often argued that voting would diminish a woman's femininity, and lower class supporters answered that if working in a factory under horrid physical conditions did not diminish femininity, neither would casting a ballot.

Between the lines of all prosuffrage arguments lay the argument that women were more moral than men. If you gave women the vote, the nation would benefit. The government, national or local, was really a family and would benefit from the mothering of women voters. Nineteenth-century feminists had argued for their rights because of their humanity; the 20th-century suffragists argued for the vote on the basis of their maternity.

Following World War I, the Nineteenth Amendment gave women the vote, but the moral, maternal arguments came back to haunt feminists. America did not particularly become more moral in the 1920s. Women voters did not deliver a better society; along with men, they gave us Warren Harding, Calvin Coolidge, and Herbert Hoover. Moreover, the Jazz Age featured crime, bootleg liquor, and a move away from conventional morality.

It turned out that very few women ran for political office. Even more distressing, there was no identifiable women's vote. Women in Iowa voted differently than those in Texas. Rich women voted unlike poor women. Women tended to vote as their male relatives did or vice-versa. This should not have surprised feminists. States that gave women the vote earlier, such as Montana, Washington, and Utah, had already showed the same results. Clearly, women should have voted. Now almost everyone agreed. Politically, however, women were not of one mind and clearly unable to shape the nation.

Moving toward the vote had held disparate feminist groups together. Winning the vote broke up the coalition. Suffrage leaders basked in glory and had become role models for some younger women, but there now seemed little left for them to do. Suffrage signaled most women that the final battle had been won. From here on everything would fall into place naturally. The surviving feminist groups continued to struggle for equality across the board in the 1920s and even introduced an equal rights amendment. However, not until the 1960s would they attract the numbers and media attention that would once again make them a national political force.

There were politically active and successful women in the period, 1920 to 1960, but they were not part of a woman's movement and did not speak for women. Women were also a very small minority in Congress. After the first congresswoman, Jeanette Rankin from Montana in 1916, another three were elected from 1920 to 1924. In 1924, three more congresswomen took office—perhaps the first real professional woman politicians. Of the sixteen additional congresswomen serving from 1920 to 1940, seven were widows who took their husband's seat and ten were not reelected. The first woman U.S. senator was appointed, but served only two days. The second, Hattie Caraway, took her husband's Arkansas seat and won reelection in 1938, but lost to William Fulbright in 1944.[9]

Women gained precious little politically from suffrage early on. More importantly, in the wake of the suffrage struggle they suffered cultural defeats that would effectively neutralize feminism for four decades. The generation of young women who came of age with the suffrage movement, from 1900 to 1920, often identified with suffragists or women social reformers such as Jane Adams, the settlement house worker. Both feminists and social workers were admired as exciting heroines and role models.

The young women of the 1920s ignored these older role models, generally finding the older suffrage leaders stodgy and old-fashioned. Moreover, they thought the older women impossibly prudish about sex. Alternatively, the suffragists did not know what to make of the young Jazz Age "flapper." They had fought to free the next generation of women, but not just so they could have a good time.

The young flappers found excitement, not in struggling against social barriers, but in breaking cultural taboos. They revolted against social conventions. They insisted on the right to smoke, drink, choose sexual partners, and live alone or with roommates. The latch key and diaphragm in the purse were perfect symbols of the new youthful feminine freedom in the 1920s.

The younger set also had new heroines. They venerated female athletes and above all glamorous movie stars. Politics were irrelevant to most younger women; they were interested only in cultural revolt and reform. The older feminists found most flappers revolting only in a pejorative sense. They viewed them very much as many contemporary parents see their supposedly spoiled teenagers. This generation gap effectively killed any hope of a new feminist movement.

There were women who were reformers, new dealers, socialists, labor leaders, and communists from 1920 to 1960. But they were not women reformers or activists, but reformers who happened to be women. The suffrage leaders could not see that suffrage was the only thing holding their coalition together and that once gained the woman's movement would dissolve. They were never able to fathom the cultural and generational disaster that overtook feminism. The cult of youth only first appeared in the 1920s, and, thus, the generation gap was strikingly new. Before 1920, young people wanted to appear older in the way they dressed and acted. After 1920 adults increasingly wanted to appear young.

The young were now on top culturally, but this hardly liberated young women. Older feminists had tried to liberate women from the home while leaving marriage and family life intact. Young women were somewhat liberated culturally, but usually found that as they got older the only viable alternatives were traditional marriage and homemaking. In the 1930s, the Great Depression drove home this point more forcefully. Youth was a passing condition; it now offered cultural prestige, but not permanent gain or security. Teenagers have been learning this ever since the 1920s.

The older feminists were devastated by the results of their success. They had fought the good fight and they had won the battle, but they had lost the cultural and generational war. The younger generation could not be attracted to feminism. As long as the cultural generation gap remained, feminism was dead as a national force. Only when a new generation of, countercultural feminist women appeared in the 1960s would feminism be reborn.[10] These women would be the first feminists to carry out a consciously countercultural movement.

2

New Left Feminism: Countercultural Focus, 1960–1972

The argument over when the 1960s women's liberation movement began will likely never be settled satisfactorily. It is like asking when post–Civil War reconstruction of the South started. The answers depend too much on definition and what part of the movement one is talking about. There were clearly women's movements prior to 1960, just as there were student movements and peace movements before the sixties. However, these feminist movements were small, unpublicized, and, after 1954, overshadowed by the burgeoning civil rights crusade.

Although the term "women's liberation" was not commonly used until 1968, some date the sixties movement from John Kennedy's administration. They argue that Kennedy shrewdly tried to attract politically active women by establishing the first Federal Commission on the Status of Women. The commission was headed by Eleanor Roosevelt, but was actually largely directed by her assistant, Esther Peterson. It accomplished very little and its report, *American Women*, was so moderate, it did not even endorse an equal rights amendment. Kennedy played it both ways: He endorsed the majority report, but also released the more radical, dissenting minority reports. This would supposedly keep everybody happy and united behind his reelection campaign. Kennedy did act on two commission recommendations. He ended a ban on high-level federal employment of women, based on interpreting an 1870 federal law. He also endorsed an Equal Pay Act which passed Congress in June 1964. Probably Kennedy's greatest contribution to women's rights was his Committee on the Status of Women in the Federal Government and a citizen advisory group on women's status outside the government. His committee and citizen group became models for state and local governments. Eventually almost every state, city, and university had its own committee on the status of women.

Another valuable weapon for feminists was the inclusion of women in Title VII of the 1964 Civil Rights Bill. Kennedy sometimes gets credit for this because the entire Civil Rights Bill was passed as a memorial to him. However, women were included only by chance and misdirection. Title VII originally prohibited discrimination in employment on the basis of race, creed, or ethnic origin. Howard Smith, a Democratic congressman from Virginia, amended Title VII to read "or sex." He hoped this would pick up enough no votes to kill Title VII, but it passed by a narrow margin.[1]

Kennedy was an unlikely hero of women's liberation—his reputation as a womanizer, notwithstanding. He had little apparent interest in feminist issues. He only wanted to keep the women who had supported him happy and add to their numbers. The women who backed him were largely middle-aged political activists who had worked in the Democratic Party before Kennedy. Kennedy worked with them, but did not particularly change their direction. These women sought narrow procedural rights for women, especially in the areas of politics and employment. For example, they wanted equal pay, equal opportunity, and a place within the party system. They were part of a woman's rights movement, but not yet the start of a women's liberation movement.

Some suggest that Betty Friedan started women's liberation in 1963 with her best-selling book, *The Feminine Mystique*. Her exhaustive study of how domestic pressures grind women into passive participants in the daily family routine did strike a responsive chord with many housewives. Her major ideas had been presented around 1900 by Charlotte Perkins Gilman who charged that the home trapped housewives in dreary, unrewarding labor. Gilman argued that the only way to save the nuclear family was to redefine home and domesticity and thus free women. Friedan did give Gilman's ideas a modern twist by placing them securely in the modern suburban setting, and illustrating the negative influences of the modern media.

Middle-class housewives ignored Gilman, but sixty years later, Friedan's audience of suburban housewives—with time on their hands and frustration on their minds—were ready to revolt. Friedan shrewdly named their malaise, "the problem with no name." Whether the major problem was frustration, boredom, or unfulfilled career plans was not made clear, but housework clearly was not fulfilling. Friedan suggested that housewives were victims of a corporate plot to keep women in the supermarket and out of the job market through media brainwashing. Even those women who did not believe the conspiracy theory found comfort in knowing that other women were unhappy for similar reasons.[2]

In 1966, Friedan formed the National Organization for Women (N.O.W.) to organize victims of the feminine mystique. It would become (and remain) the largest, most diverse, and most powerful of the contemporary women's groups. It was also the only national feminist group that consistently invited men to join. In the 1970s and 1980s, N.O.W. changed radically with the infusion of many younger members who found N.O.W. the only viable feminist group in their area. However, in the 1960s, N.O.W. was not very diverse and did not always represent the women's liberation movement. Early N.O.W. members were usually either suburban housewives or career women. Both groups were usually middle aged and looking for support to advance or start their careers. They usually did not want to liberate women, as much as they wanted to help themselves.

If women's liberation did not stem from John Kennedy or Betty Friedan and was not even called "liberation" until 1968, where did it spring from? Inquiry should start with the term liberation. The Viet Cong guerillas in Vietnam called themselves The National Liberation Front. Nineteenth-century feminists talked about emancipating women, taking their vocabulary from antislavery diction. But emancipation suggested that women were to be freed by some third party. Liberation suggested that the oppressed would free themselves and sprang from the idiom of anticolonial rebellion. The term women's rights had always been used by feminists along with the designation, women's movement. However, liberation was the favorite term of young campus-based radicals, who constantly talked about liberating the ground they stood on. Thus, women's liberation came from the campus Left. For perhaps the first time, an important national movement was born at universities, yet women's liberation did not spring immediately from campus protests, it was the product of historic splits.

In 1964, some women in SNCC (Student Nonviolent Coordinating Committee) met to discuss common problems. The result was a position paper "On the Position of Women in SNCC," which argued that SNCC women were themselves second-class citizens of this civil rights advocacy group. Women members took the same risks as men. They could be thrown out of school, arrested, or beaten by police, yet they did not have equal access to leadership positions. Their jobs were planning meetings, serving refreshments and cleaning up after meetings—similar to a ladies' auxiliary. When they presented the position paper to the SNCC leadership, Stokeley Carmichael, the national president of SNCC, joked that the only position for women in SNCC was prone.

At that point, many young college women in SNCC left the organization. More importantly, their action galvanized women in SDS (Students for a Democratic Society). SDS was the cutting edge of New Left student activism on most campuses. Founded in 1960 in Michigan, by 1965 it constituted the strongest national voice for radical student activism. Actually there was little national control and local SDS campus chapters varied immensely, along a spectrum to the left of the Democratic Party. In era when campus activism flourished more at large prestigious universities than at smaller, less well-known colleges, strong SDS chapters existed at Harvard, Berkeley, Stanford, Chicago, Michigan, and Wisconsin.[3]

SDS focused on civil rights, student rights, and, above all, the accelerating Vietnam War. Their strategies shifted with local and national leadership changes, but they basically rejected national party politics and adopted grassroot actions to organize individuals and pressure local political power. Their basic ideology stressed creating power by organizing people who individually lacked power. They tried to act out the popular slogan—"Power to the People."

SDS had often split along racial, ethnic, class, and ideological lines, but until 1966, women's issues had not been a problem. This changed dramatically at their 1966 national convention in Chicago. Following the example of the SNCC women, a group of SDS women presented a position paper on the position of women in SDS. It essentially argued the same things that SNCC women had charged. SDS women took the same risks as SDS males but did not share leadership roles. The SDS women were jeered on the convention platform with a variety of hostile comments. Later SDS leadership would explain that although women did suffer discrimination as a class, their problems were minor compared with the problems of blacks, ethnic minorities, and third world people. Women's problems would have to wait. This became the official SDS position on feminist criticism for several years. As part of their demands, SDS women asked for a women's plank, and the refusal led to a massive exodus of SDS women.[4]

The women who walked out of SDS formed the first real women's liberation groups in Chicago and New York City in 1967 and 1968. Similar groups formed in Seattle, Detroit, and other cities. Many of the new groups left no records. Campus groups too sprang up at many universities—with or without SDS chapters to rebel against. There were women's liberation groups at Duke, the University of North Carolina, and the University of Iowa, for example. These three universities had not been famous for general student activism during the 1960s.

The full number of these maverick young women's liberationists may never be known, but the participants invariably were refugees from male-dominated campus groups. A few women students who became national leaders have left first-person recollections, and a few campus groups published positions papers. For example, after presenting women's issues to the National Conference for New Politics meeting in Chicago in 1967 and being ignored, Jo Freeman and Shulamith Firestone formed a woman's group in Chicago. In fall 1967, Firestone, later better known for her 1971 book, *The Dialectic of Sex*, went to New York City and helped found the first famous women's liberation group—New York Radical Women.

More groups, especially in New York, soon followed. They had strange names, such as Redstockings, W.I.T.C.H. (originally an acronym for Women's International Terrorist Conspiracy from Hell), B.I.T.C.H. (no translation needed), and S.C.U.M. (Society for Cutting Up Men). Unless groups were in Chicago, New York, Washington, Los Angeles, or San Francisco, the national media would not cover them. Also, when the media reported on women's liberation in New York, it often could not distinguish the serious groups with substantial memberships from the flippant ones with one or two members. W.I.T.C.H., for example, had over two dozen serious, experienced activist members, but was considered flaky by the media because of their bizarre attempts to attract media attention. W.I.T.C.H. once dressed in witch costumes and hexed the New York Stock Exchange from the trading floor at a preannounced time. The market stumbled badly that day. A reporter jokingly told a W.I.T.C.H. protestor that he found it ironic that the feminists carried brooms, which were, after all, phallic symbols. The feminist replied that he was wrong: The phallus was just a broom symbol. W.I.T.C.H. went to extremes to get media attention for their serious complaints. Their experience as campus activists had taught them how to manipulate the media with protests; however, as feminists they were often unable to get reporters to look past their antics.[5]

Reporters were often very gullible about feminism. Most never knew that S.C.U.M. only had one member—Valerie Solanas. There is no evidence that Solanas cut up anybody, but she did shoot Andy Warhol on the same 1968 day Robert Kennedy was assassinated. Solanas claimed that Warhol (the pop artist) had too much control over her life. Warhol recovered from his wounds, but perhaps women's liberation never did.

Another good example of the media using feminist protest for reader entertainment occurred at the 1968 Miss America Contest in Atlantic City. At the September pageant, members of New York Radical Women protested by staging a Myth America Contest. At one point, they labeled a trash can: "the discarded badges of femininity." Among things thrown in the barrel were spiked heels, fancy cosmetics, and a bra. The contents were then burned. Journalists picked up on this immediately and labeled the feminist protestors—bra burners. This was likely the only bra feminists ever burned in protest. Yet for the next decade feminists were often called bra burners.

Journalists had their reasons for taking feminism lightly. In many ways, the 1960s were a grim decade. The media could not joke about civil rights or Vietnam. They tended to poke fun at young "flaky" campus protesters and "shrill" women liberationists. Most feminist protesters were also young and just off the campus or still attending college. Because feminists often protested cultural traditions, that made them especially lively copy, and although racial humor was clearly off limits for mainstream newspapers and magazines, mild sexist humor was still acceptable.

Meanwhile on campus, many New Left protestors became more frustrated and aggressive after 1968. Richard Nixon became president and the Vietnam War dragged on. SDS was a bellwether as usual. The group became more radical and one of its factions, the Weathermen, had carried out violent resistance in its "Days of Rage" campaign. In general, campus violence increased during Nixon's first term, and there was increasing polarization between young protesters and middle-class America. Young feminists were now usually outside the civil rights and anti-Vietnam groups, but it was clear that they supported those protests. More importantly, feminists had learned how to protest within the New Left student movement. Their on-the-job training continued to shape their style and strategy.

Slogans such as "Power to the People," "Shut It Down," and "Make Love—Not War" did not come from feminist pens, but after 1965, these words often seemed to spring naturally from their lips. Like past woman's movements, women's liberation lacked a clear ideological focus, but if it had an intellectual heritage, it derived from New Left radicalism.

From its origin in 1960, SDS had dominated the media image of the young Left, as well as the imagination of young radicals—including women. SDS's influence on Vietnam protestors, campus reformers, and community organizers is quite clear because it devoted people, strategies, and funds to all these activities. SDS's influence on the women's liberation movement is far less clear because most links were angrily broken. Indeed, some feminists had pointedly branded SDS a prime center of leftist, male-dominated chauvinism, and the major oppressor of young radical women.

Yet SDS left its intellectual and cultural mark on women's liberation. The feminists often projected the same self-righteousness, impatience, crudeness, and paranoia so closely identified with SDS. Even the way women's liberation split, between those interested in countercultural change and those interested in radical political change, mirrored a major

SDS schism. If SDS was for some, the antithesis of what a radical feminist should be, it was still a forefather of women's liberation, just as the suffrage movement was a foremother. Ironically, young contemporary feminists were now more influenced by SDS than by suffragists.

SDS helped provide feminism not only with the righteous anger the New Left was famous for, but the organizing experience and legendary energy that often marked SDS campaigns. Above all, feminism inherited the missionary fervor—the desire to convert everyone within hearing, especially the impressionable young as they progressed through school.

New Left feminists had been badly disillusioned by their treatment by leftist male coworkers, but they still believed in the politics of change. Above all, they believed in revival psychology. They had the true revivalist faith that to see and understand evil was to hate it. They believed in confrontation, not only for the excitement and immediate sense of accomplishment, but because it brought the unconverted into an inescapable personal confrontation with social sin.

Thus, contemporary feminism remained partly a New Left crusade, no less then the student-rights struggle or the anti-Vietnam movement. Yet, feminism was both more promising and more complicated then other movements; its larger promise came from the larger number of possible recruits. Complications stemmed from the dispersion of women into all groups: Civil rights drew away black women, the Chicano movement removed Hispanic women, and so on. Family ties to husbands, children, and parents, especially among poor families, necessarily divided women's loyalties. This had been a problem for past feminists who often had to struggle against family and religious ties. Now, however, there were many more groups that expected loyalty.

In the early years, women's liberation groups made some overtures to the male Left that pointed to a reconciliation. However, SDS and other campus groups were too slow to add parts of the women's agenda to their own issues. The meeting ground should have been the Vietnam protests, because women continued to aggressively oppose the war. For example, in January 1968, New York Radical Women sent members to Washington, D.C., to march against the war. They joined five thousand women from around the country in the "Jeannette Rankin Brigade" (named after the first congresswoman). Rankin became famous in 1917 for voting against participation in World War I. In 1968, it was easier to get women to protest the war than to involve them in more subtle feminist protests. When New York Radical Women organized a cultural protest, they labeled the "burial of traditional women" at Arlington cemetery after the antiwar parade, only four hundred marchers attended.

Despite the lack of support for cultural protest at this stage, groups such as New York Radical Women moved steadily toward countercultural protest as opposed to political or economic actions. The New Left, too, had moved toward countercultural approaches after 1968. Depression over Nixon's election and the continuing Vietnam War encouraged young radicals to ignore the present and concentrate on the next generation. The new wisdom suggested that adults were hopeless, but if you got the next generation, you won it all. Slogans such as: "Don't Trust Anyone over Thirty" and "Make Love—Not War" reflected the new stress.

In the early 1960s, young radicals had a much different approach to contemporary activism. They argued that you had to liberate the ground you stood on. If you did not like the health system, you should become a doctor. If you thought the educational system ineffective, you should become a teacher. If you disliked the political system, you should enter politics. Throughout the 1960s, these early activists argued and practiced their strategy. Who was General Motors more afraid of—they asked—Ralph Nader fighting them in the courts or protestors in the streets? Who did the Pentagon fear most—demonstrators sitting on their steps or Daniel Ellsberg leaking their papers from the inside?

Counterculturalists ignored logic and simply warned: If you do not like this generation, just imagine the next one. It was comforting to believe you were winning when it looked like you were losing. Yippies such as Jerry Rubin and Abbie Hoffman agreed with law professor, Charles Reich. Whatever the shape of contemporary events, the young were startlingly different and they would carry the day. In his best-selling 1970 book, *The Greening of America*, Reich suggested that trying to defeat youth culture was like striking a marshmallow. Everywhere you struck, it pulled you in. Others suggested that capitalism had a self-destruct mechanism because it disseminated anything that made profit. Thus, if revolutionary cultural media brought profits, capitalism would produce and distribute them.[6]

Many radicals disagreed. They felt that capitalism co-opted radical ideas through mass media by diluting content and dulling fervor. For example, when protest songs were accompanied by full orchestra, art improved but the message and ardor suffered. Likewise, when President Lyndon Johnson proclaimed "We Shall Overcome," the song and slogan lost most of its meaning. And while the pacifist ballad "Universal Soldier" became a national top-ten hit, the Vietnam War accelerated.

Older leftist activists hit the counterculture more directly. They pointed out that although youth culture reflected alienation, doing your own thing was a bourgeois trait that capitalism was based on. Moreover, groovy lifestyles suggested that workers ignore the system that oppressed them rather than fight to change it.

Also, because culture is only a tool, it could become a conservative force. The Left has perpetuated the myth that cultural change by definition involved a threat to the status quo in the service of humanitarian progress. Historically, this has not always been true. For example, the Ku Klux Klan, Nazi Party, and a host of dictatorial regimes used culture to brainwash the next generation.

Young feminists did not have to work through the theory of countercultural change, they had grown up with it. Also, women's problems were peculiarly rooted in culture as opposed to politics or economics. The new women's groups did have members who argued that only a political and/or economic revolution could liberate American women. However, this group (often labeled politicos) were a small minority. Most feminists argued for cultural approaches and cultural reforms. Politicos were usually marxists, socialists, or anarchists. Cultural feminists usually had no political ideology. They refuted politicos by pointing out, for example, that although a political and economic revolution had occurred in the Soviet Union and parts of Eastern Europe, it had not liberated women there. In the Soviet Union, although women were 85 percent of the physicians, Soviet doctors were paid about the same as high school teachers. Although Soviet women engineers earned the same as men, they were hardly liberated. At home, the working Soviet wife was also expected to do the housework and care for children. Thus Soviet women, unlike men, did two or three jobs but only got paid for one.

Likewise, in Cuba during the early revolution, women served with Castro's guerrilla army and enjoyed rough equality with male revolutionaries, but once the revolution was secure, Castro proclaimed that Cuban women should return to the home and raise children for the state. Cultural feminists concluded that political and economic revolution was not the answer. Yet there was disagreement on the most important cultural problems.

The broad cultural argument had wide acceptance. Self-image was the crucial starting point. What difference would it make if women had the opportunity to become doctors, lawyers, politicians, and business executives if they did not see those vocations as appropriate for women? What good was opportunity if women did not want the end results? What good was the vote if women did not know how they wanted to use it? The problem for cultural feminists was where and how to bolster woman's self-image.

One pathbreaking group in particular helped define the strategy of cultural feminism. At a November 1968 women's conference in Chicago, members of New York Radical Women split into three discussion groups.

One group held together and back in New York became the colorful W.I.T.C.H. organization, whose most famous member, perhaps, was Robin Morgan.[7] W.I.T.C.H. carried on political campaigns with a colorful cultural flair. They were action oriented rather then introspective or theoretical. Thus, W.I.T.C.H. excelled at gaining media attention. Another of the conference groups broke up once back home. The third group, however, held together in New York and became known as Redstockings. They were led by Ellen Willis and Shulamith Firestone and became the most influential practitioners of radical feminism.

Redstockings turned inward to find the roots of cultural inferiority. They popularized consciousness-raising rap sessions and the slogan "the personal is political." Their rap sessions were used to convince women that all females had the same problems. Thus, women's individual problems were really class problems and women were an oppressed group. To prove this, Redstockings urged women to organize rap sessions which threw out questions such as What does femininity mean to you? How did you learn what was feminine as a little girl? How did your father treat you compared to your brother.

With Firestone in the lead, Redstockings worked toward a theory of feminine repression and liberation. The analysis was cultural, but the chief weapon was the solidarity of women. The Redstocking Manifesto opened by noting: "After centuries of . . . struggle, women are uniting to achieve their final liberation from male supremacy." After noting that women were "considered inferior beings, whose only purpose" was "to enhance men's lives," the manifesto proclaimed:

Because we have lived so intimately with our oppressors in isolation from each other we have been kept from seeing our personal suffering as a political condition. This creates the illusion that a woman's relationship with her man . . . can be worked out individually. In reality, every such relationship is a class relationship and the conflicts . . . can only be worked out collectively.

The Redstocking Manifesto was very New Left, both in tone and content. It represented a grassroots attempt to organize individual women around their own oppression. It stressed that consciousness raising was not "therapy . . . but the only way to ensure that a liberation program" was "based on the concrete realities" of their lives. It charged that women had been "exploited as sex objects, breeders, domestic servants, and cheap labor." The Manifesto identified men as the sole agents of their oppression, arguing that all "forms of exploitation and oppression," such as racism and imperialism, were simply an "extension of male supremacy."

Redstockings also argued that men had attempted to shift the blame for women's oppression to institutions. Their Manifesto insisted that institutions were "merely tools of the oppressor." Blaming institutions implied that "men and women were equally victimized" and obscured the fact that men benefited from exploiting women. Redstockings rejected the view that women's position resulted from "brainwashing, stupidity, or mental illness." They insisted it resulted "from continual, daily pressure from men." In sum, Redstockings argued: "We do not need to change ourselves, but to change men."[8]

The most obvious New Left influences involved Redstockings's stress on personal experience and the commitment to internal democracy. The Manifesto explained that they regarded women's "experience . . . as the basis for an analysis of" women's common situation. They rejected all "existing ideologies" as the "products of male supremacist culture." Redstockings identified "with all women" and defined their best interests "as that of the poorest, most brutally exploited women." They repudiated "all economic, racial educational or status privileges" that divided them "from other women." Moreover, Redstockings were committed to ensuring that every movement woman had "an equal chance to participate, assume responsibility, and develop her political potential."[9]

Redstockings constituted a New Left clinic on how to create power by uniting powerless people and organizing around your own oppression. Whereas SDS mostly talked about these strategies, many feminist groups put them into play successfully. Feminists also took their commitment to democratic control more seriously. For all their talk about giving "power to the people," groups such as SDS steadily moved toward small-group power plays and executive action. Participatory democracy was more a slogan than a practice in the male New Left.

Feminist groups really wrestled with the problems of elitism as opposed to participatory democracy. For example, Ti-Grace Atkinson, president of the New York N.O.W., group, formed a new organization in October 1968 called The Feminists. The Feminists combined careful analysis of sexism with egalitarian governance; for example, they devised a lottery system to prevent domination by a few leaders. The Feminists were going back to Athenian democracy. The Athenians chose their leaders by lot because they believed that the government was strong and not just the men who ran it—any male citizen could do the job. The system had not precluded the rise of dominant Athenian leaders, and the Feminists had similar problems. The media constantly sought out Atkinson to speak for the group. She felt that "the media needed stars but the movement did not."[10]

Yet when The Feminists decided to choose media spokespersons by lot, Atkinson left the group. For all their devotion to democracy, the Feminists had very discriminatory rules. One rule limited the number of married members. Another said members could be expelled if they missed meetings. The contradictions, splits, and constant formation of new groups had been common on the left and particularly in the New Left. In Europe, intellectual splits traditionally resulted in a new ideology or new political party. In America, divisions traditionally resulted in a new organization.

Yet feminists were perhaps the only New Left groups to really experience the problems of participatory democracy, because they were the only ones who actually wrestled with the practical limitations. For example, some feminist groups limited the number of times a member could speak to avoid a dominating leadership. In December 1969, Shulamith Firestone, after disagreements with the Redstockings, helped form a new, more egalitarian group—New York Radical Feminists. They insisted that when a woman joined, she had to remain in the same group she started with, so she would not be dominated by older, more experienced feminists. The subgroups were called brigades, and the first one was named The Stanton-Anthony Brigade. All brigades were supposedly equal, but the first brigade had most of the high-powered writers (such as Firestone) and tended to dominate.

There was no real answer to dominance and elitism. Some groups chose leaders by lot to make the point that all women were capable. Yet the lottery system often forced hard-working followers to become frustrated, ineffective leaders. In the final analysis, the groups needed leaders more than the media did. Powerful leadership not only inspired members, it drew new converts. More importantly, it kept the group under media coverage and added to its power and prestige. Communal direction was often the ideal, but seldom the outcome. Feminism provided no evidence that participatory democracy worked any better among egalitarian-minded women than in the male Left. However, to its credit New Left feminism did leave a record of trial-and-error practice. And perhaps some of the hundreds of women's groups we know little or nothing about actually used participatory democracy with success.

The doctrinal splits that historically plagued the Left were especially creative for women's liberation in its early years. For example, Redstockings lost members because it failed to move forward with new analysis and programs. Redstockings relied on consciousness-raising rap sessions that made women feel good about shared problems. Their refusal to blame women for sexist problems was a strategy pioneered by black activists, and it worked as personal therapy, but did not lead anywhere. Eventually, support for victims without any practical remedies supported the status quo and glorified victims. The more oppression a woman suffered, the more relative status she had within the group and the more she needed support. Redstockings had ironically stressed that consciousness raising was not therapy, but the only way to expose sexism. But the rap sessions were only a start. If continued, they could only end where they started, that is, explaining situations, not changing them.

When Shulamith Firestone left Redstockings to form The New York Radical Feminists, she worked on making the new group more action-oriented. The Radical Feminists refuted Redstockings's view that only men had to change, not women. They argued that men oppressed women for personal satisfaction and not just economic gain. In the process, men destroyed women's self-image and sense of worth. Thus, women could not change sexism unless they changed their self-image. The Radical Feminists stressed personal growth as a prelude to action. But how could sexism be attacked and what specific changes could level the playing field for men and women?

Shulamith Firestone provided perhaps the most radical and comprehensive answers in her book, *The Dialectic of Sex: The Case for Feminist Revolution*. She bent marxist dialectic to fit women as a class. Just as Marx argued that the lower class must revolt and seize the means of production to gain freedom, Firestone argued that women must control reproduction. She believed that the basic inequality of women stemmed from a division of labor based on reproduction. As long as men did not share equally in reproducing, they would always have an insurmountable social advantage. Sexual differences could never be eliminated as long as only women gave birth.

Firestone looked forward to artificial reproduction without sentimental qualms. She asserted that "since pregnancy is barbaric and childbirth hurts," artificial reproduction was humane, as well as egalitarian. If Firestone was the Marx of the feminist movement, she was nevertheless ahead of her time. Some women were willing to give up men unless they could have them on more favorable terms. Very few women were ready to settle for test-tube babies in the "brave new world" Firestone envisioned.[11]

Neither Firestone nor most radical feminists had much faith in the Sexual Revolution as a cure for anything. They believed more liberal attitudes toward premarital sex just put more pressure on women to perform. With fewer reasons to say no, women were more vulnerable to men who still sought sex without commitment. Yet, radical feminism did demystify sex and make women both more wary long term and more demanding short term in relationships with men.

In the late 1960s, radical feminists constantly joked about women who faked orgasms to please men. Feminists often asserted their right to equal sexual satisfaction in relationships with either husbands or lovers. And for the first time, men's sexual prowess was publicly criticized. Women were encouraged to share their sexual frustrations with other women. They were urged to learn about the physiology of sex and to "be in touch" with their own bodies. Feminists themselves provided popular education. For example, Ann Koedt's essay, "The Myth of the Vaginal Orgasm" (based on recent scientific research), was an underground classic long before it was published in *Notes from the First Year* (a book of radical feminist essays).[12]

Lesbianism was a far more complicated sexual issue for radical feminism. At first, heterosexual feminists tried to ignore the issue. Most moderate groups, such as N.O.W., bluntly denied there was any logical connection between feminism and lesbianism. Clearly, they feared lesbianism would harm feminist appeals to straight women. When Martin Luther King, Jr. was accused of being a communist, he replied that it was bad enough being black, let alone being black and red. Similarly, a feminist might have complained that it was bad enough being radical, let alone radical and gay.

The lesbian issue continued to surface, largely because many of the most gifted and effective feminist writers were gay or bisexual. Lesbians were probably a small minority of rank-and-file feminist members, but they were often among the most active. There were good reasons why lesbians supported feminism so energetically: They usually had the most to gain from feminist reforms and the least to lose. Lesbians were discriminated against as women, without enjoying most advantages and protections extended to women, wives, and mothers. Lesbians were almost always, by definition, full-time workers. Also, because lesbians did not need men, they had little to lose in actions that threatened or angered men.

Feminists had sometimes criticized lesbians as "man-identified," because they often copied male-female stereotypical roles in the so-called butch-femme roles in lesbian relationships. However, lesbians stressed that they were woman-identified women because they did not relate to, and were independent of, men. Lesbians stressed that they did not hate men; they loved women. Their feminist critics often argued that lesbians were not an oppressed group in the sense women were because they chose lesbianism and thus chose oppression. Women had no choice but to be women. Lesbians replied that sexual orientation was innate and not open to choice.

The lesbian argument was logically compelling. If lesbianism was not reversible, lesbians had three choices sexually—celibacy, masturbation, or lesbianism. They argued that lesbianism was the most human and socially acceptable choice. Lesbians were often not satisfied with equality within the movement: they were often depicted as superfeminists, because they were not dependent on men in any way. Men knew this, they argued, and men feared and hated lesbians for that reason.[13] Yet lesbian women depended on men who employed them, and their gay lifestyles made them perhaps more vulnerable than straight women workers. Also, although most men were very comfortable with lesbians socially, because there was no sexual tension, straight women were often very uncomfortable with lesbians. Lesbians stressed that women need not fear lesbians sexually, because lesbian sexuality was based on communication and consent, as opposed to the aggressive genital sexuality of men on the make. Nevertheless, there was often tension between gay and straight feminists.

By 1970, the contradictions inherent in antilesbianism among feminists became clear. When *Time* magazine put out a cover article on author Kate Millett in December 1970 and mentioned her bisexuality, many leading feminists took this opportunity to proclaim their support of gay feminists. Yet it took the rest of the decade for many moderate feminist groups to fully accept lesbian feminists. The tension continued, but equality for lesbians within the movement was thereafter seldom questioned in theory.

Women's liberation provided instant and steady prestige for lesbians. It allowed them more access to national media, increased funding, and encouraged academic research on lesbian issues and lifestyles. Perhaps the facilitator at a lesbian culture session at the 1979 Berkshire Woman's History Conference at Vassar College put it best. She said that a few years ago their lesbian group was meeting in the back rooms of gay bars, now here they were at Vassar.

If lesbians did not hate men, it often seemed that radical feminists did. Betty Friedan, a moderate, constantly reiterated that her group, N.O.W., did not hate men and indeed invited them to join N.O.W., for man was not the enemy. Radical feminists also stressed that they did not hate men, but they seldom said they liked them either. They often exhibited a peculiar biting ambivalence, even when describing the men with whom they worked. For example, in her introduction to *Sisterhood Is Powerful*, Robin Morgan thanks twenty women and then notes, "[S]ome mention, albeit brief should go also to three men—Kenneth Pitchford, Blake Pitchford, and John J. Simon. Without such men, this book would not have been possible. On the other hand it would not have been necessary."[14] In 1972, Erica Mann Jong caught this perfectly with her satiric piece, "Seventeen Warnings in Search of a Feminist Poem." In part, she noted:

4. Beware of the man who wants to protect you; he will protect you from everything but himself.
5. Beware of the man who loves to cook; he will fill your kitchen with greasy pots. . . .
7. Beware of the man who denounces his mother; he is a son of a bitch. . . .

13. Beware of the man who picks your dresses; he wants to wear them. . . .

16. Beware of the man who writes flowery love letters; he is preparing for years of silence.

17. Beware of the man who praises liberated women; he is planning to quit his job.[15]

This characteristic feminist satire carried over into *Ms.* magazine during the 1970s. Feminist humor was seldom self-deprecating—it was halfway between Wonder Woman and Gilda Radner. For example, in 1980 *Ms.* writer, Julia Lieblich, provided freshmen college women with "Advice for the First Year." The practical wisdom included:

Be wary of women who prefer the company of men because "they are more stimulating intellectually." These women are a dying breed and should be regarded as relics. Do not assume that the only man in the room on the first day of your women's studies class is an enlightened male. He may have walked into the wrong classroom. Wearing mascara will not make you less effective politically. It has, however, been known to smear.

Finally, Lieblich suggested that women not be too hard on a man who tried to pay the restaurant check because "he is a creature of habit." Moreover, if you (the woman) waited for him to pay the check because you were short of money, "you are not obligated to sleep with him. You are also a creature of habit and may resort to old ways occasionally as long as the guilt you feel ruins the whole evening."[16]

The easy flippant humor of the 1980 *Ms.* piece was out of place before 1973. Radical feminism appreciated some feisty humor, but found most feminist issues too serious to joke about. Radical feminism had it heyday in the period 1967 to 1972. The marches, media actions, contentious theorizing, and creative analysis in many ways represented the finest flowering of New Left politics, but radical feminism faded shortly after the New Left student movement itself declined and for many of the same reasons—especially the end of the Vietnam War. More importantly, President Nixon's overwhelming reelection in 1972 reflected a growing conservative backlash against activism in general. Yet radical feminism left a proud legacy and an emotional call for universal sisterhood that has never been equaled before or since. In its wake it left a viable middle-class women's movement that rallied around *Ms.* magazine, feisty female popular singers, television stars, and movie actresses. It also left many campus feminist groups around the nation that continued to practice their own unique brands of radical feminism. However, in the big cities there was a cultural void and loss of energy as the pioneer groups disappeared.

The New Left itself faded away between 1970 and 1972. However, the collapse of campus activism was necessarily exaggerated, because the rise of campus activism had also been wildly overstated. There remained a substantial number of white, middle-class college youths anxious to turn America away from military adventure abroad and corporate domination at home. Yet, increasingly their pillars of support were undermined. The black, Chicano, and Native American movements drew away lower-class ethnic support, and Women's Liberation drew away women, while general frustration eroded their own ranks. The Vietnam War wound down; the campuses and cities became quiet, if still untamed; and the silent majority not only broke its vow of silence, but reelected Richard Nixon and Spiro Agnew to speak for the new American majority.

Some of the more militant radicals went underground after a brief fling with violence; the peaceful activists either dropped out to meditate, started working for George McGovern, or slipped into more cosmic causes, such as organic foods. Yippie leader Jerry Rubin discovered he had been sexist. Vietnam mobilization leader Rennie Davis found that a maharishi had the answer to life's problems; SDS founder Tom Hayden married the activist Hollywood actress, Jane Fonda.

The young generation of the 1960s, brought up on contemporary protest and visions of a new world, had grown disillusioned by their failures. The next generation had long hair and blue jeans but shared little else with their predecessors. The younger kids grooved on concerts, music, and festivals as much as the last generation, but they were uninterested in cosmic meaning or even national problems. They would not mind having a Woodstock experience, they were enthusiastically for peace, and ostensibly for giving blacks an equal chance, but somehow these things were not their job. If reforms came, fine, but like the 1950s generation, 1970s youth were generally content to get along. The new stress was on observation rather than participation.

Aspects of the malaise that overtook the New Left hurt radical feminism too, but it did not do nearly as much damage, because the feminist movement was at an earlier stage and still filled with energy. In the New Left, these women had largely been followers; as radical feminists, they were clearly leaders. In the New Left, they had talked about organizing around your own oppression, but ended up organizing around someone else's oppression.

All the progressive movements that had gathered steam in the period before World War I and had languished in the socially sterile 1920s came back in the 1930s under the stimulus of economic depression. All the movements came back, except one—the woman's movement. Ironically, in the 1970s feminism was the only movement that remained strong after the decline of the radicalism of the sixties. Radical feminism survived in part under the stimulus of anger directed at the male left.

Feminist anger was also fueled by insults from the federal government. The Federal Bureau of Investigation (FBI), under J. Edgar Hoover, had the women's movement under surveillance as a possible threat to the nation. Yet even the FBI approached feminists in sexist ways. An FBI report noted that women liberationists often dressed like male radicals and had frizzy hair. The FBI quickly decided women's liberation was not a threat to national security, but many feminists continued to believe they were under surveillance.

Above all, anger kept feminists going. They were angry at the avant-garde male left, and they felt stupid when reviewing their role in the New Left. For example, Leah Fritz, a young feminist activist, saw her relationship to the male left as follows

To leftist men I was eventually to become an anomaly. Since I was neither a passive beauty they could feast their eyes on, nor an earth mother to nurture them, . . . what the hell was I doing drinking wine at their penthouse parties. . . .

"You bore me woman" was the look they threw me. But I didn't stay to catch it and I wondered at those women who continued to hang around, darting between insults to find the correct leftist position.[17]

Robin Morgan said "goodbye to all that" New Left male chauvinism in 1970, when *RAT*, a New York underground newspaper, let feminists write one entire issue. Morgan noted: "We have met the enemy and he's our friend." She continued to say good-bye to the male left in this long article. For example:

White males are most responsible for the destruction of human life. . . . Yet who is controlling the supposed revolution to change all that? White males . . . Goodbye to the "straight" male-dominated Left . . . who will allow that some workers are women, but won't see all women (say housewives) as workers. . . . Goodbye to Hip Culture and the so-called Sexual Revolution, which has functioned toward women's freedom as did the Reconstruction toward former slaves. . . .

Goodbye to lovely pro-Women's Liberation Paul Krassner, with all his astonished anger that women have lost their sense of humor. . . .

Let it all hang out. Let it seem bitchy, catty, dykey, frustrated, crazy, Solanisesque, nutty, frigid, ridiculous, bitter, embarrassing, man-hating, libelous, pure, unfair, envious, intuitive, low-down, stupid, petty, liberating. We are the women that men have warned us about.

Goodbye goodbye forever, counterfeit Left . . . male-dominated . . . reflection of the Amerikan Nightmare. Women are the real Left. We are rising, powerful in our unclean bodies. . . . We are rising with a fury older and potentially greater than any force in history, and this time we will be free or no one will survive. Power to all the people or to none.[18]

The vitriolic tone suggested that the radical feminists were almost as mad at themselves for being subordinate so long as they were angry at New Left males. Morgan deals with this indirectly when talking about those women who supported the radical SDS splinter group, The Weathermen. She says: "Left Out—not Right On—to the Weather Sisters who, and they know better—they know, reject their own radical feminism for that last desperate grab at male approval that we all know so well, for claiming that the machismo style and the gratuitous violence is their own." But if radical feminists took several years to recognize their position, why wonder about Weatherwomen supporting male comrades at the hour of their greatest need?

The greatest irony of "Goodbye to All That" is for all the rejection and ridicule, Morgan's style is classically New Left. Its profanity, wicked satire, vivid images, black humor, and even its unevenness, all mark it as New Left rhetoric. The piece ends with the phrases, "Free Kathleen Cleaver," "Free Robin Morgan," and eighteen other women associated with male New Left or establishment political figures, but radical feminists such as Morgan would never free themselves from their New Left upbringing. Although feminists prefer and use the term radical feminists to describe women's liberation groups from 1968 to 1975, the term New Left feminists would be a more accurate label. The radical feminist rejection of their New Left heritage might not have been logical, but it fueled an important part of women's liberation. Perhaps feminists should have been glad that New Left men had not been more sensitive to movement sexism. If halfhearted compromises had satisfied leftist women, there might not have been a radical feminist movement in the 1960s.

Although radical feminism waned in the mid 1970s, the women's movement continued to grow, but now it grew in well-established patterns. There were far fewer wild creative surges. Radical feminism turned more conservative—in part a victim of its own success. It, after all, continued to make gains when most of the Left was still licking its wounds. Progress in abortion rights, equal pay, and job discrimination were the obvious gains, but perhaps the most important gains were cultural and harder to see. Everyone noticed that there were dozens of commissions, committees, and conferences on the status of women. Much more hidden were the private networking, the explosion of women's studies, and the rise of aggressive feminist cultural criticism.

The ERA remained the one political goal that eluded women's liberation. The ERA had been in most Democratic and Republican Party platforms since 1940, but party pros had ignored it. Now political pros usually pushed it, but a minority of conservative states blocked it. The justice of the ERA seemed self-evident, but opponents had some interesting objections. Conservatives warned that nobody could forecast how the Supreme Court might interpret ERA, and they forecast that ERA would bring women into a mandatory draft in wartime and perhaps mandate unisexual rest rooms. If mixed-sex washrooms were not likely, the draft issue was plausible. Perhaps the strangest argument against ERA came from lower class women with left-wing politics. They argued that ERA would make protections for women workers only, illegal. Thus, if women workers received cab fare when working late in dangerous areas, male workers could demand equal protection under ERA. Some women warned that employers would react, not by extending benefits to men, but by discontinuing benefits altogether. ERA will likely pass someday. In the meantime, it has kept women's groups almost totally united on at least one issue. As such, it might temporarily be worth more as something to seek, rather than a victory to celebrate.

Women's studies often divided the academic world, but it furnished women's liberation with a steady stream of new recruits. College women were not naturally drawn to women's issues. As a popular minority, they were sought after as dates, encouraged by parents, and generally treated equally by instructors and the university. Not surprisingly, the vast majority of complaints of university sexism come from staff and faculty. Conventional wisdom suggested that only when women have faced job discrimination, suffered from an unequal marriage, or endured sexual harassment would they be ready for women's liberation.

Yet, women's studies did recruit young women students. The classes were liberating in style as much as content. For most women, these classes were the only ones in which they formed the majority. The average class enrolled only 20 percent men. Women's studies classes were also much more likely to use open discussion on sensitive social issues. Instructors experimented with new testing techniques, such as mandatory individual journals. The result was a proliferation of women's campus groups and an infusion of college students into women's community groups (often the local N.O.W. chapter).

If feminism was increasingly irrelevant to the average college woman, it was because the woman's movement had accomplished so much in a short time. However, women's studies classes were problem oriented. They seldom spent as much time analyzing past victories as discussing unresolved problems. While Madison Avenue advertisers tried to convince women that they had "come a long way," women's studies stressed that they had a long way to go.[19]

Women's studies were not usually very objective, but for a long time academia and students accepted this as natural. The typical women's studies class featured a woman instructor with a strong feminist background, required reading by leading feminist authors, and topics organized around feminist issues. Thus, women's history courses tended to be a history of feminism, rather than a history of women. There was a certain logic to this bias. Without the recent feminist movement, there would be no women's studies and no history of women course.

When challenged, feminist historians often testily replied that standard history courses were similarly men's studies course, because they ignored women's history. It was more true that liberal arts courses in general had a liberal bias, and thus it was not relevant to attack bias only in women's studies. The real problem was that not enough conservatives choose to teach liberal arts and almost all women studies teachers are feminists. This situation has received much more attention since 1989, when conservatives effectively raised the issue of political correctness. Since 1990, Accuracy in Academe, a conservative companion group to Accuracy in Media, has given many examples of women's studies classes that they felt brainwashed students on issues such as abortion and lesbianism.

Bias aside, women's studies were often a boon for professors and universities, even though relatively few students took women's studies classes and even fewer pursued women's studies majors. Women's groups grew closer to campuses, and women in general found a university with a women's center, a friendlier place to study or visit. Academic publishers were quick to realize the market for feminist studies and feminist scholars were very energetic and aggressive in forming new feminist groups. Also, these new professional organizations often founded their own feminist journals.

The biggest scholarly bonus was the interdisciplinary nature of women's studies. Especially in history, sociology, political science, philosophy, and English, feminist scholars opened new avenues of approach. They organized their own conferences and became a significant part of traditional academic conferences. Feminists necessarily linked past and present and pursued problems across academic boundaries. Feminist scholarship also infused more energy into the serious study of popular culture. Academic approaches to popular culture had begun in earnest during the 1960s. Innovative scholars had argued that mass culture was the new environment and that those who believed people were shaped by their environment had to take popular culture seriously. Feminist scholars needed little convincing. They often saw popular culture as one key to the next generation. The interdisciplinary approaches also encouraged another academic tendency—networking. Women scholars had good reason to organize, academic interests aside. Women's studies just made it easier and somewhat less threatening to the academy. There had been black caucuses before, but they had been mostly students since there were few black faculty. Women faculty, however, represented a large minority. The issues were obvious: Women were underpaid, underpromoted, and underrepresented as administrators. Women made slow gains across the board in these areas during the 1970s and 1980s, but, recently, networking has created a backlash of male faculty resentment in an era of declining faculty compensation.

Affirmative action has been a bigger boon for academic women than for minorities and has slowly increased women faculty nationwide. Although there are strategic ways around affirmative action hiring, few universities work these angles. When a college narrows down to two or three candidates, their credentials are so close that almost inevitably the woman or minority contender is offered the job. For under affirmative action rules, there must be a clear difference between the candidates and the burden of proof is on the employer, not the candidate.

Women's liberation has clearly helped women in academia. It is less clear how much academia has helped women's liberation. In the 1970s, when radical feminism faded, women's studies had its greatest growth. Moreover, feminist scholars created the new cultural and economic battleground with careful economic studies and creative cultural analysis. A close connection developed between academic feminists and mainstream public feminism. N.O.W. groups often used college teachers as speakers and resource persons, and academic feminists invited public feminist leaders to guest lecture in college classes. *Ms.* magazine also used many academic writers during the 1970s and 1980s and had strong academic support.

Feminist scholars traced the early women's liberation movement and created an instant history with new contemporary feminist heroines. They also collected and publicized the research, actions, and musings of feminists on secluded campuses and in towns around America. They extended feminist concerns from urban to rural areas and to lower class, ethnic, and even Third World women. Academic feminist conferences were a panorama of feminist interests. There was something for everybody.

Although feminist political organizing and group memberships dwindled during the seventies and eighties, feminist cultural criticism and countercultural approaches continued to blossom at universities. Although factional strife was endemic among radical feminists, the unspoken tie was the cultural attack. An unfortunate terminology confused feminist arguments. Those women who eventually argued for a national female culture as opposed to male culture have been labeled cultural feminists. This obscures the peculiar New Left cultural approaches common to all radical feminists.

The so-called "nationalist" feminists were no more cultural than some others—they were separatists. They argued that women could not develop fully while dominated by male culture. This group should have been called gender separatists.[20] They had their counterparts in the black, Chicano, and Native American movements. They did not seek to change, reform, or use the prevailing mass culture, they wished to escape it and create a new one.

But was a new culture a step forward or just escape? You could control your own culture locally and still be controlled by the large more powerful national culture. Blacks might control the ghettos and Native Americans the reservation, but they still ended up dealing with state universities, television, and Hollywood films. Radical feminists and New Left activists had used cultural approaches creatively to change society and/or make their point. In truth, all radical feminists were cultural feminists.

The New Left had used cultural strategies to lighten up tedious confrontations, amuse themselves, and confound the opposition. Although the cultural actions were often planned for fun, they sometimes were very successful. For example, when students at the University of California at Berkeley demonstrated for day care in the late 1960s, instead of a mass demonstration they just asked anyone who had small children to bring them to campus on demonstration day. Another example is how left-wing campus activists protested CIA recruitment at various colleges. Some groups simply picketed the CIA interview sites. However, more creative protestors signed up for CIA job interviews and dressed up as hit men and soldiers of fortune. They carried signs such as "I want to kill" and "Mafia, today—CIA tomorrow" and carried violin cases. My earliest recollection of such cultural tactics was as a student at the University of Chicago in 1959. Students planned a demonstration against the Marines recruiting on campus. Instead of picketing the Marine recruiter or staging an antiwar demonstration, they staged a prowar demonstration. They carried signs such as "Guns for the Arabs" and "A Final Solution to the Peace Problem." In the middle of this "war" demonstration was the Marine recruiter, looking as befuddled as other establishment figures would look under countercultural attack in the next decade.[21]

Whether radical feminists were politicos, lesbian activists, cultural nationalists, or mainstream feminists, they used countercultural methods naturally and with abandon. Cultural reforms and satires were as common in *Ms.* magazine as in the smallest underground feminist newsletter. Feminists played off popular and traditional culture in highlighting the condition and status of women. Not surprisingly, the first regular issue of *Ms.* magazine featured Wonder Woman, the comic-book heroine, on the cover.[22]

The most outrageous and creative satires usually came from the direct New Left splinter groups in the period 1969 to 1972. For example, the Media Women group in San Francisco turned the fairy tale, "Sleeping Beauty," into a feminist fable titled "The Story of Sleeping Handsome." It began: "Once upon a time in a queendom far away there lived a baby prince named-Handsome. His Mother, Queen Goodness was a wise ruler, but stern parent. His Father, King Helpmate was good looking and a very efficient homemaker."

After relating the story of the famous curse put on the prince by a "wicked wizard," the fable noted that Handsome had grown into a "lovely young man" with "beautiful blonde hair and cute dimples," but he was "careful not to appear smart" because as all "marriageable young boys" knew, "sounding intelligent would not have been masculine." At age twenty, Handsome falls into his sleep, but is rescued by Princess Charming, "a strong and wise ruler of a neighboring queendom," who brings him out of his permanent slumber with a kiss. Prince Handsome then awakens and exclaims: "At last my princess has come." The fable concludes:

And so Princess Charming carried Prince Handsome away to her castle where they were married . . . as woman and husband. Prince Handsome fulfilled his manly destiny by cooking, sewing, and spinning, keeping his mouth shut and waiting till Princess Charming finished her important business and had time for him. They were both very very happy.[23]

Whereas the New Left often used cultural and countercultural strategies indiscriminately to shock and outrage the establishment, and thus get the attention of the young, feminists were generally more purposeful. Feminist cultural strategy invariably tried to expose and correct sexist cultural conditioning. This involved cultural theories, as well as practice. Even the theories of antifeminists sometimes proved helpful.

For example, Bruno Bettleheim, an enemy of feminism, ironically proposed a theory that envisioned Betty Friedan's problem-with-no-name malady, a decade before her book, *The Feminine Mystique*. In the 1950s, Bettleheim suggested that America created numbers of unhappy housewives because American women were treated inconsistently. In grade school, women were encouraged to excel as students and compete with males. Up through the first two years of high school, girls were, on average, better students than boys. Then social experience taught girls that if they appeared too bright and successful as students they were not as attractive to boys. Thus, many girls started to excel less or feign relative ignorance. Bettleheim also argued that girls had greater social maturity than boys, but using it also made them less popular. Thus, around boys, girls sometimes cleverly appeared immature. Boys had no similar problems. If they were bright, achieving, and socially mature, this made them more attractive to girls their age.[24]

The final result, noted Bettleheim, was that men passed women in average academic achievement in college, and they often married women with less academic accomplishment, who were nevertheless superior in intellect and social maturity. Yet after years of child rearing and housework, while the husband advanced his career and knowledge, housewives were unable to assert their felt superiority. Indeed, in many cases that superiority had been erased. These women became frustrated, and Bettleheim argued this caused many American marital problems and accounted for America's skyrocketing divorce rate.

Bettleheim's solution was hardly acceptable to feminists. He urged that American culture consistently signal women from birth that they would have a secondary role in society. Girls would know they were being educated and groomed to be wives and mothers, and not to compete with men. This, Bettleheim argued, was the way culture worked in South America and most parts of Europe. There girls did not receive inconsistent signals, first to compete and excel and then later to accept a secondary, helpmate position to men. Although feminists obviously rejected Bettleheim's solution, they accepted his definition of the problems, which later became known as the female fear-of-success syndrome.

Another perceptive broad cultural theory with important countercultural implications appeared in Susan Sontag's essay, "The Double Standard of Aging." Sontag argued that no matter how much progress women might make economically, politically, and intellectually, they were building on sand because of unspoken cultural inferiority. Her arguments clearly borrowed from Malcolm X's views of black cultural pride as the basis for progress. Sontag substituted woman's inferior position in the aging process for general cultural inferiority.

Sontag saw a double standard of aging, not only because women were supposed to be beautiful and youthful attractiveness fades, but because men got "power compensations" as they aged, and women often did not. As men became higher salaried and more competent, they become more attractive to women, even while losing youthful attractiveness. Women developed skills as homemakers and lovers early on. Housewives did not gain more prestige with experience, while their beauty inevitably faded.

Sontag noted that men too lost youthful beauty, but they were able to trade in one kind of attractiveness for another more mature type. Thus, if men's hair turned gray, they were often described as distinguished looking. When men got facial wrinkles, these were often said to add character to their face. Women, however, must fear every wrinkle and every gray hair for women had to appear young all their lives. Thus, women were locked into a struggle to stay perpetually young—a struggle that they could never win. Men suffered far less from growing old, as long as they retained their economic or professional status.

The cultural results encouraged older men to date and marry younger women, but not the reverse, even though women lived longer than men and women reached their sexual peak later than men. The double standard also explained why female movie stars were finished as sexy leading ladies at age forty, whereas leading men, such as John Wayne and Cary Grant, played sexy leading men until age sixty or more. Sontag suggested that until women confronted this basic cultural inferiority, other gains would be elusive.[25]

Feminists also insisted that body language had political ramifications. When a man opened a door for a healthy woman, he was really asserting physical superiority, and women were admitting they were too weak to take care of themselves. When men put their arms around women coworkers, they were asserting dominance. Some radical feminists urged women to resist traditional body language and custom by duplicating them. For example, in her essay, "The Politics of Touch," Nancy Henley suggested that when men put an arm on a woman's shoulder, she should reciprocate. Men would then get the point without any verbal argument. Her research suggested that men touch women about twice as much as women touch men, and this underscored dominance. For Henley, touch was just "one more tool" men used to "keep women in their place."[26]

Semantics were one of the earliest cultural points of attack. Starting with Ms. as a generic title for women, feminists moved on to replace chairman with chair, spokesman with spokesperson, and mankind with humankind. Feminists pointed out that women were a semantic appendage of men as in woman and female. Words subtly made women appear weak, silly, or both. For example, male athletic teams were aggressively named Tigers, Bears, and so on. Female teams were named Tigerettes, Mama Bears, or Michigams.[27] The male left poked fun at feminist semantics almost as much as middle America, yet it was they who had pioneered a revolutionary semantics in which police became pigs and America became Amerika. "Say the word and be like me," the Beatles had sung, "say the word and you'll be free." The feminists had different words, but they had learned the power of the words from the New Left. Many feminists literally believed that the word was father to the sexist deed. Some male-centered semantics were just silly, such as the textbook phrase: "Menstrual pain accounts for an enormous loss of manpower hours." But other male lingo was degrading. Male phrases describing women as birds, chick, dogs, and foxes were not difficult to critique. The subtle difference between what the term bachelor suggested about a man as opposed to what "spinster" suggested about a woman was more difficult. Yet feminists often conveniently ignored the ways language maligned men. For example, the words maniac, manhandle, manipulate, manure, and manslaughter hardly gave a positive image. Yet feminists usually met such criticism by asking if men had cultural image problems, why was there no men's liberation movement?

Of course most left-wing men had thought of the New Left as a men's movement with women auxiliaries. The New Left was supposed to liberate all oppressed people, but the movement thought of people only in terms of class and race, not gender. However, they did come to think of youth as a class. The simple theory of countercultural change posited the next generation as a group that could be radicalized culturally and thereby alienated socially and politically. Cultural feminists simply substituted women for youth and argued the same thing. However, feminists were more optimistic about using culture to radicalize older women, as well as younger ones.

For the New Left, the counterculture was a hazy, romantic substitute for all the things it failed to accomplish through politics. It acknowledged that the battle likely had been lost, but suggested that the generational war would bring inevitable victory out of political failure. Cultural revolution brought counterculturists a new mystical prestige. At the Chicago Seven Trial in 1969, defendant Abbie Hoffman was asked to tell the court his present occupation. He proudly replied: "I am a cultural revolutionary."[28]

Yippies such as Hoffman and Jerry Rubin often made countercultural theory seem juvenile. However, the theory was in part grounded in Herbert Marcuse's tedious philosophy. Marcuse, a refugee from European fascism, argued that strong national states and systems control individuals through culture rather than politics. The national elites, whether in America or the Soviet Union or nazi Germany, impose a "false consciousness" on the masses. This manipulation is hidden by a comprehensive cultural system of propaganda and miseducation, and is so effective that people come to love their oppression, for they cannot think outside the terms of the culture. The only hope for reform lay in shocking people into exploring new cultural norms.

Thus, for Marcuse economic freedom meant freedom from the manipulative economic system. Freedom of thought meant freedom from media and state propaganda and miseducation. New Left followers of Marcuse logically rejected old left theorists because they still defended the socialist state as exemplified by the Soviet Union. The New Left found the Soviets even more bureaucratic and culturally resistant than America. Marcuse wrote about people caught in a single dimension of thought. If anything, Soviets were more one dimensional than the dreariest American bureaucrats.[29]

Radical feminist philosophy and strategy fit neatly inside Marcuse's thesis. Feminists saw women as the picture within the big picture. They had been culturally brainwashed through propaganda to believe in their own inferiority. They too were victims of a false consciousness. Women had to learn to think outside the prevalent system of thought—to escape the dimension they were trapped in. For feminists, the male-dominated culture was a state within a state. The problem was whether women should break the bonds of male culture and expose those bonds, or create a new, women-centered culture. Another dilemma was whether to try to change men or just women. In practice, feminists attempted all of the above. They exposed sexism, tried to correct it, and tried to form new cultural and social institutions. Countercultural approaches were a natural strategy for feminists. Although they picked up countercultural experience in the New Left, they used it much more extensively and effectively than the male Left. After three decades of women's liberation, there are hardly any cultural institutions, vehicles, or art forms that have not been subject to intense feminist criticism and reform.

Feminists were particularly active in reforming popular culture. Increasingly, they realized that they themselves had been shaped by the media. Film, music, television, and advertising were not only the country of the young, they were the modern cultural environment. These countercultural radicals fit securely into a tradition that historian Christopher Lasch had called the "new radicalism." The new radicals that Lasch described were intellectuals such as Jane Adams, Lincoln Steffens, and Norman Mailer. They distrusted middle-class culture, felt alienated from that culture, and were interested in improving the "quality of American culture as a whole." Their mixing and confusion of politics and culture was peculiar to this new radicalism. Lasch identified the past new radicalism from the vantage point of 1965, and he was clearly surrounded by New Left activists with the same approach. However, the intellectuals Lasch wrote about were a very small minority of activists. By the late 1960s, the new radicalism was everywhere triumphant among youth and could be seen from all corners of the counterculture. Cultural feminists were perhaps the clearest examples of these new radicals.[30]

Earlier in the century, American culture had been very diverse and amorphous, which made it hard to identify and harder to change. Mass media changed that. Film, radio, sound recordings, television, and advertising all provided an increasingly powerful and increasingly national mass culture. After 1945, it became clear that national media were the cultural battle-

grounds. But because radical feminists had been shaped by the media, they sometimes had their toughest battles with themselves. To paraphrase Jerry Farber's analogy between blacks and students in America: For women, "as for black people, the hardest battle" was not "with Mr. Charlie"; it was with "what Mr. Charlie" had "done to your mind."[31]

The New Left had talked a lot about creating a new culture and freeing your mind and "getting your head straight." But they seldom worked at either goal. The male Left, such as the Yippies, were usually long on theory and slogan, but short on practice. Feminists tested the New Left theories about culture and were stronger on practice than theory. Freeing one's mind from a male-dominated mass culture became central to women's liberation. Music, film, and television suddenly became cultural war zones for feminists. At stake were the hearts and minds of the next generation. Those hearts and minds were increasingly mesmerized by songs, ads, motion pictures, and television programs.

PART II

Cultural Liberation: Developing a Modern Feminist Counterculture

3

Songs of Sisterhood: Music as a Countercultural Tool

Women have always used music in America, and, thus, modern feminist singers had a heritage. From the beginning, women sang about their joys and problems. Like many contemporary popular songs, the early ballads were overwhelmingly personal and lacked broad social goals. Indeed, until this century American music has usually been narrowly topical, and because topical songs are, by definition, custom made for a particular time and place, they remain rigid period pieces. There have been few classics of American music. Stephen Foster could hardly become a Melville, questions of talent aside. Foster's music furnishes nostalgia, not art.

In the past, women mostly sang folk songs. Yet, there is little agreement about what folk music is. Folksinger Pete Seeger simply suggests that "if folks sing them, they are folksongs." Folklorists might agree that folk songs are older songs, usually of unknown authorship, passed down by oral tradition in several versions, and changed and altered by various folk musicians. However, when folk music became popular on college campuses in the 1960s, folk music became anything that appeared folky in style or content: Folk songs were identified as ballads that told a story and focused on the basic aspects of life. Moreover, folk music projected an image of both honesty and community. The folksinger traditonally sang to and with his or her own community, whereas modern folksingers often sang to strangers, but they created a feeling of shared intimacy.

It was not surprising that folk music became popular with 1960s college students in general and activists in particular. Genuine feelings, considered corny in the 1950s, became more acceptable in the morally charged civil rights era. Thus, in 1962 *Time* magazine described folksinger Carolyn Hester as a person with "a gift for appearing as if she were delivering the truth every time she" sang. And in 1964, a Harvard student explained that he listened to folk music because it was "honest," because it told true "stories about real life," and because it did not "mince words." Defining folk music was irrelevant. Folk music could be subdivided by historical era, category, and region, but it could not be defined. Folk music was clearly nonexclusive; it was available to all comers.[1]

Young feminists had already experienced folk music in the New Left as protest music—an important genre of the sixties folk revival. Protest music began as a merger of topical political songs and union songs, fused together by union organizer Woody Guthrie in the 1930s. Guthrie, a southwesterner, planted his musical style in New York City, after World War II. There it rather hibernated until the cataclysmic events of the 1960s called a new generation of folk guitarists to arms. Northern songwriters, such as Bob Dylan and Phil Ochs, picked up on the folk tradition and spun out protest songs against racism, the arms race, and middle-class conformity.

As the commercial success increased, the protest characteristics were diluted, but protest ballads continued to supply the most popular music on campus. For example, in 1961 *Newsweek* reported: "Basically the schools and students that support causes support folk music. Find a campus that breeds Freedom Riders, anti-Birch demonstrators, and anti-bomb societies, and you'll find a folk group. The connection is not fortuitous."[2]

By 1965, the merger of rock-and-roll with folk songs, which the music industry christened "folk-rock," brought message songs to the high school crowd, as well as the top ten charts. There was a media vogue for thoughtful songs such as "Universal Soldier" and also for idiotic songs such as "Eve of Destruction." Increasingly, it appeared that protest songs had been poisoned by their own success. As civil rights, antiwar, and student power movements created their own songs, the guitar-strumming, singing demonstrator became a national stereotype. Once the prototype was established, commercial entertainers turned out scores of protest songs that were technically pleasing, general enough to attract diverse tastes, and above all profitable. Originally protest songs grew out of a concrete social situation that called for redress, now they were more likely an expression of individual lifestyle. The most popular folk-rock songs of Bob Dylan and Paul Simon, for example, had by 1968 evaporated into an existentialist haze. By attempting to be all things to all people, the ballads became do-it-yourself protest songs. One could read whatever one wanted into the lines. The tendency was to treat protest music as a lifestyle, divorced from specific goals. By saying everything, the songs, in effect, said nothing.

Another symptom of the breakdown of meaning lay in the relationships between the performer, the song, and the audience. One primary characteristic of traditional folk-protest singers was the inclination to spend as much time introducing and explaining the song as singing it. If the contemporary singers spoke to the audience at all, they tended to talk about everything but the song. It was no longer stylish to sing directly about social evils. The young ears that strained to pick up the vibrations of protest music were usually already convinced that the nation was hung up, corrupt, and decaying. They only wanted to know how to live with the situation. Also, somewhere along the way, folk-protest was swallowed by the general musical category called rock. Musically, rock had assimilated the whole of American music, from ragtime to gospel, and thus folk-protest was hardly the only genre to be devoured, yet there was something especially sad in its demise. Here and there, record stores began filing folk-protest albums in with those of the rock superstars. There was surely no other place for a Bob Dylan, but it somehow seemed sacrilegious to find Joan Baez albums stacked in front of those of the theatrical transvestite, David Bowie, or to see Phil Ochs's protest-song albums sandwiched between Procul Harum records and those of Nico and the Velvet Underground.

Folk-protest had its commercial side, but it also had a proud heritage and left an important social legacy. Rock, however, consumed all and left nothing but the music. From folk-rock to acid-rock to country-rock, the music moved on but in no particular direction. From single performers to small groups to superbands and back again, the rock musicians moved around but not toward anything. Rock reflected a great deal about the people who created and supported it, but it lacked any tangible reason for being.

Protest and topical music declined because the combination of social commitment and folk music was increasingly ridiculed by alienated artists who felt that politics was hopeless. In 1970, Gordon Friesen, a folk critic, complained that although a number of good protest songs were being written, many folksingers sold out by singing "meaningless fluff about . . . clouds, flowers, butterflies . . . Suzannes . . . and the like." Indeed some former topical singers even avoided the term folksinger by describing themselves as singers of contemporary art songs. Joni Mitchell, a popular folksinger, confessed in 1967 that she felt "helpless" when she thought about Vietnam. She simply wrote about what happened to her. And Tim Hardin, another gifted singer-songwriter said that he "was too involved" in his personal life "to write about the world." Perhaps, a 1970 *New Yorker* cartoon summed up the new attitude best. It depicted a young female folksinger (guitar in hand) about to begin her performance at a coffeehouse. Before commencing, she advises her audience that since her songs had no "social or political significance" she would like to assure them that she opposed the Vietnamese War and favored legalizing marijuana, boycotting California grapes, and federal control of the economy.[3]

Because radical feminists separated from the New Left, just as topical music declined, they escaped the malaise. Feminist songwriters felt everything they wrote broke new ground. Whether they performed traditional songs, wrote topical ballads, or wrote about their own experiences, they felt they were speaking to the condition of all women. In the early 1960s, most of the best-known folk and protest songs were written by men, such as Bob Dylan, Phil Ochs, and Paul Simon, but were often sung by popular women folksingers, such as Joan Baez and Judy Collins. The women's liberation movement greatly encouraged women songwriters. In 1976, the introduction to *All Our Lives: A Women's Songbook* summed it up: "As women and as feminists who love folk music and who love to sing, we have produced this book as a reflection of our own struggles in a society which still has so little room for a woman with a mind of her own—even less for a woman with a song of her own." The songbook split between traditional songs with both positive and negative images of women and contemporary feminist ballads. The traditional songs were largely courting songs such as "Beware O Take Care," which warns about young men, and "I'll Not Marry at All," which asserts independence from unfaithful husbands.[4] Roughly 90 percent of the 18th- and 19th-century courting songs are complaints by women about the infidelity of men. The other 10 percent are mostly complaints by men about shrewish wives, such as "The Farmer's Cursed Wife," which complains about a wife so fierce, even the devil would not take her. Although women could not properly talk about men's infidelities in public or print before 1900, they did sing about them in traditional folksongs.

Traditional songs also furnished a bridge between women's liberation and the suffrage movement. The suffragist obsession with procedural rights, along with their fevered moral righteousness, pervade suffrage ballads. Songs such as "Let Us All Speak Our Minds," "The Suffrage Flag," "Giving the Ballot to the Mothers," and "She Wore a Yellow Ribbon" give the same clear message: The nation was an extended family, and the body politic, whether local or state, needed mothering. Tactical, ideological, and class differences divided the suffragists, but the maternal wrath and self-righteousness common to all wings of the movement shine through the songs.[5]

Compared with the suffrage ballads, the recent women's liberation songs are much more diverse. They range from worker's songs to ballads of cultural pride and psychological independence. The mood is much more strident; the goals are much more fundamental. Songs such as "The Modern Union Maid" (a parody of Woody Guthrie's 1936 ballad), "Stand and Be Counted" (a marching song), "The Freedom Ladies" (with its firm, but good-natured, declaration of independence), and "Papa" (a put-down of sexist male rock musicians by the Chicago Women's Liberation Rock Band) all capture the verve and complexity of the modern feminists.[6]

Contemporary feminists were brought up on protest music and rock, and they knew music's great potential influence. Youth were into music as nothing else. If feminists wanted to reach the next generation, music was clearly the best countercultural tool. As rock performer Frank Zappa noted, many sixties youths were not loyal to flag, country, or doctrine, but only to the music. Never before in history had music meant so much to a generation. The new music, and the records and tapes that disseminated it, had become the real alternate media as opposed to the underground press. If there was a counterculture, surely it lived between the microgrooves.

As the power of popular music became clearer, it had become an ideological battleground. The political right-wing attacked rock music for encouraging and glorifying drug use and criticized protest music for brainwashing youth. For example, in 1966, Rev. David Noebel of Tulsa's Christian Crusade did not agree with Francis Bacon that "generally music feedeth the disposition of the spirit which it findeth." On the contrary, he seemed obsessed with Alexander Pope's observation: "What will a child learn sooner than a song?" In a long, overdocumented book titled *Rhythm, Riots, and Revolution* and a short pamphlet titled *Communism, Hypnotism and the Beatles,* Noebel charged that protest songs in particular and folk and rock music in general were part of a communist plot to subvert America's youth. Although Noebel's specific charges leaned toward the ridiculous, as a frightened, fundamentalist patriot, he was one of the few individuals who grasped the immense power of the music.[7]

Feminists found it easy to believe in music's hypnotic and possibly negative influence. As they tried to create prowoman music, they were forced to confront the images of women in recent popular music—especially rock. The result was a new school of feminist critics who examined all types of popular music for sexist imagery and found much of the recent musical heritage suspect.

Music has always been suspect. Philosophers and politicians from Plato to Spiro Agnew have warned about its sinister effects, but its critics were usually entrenched power brokers who feared that songs might stir the masses, corrupt individuals, or provide a proletarian rallying point. For example, in recent years American conservatives identified communal folk singing with communism and rock music with youthful radicalism. Of course, right-wing groups such as the Ku Klux Klan used organizing songs, and although country-and-western lyrics have often been conservative, they, too, were proletarian and antiestablishment in origin. Thus, contemporary attacks on sexist popular music are something new. The feminist criticism is quite familiar to those brought up on right-wing musical paranoia, but now it is the agitators who accuse the establishment of using music to brainwash the masses. Did the communists infiltrate folk music? Did drug pushers shape rock? Regardless, feminists point out that men control all music. For some critics, the musicians, singers, disc jockeys, songwriters, and record producers represented one huge chauvinist conspiracy that dwarfed right-wing communist nightmares. For example, Betsy Greiner-Shumick warned:

Wherever we are, we are surrounded by music. Whether it be Muzak of the supermarket and dentist's office, or the bus driver's radio, we are its captive.... It is simple. It is sexy. It is accessible. The trouble is that over the years the message that it hammers into us is male sexual superiority. . . . Pop music is propaganda.[8]

The specific charges were legion. Male disc jockeys insulted their female audience with housewife jokes and stupid giveaways. Because few women were big pop stars and even fewer were writers, most songs portrayed women as "love objects, mothers, nags, tramps, homewreckers, honky tonk angels, regular angels, wicked witches, wives, bitches, sweethearts, babies, pets, illusive, abusive and dead."[9] Moreover, it was difficult for chauvinist writers to redeem themselves. For example, whereas older Bob Dylan songs were attacked for putting down women as bitches, his newer songs were criticized for putting women up on a pedestal. Early on, Dylan sang boldly about his individual predatory male freedom; later, he sang gently about the love and joys of the nuclear family. However, for feminist critics, Dylan simply exhibits both sides of the sexist coin.[10]

Feminists were quick to confess that they had been taken in by rock music because it had challenged the status quo. But like Saul on the road, each sooner or later had a conversion experience and came to see that rock culture was only a groovy microcosm of the brutal larger society, which, according to Cheryl Helm, had "ruthlessly amplified" the rule of "male supremacy." Post–1965 rock supposedly trapped women between the conventional roles of "sweethearts, wives and mothers" and a new identity as "liberated chicks whose sole purpose was to gratify the demands of any and all men." Helm, like other feminist critics, concluded that although times have changed, rock had not. Indeed, it remained "written, produced, packaged, and sold by men who regard women (on or off stage) as exploitable, expendable commodities."[11]

The struggle against sexist music included consciousness raising, alternative music, working within establishment media, and direct consumer protest. Successful consciousness raising could make a woman feel that listening to Tom Jones sing "She's a Lady" was the equivalent of an African American listening to "Old Black Joe." Feminist singers on independent labels operated as alternate media, although independent-minded stars, such as Helen Reddy and Bette Midler, sometimes worked within the industry. Consumer protests, such as complaints about the content of radio music and the lack of female disc jockeys, were also a possibility. Pressing for feminist-oriented DJs was particularly important, because they had direct control over the music. Although there were a few women announcers in the large urban areas, feminist critic Jean Hunter was probably justified in noting that the last famous woman DJ was Tokyo Rose.[12]

Most feminist, musical energy has centered on producing and encouraging alternative music. Working within the system had not proved very effective. Unfortunately, whenever a Janis Joplin, Carole King, or even a Helen Reddy made it big, their focus invariably shifted to musical production rather than content and effect. For example, in 1972, Helen Reddy rose to stardom on the strength of her hit single, "I Am Woman." Heralded as the anthem of women's liberation, the song sold twenty-five thousand copies a day for months and was followed by an *I Am Woman* album. Reddy noted that the best thing about the record was that she "had a chance to raise consciousness among American women en masse," but she also valued the economic security that went with success and allowed her to be herself. As a woman, she would "always feel pressures"; however, a plush Hollywood home with swimming pool and his-and-her Mercedes cars in the garage obviously eased her stress substantially.[13] Thus, feminists bitterly complained that, unfortunately, feminist music was either inaccessible to masses of women or controlled by men. Either a local feminist singer made a record and sold thirty-five "copies to her friends" because nobody had heard of her, or Helen Reddy sold a "million copies of 'I Am Woman' and the women's movement," which made her record successful, received "not one penny" of the millions the record produced.[14]

Not surprisingly, many feminist singers stressed the need to create music apart from men. When Ellen Shumsky left "an all-woman environment" to attend a 1970 folk festival, she was shocked by the subtle and direct sexism of the singers, lyrics, and situations. Particularly noxious to Shumsky were the male-female performing duos. She generally found the female partner to be totally supportive. "The man almost invariably introduced and commented on the songs. When the woman did speak, the man seemed to need to verify what she said." When a male performer noted that he was going to sing "a fine male chauvinist verse," the audience (including most women) just laughed. At another folk festival, Shumsky attended a "women's workshop" and found that all the songs concerned women's relationships to men. She felt that although men sang of "their quests and struggles and perceptions and feelings," women sang and looked "through the filter of men's experience." She concluded that women would not really grow until they "looked in the mirror" and described themselves, and this could only occur apart from men. According to Shumsky, something happened "to women in a space absent of men." They were forced "to rely on themselves and reach deep in themselves to cope and create, and they" blossomed.[15]

Clearly one way to accomplish this was through small alternative record companies, and this process proved successful. Olivia Records was a good example of such a group. In 1974, the pioneer company described itself as "a five-woman collective." Its goals were to create an alternative economic group "with hiring and salary based on need and decided by the workers," and to present "high-quality women's music" for the public. They defined women's music as that "which speaks honestly and realistically about women's lives," while stressing women's needs, anger, fears, dreams, and relationships with other women. In short, Olivia intended to provide feminist musicians an opportunity to record something other than heterosexual blues. According to Olivia member Ginny Berson, the top forty hits suggested that "the only thing women did was supply sex and then complain because 'he left me' or be glad because 'he didn't leave me.' "[16]

Yet most of the small, feminist-oriented, alternative record companies were less interested in ideological pronouncements than in just making music. As a result, since 1972 they have produced a number of innovative records which largely defy categorization. Early on there were hard-core, rather humorless albums, such as *Reviving a Dream: Songs for Women's Liberation*, put out by Femme Records in 1972, and *Mountain Moving Day*, released by Rounder Records, but there was also the whimsical collection of old and new folk songs about women titled *Virgo Rising: The Once and Future Woman*, put out by Thunderbird Records. *Reviving a Dream* was an older, 1950s civil-rights style protest record. The songs were written, produced, and sung by Ruth Batchelor, a New York feminist, and she was aided by a strident chorus, titled the "Voices of Liberation." The songs ranged from a solidarity, union-style hymn, "Stand and Be Counted" to "The Princess" (an anti–fairy tale which describes a cast-off wife) to "Barefoot and Pregnant" (a tale of rural, poor white, male chauvinism). Batchelor's songs were too straightforward to be musically interesting, and the lyrics were too obvious to stir the imagination. However, here and there was a memorable line, and the album had an infectious spirit and gusto throughout.[17] *Mountain Moving Day* was musically exciting, if technically disappointing. One side of the album belonged to The Chicago Women's Liberation Rock Band, the other featured The New Women's Liberation Rock Band. Although both groups were out to show that women could play good rock, they only established that some women played only mediocre rock. Nevertheless, the recording was lively and sassy and clearly supported both bands as the self-proclaimed "agit-rock arm" of their respective local women's movements. The record notes proclaimed that the bands intended to "use the power of rock to transform our present world" into a vision of "what the world could be like," and at the same time to create music that embodied "the radical, feminist, humanitarian vision" they shared. At first glance, lines such as "Jodi wants to tell the boss to get off" (from a ballad titled "Secretary") and "papa don't lay that shit on me" (from "Papa," a song-title pseudonym for male rock stars), did not seem particularly humanitarian. Yet, in context the angry phrases made their point forcefully. The problem here was musical. With the exception of "Papa," the songs just did not work musically. There was too much chanting , too much lyric repetition, and too little melody and arrangement. The result was often close to cheerleading. Song titles such as "Ain't Gonna Marry," "Abortion Song," and "Sister Witch" tell you what was being cheered.[18]

The subtleness the latter two records lacked was there to spare on *Virgo Rising: The Once and Future Woman*.[19] The album featured a delightful, insightful anthology of songs for and about women, and was performed by six different singers and groups. The artists included both professionals and amateurs who ranged in age from seventeen to seventy-two. Janet Smith, a west coast folksinger, was the best of a good lot. Smith's rendition of her own songs, "Freedom Ladies March," "Talking Want Ad," and "Mama's Peaches," included clever feminist barbs, tastefully set to music. Charley's Aunts, a trio of sisters, added verve with a parody of Woody Guthrie's classic "Union Maid" ballad and the venerable folksinger Malvina Reynolds contributed three of her older, droll, prowoman songs. For good reasons, feminists greeted *Virgo Rising* with enthusiasm. One record reviewer noted: "I love it. I get dizzy, giggly high and strong-laughing, loving high on it. There are songs to diaper babies by, songs to rivet or sculpt by, to drink or type or draw up the terms of your divorce by."[20]

In the case of the album *Hazel and Alice* (released in 1973), effective feminist songs came in a musical package that easily stood on its own musical artistry. As released by Rounder Records in 1973, the album featured Hazel Dickens and Alice Gerard, both skilled bluegrass musicians with

roots deep into traditional rural music. On one album side, they sang traditional bluegrass as well as anybody; on the other side, they turned to their
own compositions and shone equally well. Easily the best of their originals
were two feminist tunes—Alice Gerard's "Custom Made Woman Blues"
and Hazel Dickens's "Don't Put Her Down You Helped Put Her There." The
first song covered the problems of a rural wife trying to follow *Cosmopolitan* magazine advice on how to hold her man, and the second ballad puts the
blame for the bar floozy squarely on her male companions.[21]

Hazel and Alice, with its rural, family, working-class orientation, neatly
bridged the gap between the consciousness-raising, countercultural feminist records and those of the more overtly political socialist Left. The rem-
nants of America's young Left had increasingly realized the threat that
women's liberation posed to their already declining ranks. Not surprisingly,
after 1972 the New Left began to stress women as a specially oppressed
group. The oppressor, of course, was always the unfeeling capitalist state.
Two good examples of the new relationship between socialism and feminism were Barbara Dane's album *I Hate the Capitalist System* (1973) and
the Red Star Singers's album *The Force of Life* (1974), both released by
Paredon Records.[22] Barbara Dane's album proceeded roughly from the union songs of the 1930s (such as the title song) to ballads of the 1960s such as
the North Vietnamese "Song of the Coats" and a Dane song titled "The Kent
State Massacre." Yet, interestingly enough the album ended with "Working
Class Woman," a ballad written by Dane and others in 1973 and filled with
women's liberation themes within a socialist context. The song's heroine
works in a factory, and although her "kids are in high school," the boss calls
her "girl." Despite her many problems, the song's heroine always sees a
brighter future for women. One verse ends: "But I'm a hard-working
woman, and the future is mine." Another suggests that if the boss controls
today, tomorrow is hers, and the final verse proclaims and thrice repeats:
"I'm a working class woman and the future is mine." Barbara Dane's
rough-hewn, stoic voice was quite suited to her material here, and the songs
successfully reflected the continuity of working-class problems from the
1930s through the 1970s.

The Force of Life was a much livelier album with a totally contemporary
anger. The Red Star Singers came on as a cross between the Yippies and the
Stanford SDS with a few socialist and third world women thrown in for
good measure. The songs were all irresistibly upbeat and hit hard at the image of the oppressive national State. Songs such as "Belly of the Monster,"
"Pig Nixon," and "Vietnam Will Win" quickly told you where the Red Star
Singers were politically. Each album side also featured a militant women's
liberation song—"I Still Ain't Satisfied" on one side and "The Women's

Health Song" on the other. These songs mocked the progress of women's liberation as "co-optation." One line, for example, declared: "I ain't askin' for crumbs, I want the whole meal."

In a somewhat different category was a musically top-notch 1974 album called *Lavender Jane Loves Women*, released by Women's Wax Works in New York. The frankly and aggressively lesbian songs were sung by Lavender Jane, a musical trio consisting of Alix Dobkin, Kay Gardner, and Patches Attom. Dobkin was the musical mind behind this record, and her pithy lyrics and expressive professional voice were very effective at registering lesbian pride.[23] Highlights of the album were "Fantasy Girl" with its rich satire and "The View from Gay Head" with its claim of lesbian superiority. The album consciously blended lesbian and feminist concerns, but its most striking characteristic was the ability to shatter popular lesbian stereotypes. The songs tended to depict the lesbian as a superfeminist, but exhibited a wide range, from organizing songs to love ballads.

The most talented and hardest to characterize of the early feminist singers was Holly Near. Her two 1974 Redwood label albums, *Hang in There* and *Holly Near: A Live Album*, showed steady growth and brilliant talents as both songwriter and singer.[24] *The Hang in There* album stressed songs against the Vietnam War, but it included two sensitive feminist songs—"It's More Important to Me" (about how competition for men drives women apart) and "Strong" (a ballad about the social conditioning of women). The second "live album" fulfilled the promises of the first. Here and there, her lyrics were too forced and mushy, but her voice, style, and inflections carried even the weaker songs. Fully half of the second album's songs were feminist, and others considered the strengths and weaknesses of male-female relationships. Near's voice is wide ranging and expressive. On highs, she sounds very much like Joni Mitchell; in the lower registers, she can belt out lyrics like Helen Reddy, but her voice inflections are strikingly varied and emotive. Her live album, *Feeling Better*, a satire on high school, sex-role expectations, was the best showcase for her talents. Near was easily the early artistic leader of the feminist singers.

On balance, the early music of women's liberation was far better than one would have expected. Art and politics are often joined, but seldom compatible, and women's liberation music was necessarily political. Yet political mission often fuels the imagination, and audience enthusiasm can provide effective creative incentives. Considering the political pressures, the most surprising thing about early feminist music was its rich variety. Feminist critics have sometime patronized women who made their musical mark in traditional ways—with acoustic guitar and piano accompaniment, for example. The big challenge has been to prove that women can play rock and that hard rock need not be sexist to be good. Ironically, the best feminist music has largely followed women's traditional musical forms. Yet those feminist singers who followed in the musical footsteps of Joan Baez, Joni Mitchell, Judy Collins, and Carole King have not been put down in practice. For one thing, the women's movement stressed the need to support all women artists. For another, feminists realized the potential that quality feminist music offered for making new recruits think seriously about the women's movement. Feminists also appreciated the striking way music raised specific issues and the enthusiasm it engendered at live rallies. The largely traditional women the movement hoped to attract were more likely to seriously consider a subtle, sensitive, well-done ballad than a second-rate, derivative rock number. The woman rock musician generally got more attention, but often drew attention to herself at the expense of her music.

Feminism quickly concluded that the power of music was its ability to communicate rather than its ability to shock or cross male boundaries. As Barbara Dane explained:

We need to control our own culture again. . . . We've been taught to think of "culture" in two wrong ways: Either as something too far above us, like the so-called classics, or as something frivolous, made for escaping our day-to-day problems. It's neither of these, but it's the stuff of which human communication is made, that which expresses the connection between us all.[25]

Women's liberation music seemed to hit its first peak in 1974. In February 1974, *Paid My Dues*, "the first feminist journal of women and music," appeared, and in June 1974, the first National Women's Music Festival took place in Champaign-Urbana on the campus of the University of Illinois. The festival did not attract many big name acts, and *Paid My Dues* failed to attract many subscribers, but both were models. Soon there were other local and national music festivals, and suddenly there were articles in many alternative and mainstream magazines on women and popular music. After 1974, there was less criticism of negative images in male music and more talk about women creating their own images in their own music. For example, in 1976 the *All Our Lives* songbook argued for a woman's culture because culture was "a subtle form of power" that shaped ideas, and those who controlled culture had largely been men who had "seen women as objects." They had created many of the ideas women held about themselves as women. The songbook editors felt that the "general feeling about women and creativity" suggested: "Men create culture, women create children, and women who seriously try to create anything other than children are deviants who can never be truly fulfilled." They urged women musicians to learn musical technique from men, but not to pick up their ruthlessness or the oppressive way most male musicians related to their audiences. As for men, they could not be expected to be comfortable with women's music, for they would just be "eavesdroppers" in a woman's culture.[26]

The songbook had included traditional folksongs to place women's music in an historical perspective, but clearly its heart was with the contemporary feminist songwriters. The editors acknowledged that most women still lacked the technical expertise for excellent rock and that they would have to concentrate on folk music. However, they thought that had advantages, because folk music was for people to sing rather than for superstars to dub and redub in a studio. They defined folk music as both traditional and contemporary songs, "simply accompanied."

Folk music had other advantages for feminists. The public had been "taught to want honey-throated pristine girls-next-door singing ballads, bluesy wronged lovers, or back up choruses." With folk music, however, feminists could "reach people in small, comfortable and unadulterated ways." The problem was musical content. What were the characteristics of women's songs? The songbook editors had no clear answer, but they defined women's songs in either of two categories: "traditional women's songs (those sung about or by women, with particular emphasis on . . . women)" or "feminist songs (those written since the recent" women's movement) which raised "specifically feminist issues." Traditional songs could be love songs or lullabies, but they had to give a sense of woman's past. Feminist songs should express "self-definition, collective struggles and solutions to women's problems." The latter songs could unite the movement, the editors argued, because they reinforced "the solidarity that women in the movement" felt. Furthermore, they could "serve as the first flash of insight for women who" had "not yet thought much about" the women's movement.[27]

The *All Our Lives* songbook tried to use music as a tool, but it overcomplicated its use. It tried to fit often powerful and compelling new and old music into a cultural ideology. This had been the bane of the radical feminist groups throughout the period 1967 to 1973. They insisted on a full-blown theory for all their actions, tactics, and techniques. Simple success and satisfaction were not enough. Everything had to be part of a wider comprehensive plan. Luckily, women's music could not be categorized, theorized, or confined, any more than folk-protest music could. Women's music was wild, diverse, and usually out of step with theory. Ironically, the songbook itself proved this. It included a spectrum of traditional songs, mixed with subtle vocational protests such as Peggy Seeger's "I'm Gonna Be an Engineer." There were also aggressively lesbian songs, such as Meg Christian's

"Ode to a Gym Teacher, " and riotously funny songs, such as Ca Berman's "The Armpit Song." The last verse of "The Armpit Song" noted that most people didn't shave their head and "if pits were" supposed "to be bare" people would "shed." It concluded that it's "lovely" to have hair there, "for what's an armpit without the hair?"[28] On balance, the lively songs and angry feminist music critics rose above the terse formulas and rationales. In the period after 1976, women's music grew even more diverse and crossed all theoretical lines and actual genres. Women's music had a life of its own, or more precisely, lives of its own, which depended on the individual artist and not the mass movement.

That life and those lives are best traced through Ladyslipper, Inc.—a North Carolina non-profit corporation, founded in 1976 to distribute women's records and promote women's concerts. By 1984, Ladyslipper was also producing records, but its main function was widely circulating their "Ladyslipper Catalog" and "Resource Guide of Records and Tapes by Women." This catalog was a cornucopia of lore and information about the many women artists recording for alternative companies. Ladyslipper sold records and facilitated concert appearances for almost every woman musician who had recorded. Their name came from the exquisite North American orchid on the endangered species list.

Ladyslipper, Inc. was far from an endangered business. With a staff that grew from two full-time workers to a dozen full and part-time workers, they became the center of women's music just as *Ms.* magazine was the center of women's liberation. Their catalog grew from twenty-eight pages in 1980 to forty-five pages in 1984 and to seventy-nine pages in 1986.[29] By 1980, the catalog already had seven categories of women's music, including classical, jazz, and blues, besides the four folk fields. The 1984 catalog added the additional categories of New Age, Punk and New Wave, Rock, Calypso and Reggae, Gospel, Soul, and Disco. The 1986 catalog featured the new categories of Comedy, Girl Groups, Country, and Children. It also split the international folk category into seven ethnic or national areas.

The most interesting and most diverse category was the feminist music listing. The 1980 catalog called it "Women's Music & Music of Special Interest to Feminists." It included the pioneer women's liberation albums from the early 1970s, such as *Mountain Moving Day*; older women topical folk singer albums, such as those of Peggy Seeger and Malvina Reynolds; and the work of the first new feminist stars, such as Holly Near and Alix Dobkin. It also featured records of newer feminist topical singers, such as Willie Tyson and Kristin Lems, who had worked their way through the movement by singing live for women's groups. Tyson's first three albums, *Full Count*, *Debutante*, and *Willie Tyson*, showcased her raucous satire;

they included songs such as "Witching Hour," "Debutante Ball," "You'd Look Swell in Nothing," "Mommy," and "Will There Be Muzak in Heaven." Kristin Lems, a founder of the National Women's Music Festival in 1974, did more straight topical music with a cutting satiric edge. Her "Ballad of the ERA" was an instant classic, although she became equally well known later for her satire on breast fetishism, "Mammary Glands." Aggressively lesbian albums, such as Alix Dobkin's *Living with Lesbians* and a seven-woman German band album, *Flying Lesbians*, were always listed under the general feminist listing. This clearly showed that Ladyslipper felt lesbians were an integral part of the feminist movement rather than a separate category.[30]

Despite their openness to many kinds of women's music, the Ladyslipper Collective could not resist answering the big question—what is women's music? In the 1984 catalog, they asserted the most important thing about women's music was the messages it sent: "It takes women seriously. It springs from a feminist consciousness, utilizing women's talent, intellect, emotion, energy, and spirit. Its production, presentation and finances are controlled by women. The essence of women's music is the integration of all these things and belongs to all of us as women."[31]

Even after two decades of women's music, it could still no more be defined than folk music. Trying to define what almost everyone agrees on leads to division, not accord. Each piece of music and each artist stands on their own merit. A song that may profoundly influence one audience or individual may leave many others untouched. Music's influence cannot be understood ideologically or statistically. For example, at a 1967 symposium in Cuba, Xuan Hong, a Viet Cong singer, defined a protest song as "militant in content, national in form and popular in idiom."[32] These criteria had little relation to American protest songs. Our most effective protest ballads have been subtle rather than militant, poetic rather than merely idiomatic, and their orientation has been universal rather than nationalistic. American protest music has invariably sought to make individuals feel guilty and responsible. However similar the goals, the music has always been very diverse. And so it is with women's music. Any music played by women or speaking to women, is women's music. Feminist music could not be limited. It was open to all.

The most serious feminist singers have usually been on the fringes of mass culture, but their influence could grow geometrically through their effect on others. The small audiences who heard them often contained many activists who influenced many others. Also, feminist songwriters constantly influenced more popular writers and singers (of either sex) with their lyrics and their own personal commitment.

Songs can only take people so far. They provide inspiration and insight, but not goals or means. Feminist musical ideologists tended to make women's music an end in itself. As Pete Seeger noted, songs after all "lie only halfway between thought and action," and unfortunately "may become a substitute for both." Yet many women embraced feminist music because it gave meaning to their lives and underscored their personal experience; it also just made them feel good. The best feminist music was both poetry and art. President John F. Kennedy cogently expressed the value of the poetic arts when he observed: "When power corrupts, poetry cleanses. For art establishes the basic human truth which must serve as the touchstone of our judgment."[33]

The best feminist songwriters were indeed a cleansing force. They had the revivalist's faith that to hear about evil was to hate it. Their songs radicalized some women who had never been influenced by political appeals. Their audience extended far beyond the concert stage or feminist meeting hall. It was both private and national. The music's influence could not be effectively traced anymore than the content or style could be defined. One woman's feminist song was another woman's pop standard. Similarly, a heterosexual love song sung by a lesbian was a lesbian love song.

By 1986, the Ladyslipper catalog generally gave up on rigid definition and offered a much wider range of musical fare—including some major record label stars such as Tina Turner and Diana Ross. Also included were mainstream folk stars such as Joni Mitchell, Laura Nyro, and Phoebe Snow. Records by Bette Midler, Cher, Cyndi Lauper, Bonnie Raitt, and Janis Joplin all appeared in the rock section, along with virtually unknown women rockers such as Marsha Chapman.

Another early center of women's music was Olivia Records, founded in 1973 by a women's collective. Olivia was an all-woman company. They made a point of doing without men, even if that meant a temporary lower level of performance. They were out to show that women were competent by themselves. Olivia applied feminist principles to business. For example, their concert productions regularly supplied child care for ticket holders. They were about halfway between a business and a feminist organization. In 1983, after a year of modest success, one could become an Olivia "member" for $25 and receive one album and a T-shirt. For $100, one could be a sponsoring member and receive four albums and a T-shirt. Prospective customers were asked to join Olivia "in developing women's music." It was not too far-fetched. One satisfied customer wrote back: "Women all over the country are somehow united through the music of your female artists."[34] In the 1970s especially, Olivia had several of the freshest, liveliest, new feminist artists. The Olivia group included Meg Christian, Cris Williamson,

Teresa Trull, Bebe K'Roche, Linda Tillery, and a young, relatively unknown named Bonnie Raitt. The two stars of the Olivia operation were Meg
Christian and Cris Williamson. Christian's first album, *I Know You Know*,
was the first feminist classic, and Cris Williamson's album, *The Changer
and the Changed*, was the big best-seller of alternative women's music.
Williamson was perhaps the Bob Dylan of feminism. Her ballads were subtle, often whimsical, and open to interpretation. Olivia billed itself as "the
largest women's recording company." More importantly, it was the first collective to put out interesting, original feminist music. That it accomplished
this without the help of any men was probably irrelevant, but this added to
its mystique. As women's music grew in the 1970s, both on the alternative
side and in some mainstream areas, Olivia became just another record company, whose earliest pioneer albums were still its most important ones.

The one early feminist singer who reached out most effectively to other
groups was Holly Near. Although she was a prolesbian feminist, she never
allowed either lesbianism or feminism to define her interests or songs. During the Vietnam War, Near toured with Jane Fonda and Donald Sutherland
on their infamous antiwar coffeehouse shows for American troops in both
Asia and America. In the 1980s, she teamed with Ronnie Gilbert, an older
left-wing folksinger who had sung with Pete Seeger in the 1950s. Near and
Gilbert's songs were a mélange of social activism, and their alliance healed
wounds between feminists and the old Left. In 1984, she also toured with a
seven-man Latin American group, Inti-Illuminatti, singing against President Reagan's South American policies. The alliance with men bothered
some feminists, but Near had always musically collaborated with a child-
hood friend, Jeff Langley. Her own record company, Redwood Records, used
her success to record another dozen male and female artists from various cultures. She calls herself a "cultural worker," and her work has garnered respect across the liberal-activist political spectrum. In January 1985, *Ms.*
magazine gave her an achievement award "for creativity as a composer, performer, and lyricist . . . and as a woman who lives the message she teaches."[35]

If alternative feminist music was a triumph of women's liberation and an
effective countercultural tool, mainstream music presented much more
mixed results. At first glance, it seemed that there was nowhere to go but up
for women music stars. Female rock stars in the 1950s and 1960s were
stereotypically cute and sexy. Connie Francis and Brenda Lee offered good
examples. The 1960s girl groups, such as the Shirelles and Ronnettes, had
high heels and beehive hair, but projected a similar, if updated, cute sexiness. They often sang stupid lyrics because record producers thought dumb
was cute. Looking sexy, acting dumb, and sounding cute helped sell records—according to conventional wisdom.

The folk music boom of the middle 1960s helped change women's image in several ways. The archetypical female folksinger was a Joan Baez or a Judy Collins. They were not cute and sexy; they were saintly and outspoken. Clearly identified with progressive politics, the female folksinger enjoyed a rough equality with male folkies. As a detached observer of traditional songs, women could sing men's songs and vice-versa. Indeed, on traditional songs female singers seemed preferable. However, with contemporary folk songs and topical music, men took the lead. Bob Dylan, Phil Ochs, and Tom Paxton led the way, although singers such as Baez and Collins later developed the confidence to write their own songs. The women always had the lead in performance. Baez and Collins sang folk songs beautifully; most male performers just sang beautiful folk songs, although male guitar accompaniment was usually superior. As women folksingers sang the roles of cowboys, soldiers, and whalers, they broke taboos on what kinds of songs women could sing. When Judy Collins changed the ballad "Man of Constant Sorrow" to "Maid of Constant Sorrow," she helped make it easier for Janis Joplin to role-reverse the hit, "Me and Bobby McGee" a decade later. Kris Kristofferson had originally written "Bobby McGee" to be sung by a man.

Another confidence builder was folk instrumentation. Female music stars did not usually play instruments before 1960. Almost every woman folksinger, however, played at least passable acoustic guitar, and some were among the best guitarists. Even Janis Joplin started her career playing her own acoustic guitar accompaniment. Judy Collins was proficient on several instruments and had strong classical training in piano. This meant that women were no longer band add ons; they were often one-woman bands. The tradition continued. For example, in the 1970s Joni Mitchell became a gifted guitar player with a penchant for open tunings, and she also became a solid pianist. Her restlessness later took her musical skills into jazz and she continued to excel. Bonnie Raitt, starting in 1971, steadily increased her blues-guitar mastery in a field previously reserved for men. Raitt also played the electric Fender Stratocaster guitar with both skill and wild abandon. Although rock was a male province except for the occasional Grace Slick (of The Jefferson Airplane group) or Janis Joplin, female folksingers not only held their own, but were actually gaining on men.

The next generation of female folksingers sported long hair and simple dress, but had little else in common with Joan Baez and company. Emmylou Harris, Maria Muldaur, and Linda Ronstadt were sweet instead of saintly, and they generated considerably less social voltage. They sang about romance and their personal experiences rather than social issues. Their relative blandness contributed to the difficulty of separating them from country or general pop singers. Perhaps Melanie (Safka) with her liberal political leanings and saccharine cute ditties was halfway between the old and the new woman folksingers. Melanie was neither saintly or sexy; she was simply the nice girl next door.

Yet amidst the girl groups, folk madonnas, and sexy ladies came solid lyrics by artful women songwriters. Carole King wrote "One Fine Day" and thereafter became the modern Irving Berlin of soft rock with hit after hit. Other artists covered many of her songs, but her 1971 *Tapestry* album was a blockbuster. Cynthia Weil wrote "Uptown" and a host of other meaningful songs. Joni Mitchell wrote critically acclaimed ballads such as "The Circle Game," and "Both Sides Now." Mitchell's songs were popularized by others such as Judy Collins, but Mitchell established herself as a sensitive, artistic singer-songwriter on a par with the other two famous Canadian folk songwriters—Gordon Lightfoot and Leonard Cohen. Women such as King, Weil, Mitchell, and Collins had mainstream success, not because they were sexy, but because their music was good. The same could be said of the first female rock singers—Grace Slick and Janis Joplin. All these women were played by serious FM music stations, while AM stations generally kept playing sexy girl groups, such as the Supremes and Martha and the Vandellas.

The women's movement opened the door for new types of female singers in the 1970s. For example, it fostered the career of Helen Reddy, the Australian who catapulted to the top of the charts with the song, "I Am Woman." Thereafter, Reddy spun out hit after hit with songs about isolated, alienated women on the fringe of society and the edge of desperation. Whether it was "Delta Dawn," waiting decades for the man who never came; "Angie Baby" who related only to the radio, "Georgy Girl" who was generally flaky; or sad-eyed ladies of the lowlands such as "Eleanor Rigby," "Ruby Tuesday," or "Suzanne," these women were hurting. But such songs usually did not show who hurt these victims—men, society, or themselves. Reddy was mostly a conventional careerist, but it suddenly paid to be identified with women's liberation. Reddy got rid of her wig and padded bra and now appeared braless in simple, natural clothes. She said that she "used to feel like a female impersonator." Evidently, her identification with the woman's movement put her in a special class. The NBC-TV network agreed that she would not have to wear a bra, but she would have to shave her armpits.[36]

Other popular woman singers broke other barriers. Bette Midler made it easier for women to be comedic. Deborah Harry, lead singer of the British group, Blondie, pioneered demonic independence, and a more mature Linda Ronstadt projected philosophical independence. It became increasingly difficult to make general comments about popular women singers. Black women singers had often projected an aggressive independence as blues singers. Now they could carry those attitudes over from rhythm and blues into mainstream music. By the 1980s, a strutting Tina Turner consistently projected the strong woman motif, and the Pointer Sisters (June, Ruth, and Anita) made the sassy woman popular. Even Donna Summer who in the 1970s had been the quintessential, burlesque disco queen was singing strong woman songs in the 1980s—such as her big hit, "She Works Hard for the Money."

Rock musicianship was the real 1970s frontier for women. Women could play folk guitar, blues guitar and even electric blues guitar, but could they play hard electric rock? The earliest notable slide-guitar player was Ellen McIllwaine, who put out her first record in 1968. But her excellent work was appreciated more by professionals than the record-buying public. Suzi Quatro, a bassist, played decent hard rock, but was more famous for her black leather outfits and appearances on the *Happy Days* TV show as Fonzie's sidekick—Leather Tuscadero. Her albums sold well from 1973 on, but she was not taken seriously as a rocker. Some previously all acoustic singer guitarists, such as Joni Mitchell and Bonnie Raitt, plugged in during the 1970s. Raitt even mastered the Fender Stratocaster. Yet the few serious women electric guitarists were not well known. Tessa Pollit, "Poison" Ivy Rorschach, and Lydia Lunch played good rock guitar throughout the seventies, but were not generally well known.

All-woman rock bands fared better. The Runaways, Heart, and The Go Gos, for example, sold well and got plenty of media attention. However, it was not their music, but their novelty that got them noticed. Their music was at least average, but clearly not state of the art. Joan Jett was one of the hardest woman rockers of all, but without her hard, slightly trashy sexuality, she was just another act.

Women rockers had a sexuality problem. Male rockers such as Mick Jagger or Rod Stewart could be as trashily sexual as they wanted. Indeed, they were imitating sexy women on stage as a type of female impersonator. In contrast, women rockers who tried to be sexy were often classified as trashy. When Tina Turner played the sexy performer to the hilt and did it well, she was typed as raunchy. When Mick Jagger did a crude imitation of Turner, in almost transvestite costume, he supposedly exhibited great showmanship. Rod Stewart and Tom Jones could tease women with tight pants and loose lyrics; however, when women did the same, from Joan Jett to Madonna, they were usually seen as sleazy or slutish.

Most feminist musicians were not satisfied with the progress—especially in hard rock. In 1979, Pamela Brandt complained that although in 1976 her woman's rock group, The Deadly Nightshade, had hit the top 100 chart of Billboard magazine, unfortunately they were number eighty-one on a list that included only nineteen and a half women. The half was Toni Tennile, without her Captain. Brandt bitterly noted: "Our politicized disco version of the 'Theme from Mary Hartman, Mary Hartman' bulleted clear on up to number seventy-nine, and shortly thereafter was available in supermarkets packaged two-for-a-dollar with 'The Singing Dogs Greatest Hits.' And as the tail will sometimes wag the dog, my band followed its record down the tubes."[37] Brandt titled her essay, "At the Top of the Charts . . . but Are They Playing Our Song?" Her answer was largely no. Brandt acknowledged that record customers were dancing "to an increasing number of drummers," but wondered whether feminists should plunk down their "Susan B. Anthony dollars" for "all those different drummers playing the same old beat." Brandt would not settle for "anything less than the classic feminist rock fantasy personified." She meant some woman who would satisfy critic Ellen Willis's call for "art so powerful that men and . . . society in general will have to come to terms with it." For the "trashier feminists," this dream creator's music would also be "terrific to dance to." Brant's dream rocker was "sexy, but not sexist." Although admitting her fantasy woman was not here yet, she noted how well women were doing. In June 1979, disco queen Donna Summer had become the first female singer to have both a number one single and number one album "on three separate occasions." Only eight women had ever accomplished that trick even once; among them were "Janis Joplin, Barbra Streisand, and the Singing Nun."[38]

Brandt also perceptively pointed out that Bonnie Raitt had become a virtuoso of bottleneck guitar and had a "rich sleepy" sleazy voice that should make her a superstar. A decade later, Raitt won a Grammy award, but in 1979, Brandt noted Raitt's records sold "closer to a cult figure's 250,000" rather "than a superstar's million." She thought Raitt's problem was that she projected an "ass-kicking" strength rather than the more commercial "vulnerability" of a Linda Ronstadt. Brandt's female favorites in 1979 were an eclectic trio of sisters called The Roches (their real name) and Rickie Lee Jones, the hip California singer whose first album, *Rickie Lee Jones* soared to the top of the chart without "any sexist lyrics whatsoever." However, by the time Bonnie Raitt went to the top of the charts in 1990, Rickie Jones and the Roches were only cult singers. They had simply changed places. In any case, Brandt was still "holding out" for a female singer "with the perfect balance of art, politics, and trash." Brandt admitted that she hadn't shown up yet, but warned that "she's coming."[39]

If the 1980s never supplied the perfect woman rocker, it came up with many pretenders and several short-term flashes that warmed some feminist hearts and rankled others. In the 1970s, it became increasingly difficult to type singers by musical genre. The lines were fluid in the seventies and largely irrelevant in the eighties. For example, in 1974 The Country Music Association named Olivia Newton John, the Australian pop singer, its Female Vocalist of the Year. That same year, Anne Murray, the Canadian pop singer, received a Grammy Award as the top country artist. Country music stars joined together to protest, but country artists were themselves so diverse that no effective protest could be mounted. Country artists got their revenge by increasingly crossing over into pop. For example, Dolly Parton crossed over into pop with hits such as "Here You Come Again," and Lynn Anderson had already crossed over with "I Never Promised You a Rose Garden" in 1970.

There were woman singers you could still clearly call country, and country music itself became more widely accepted in the late 1970s. Its commercial success, the many crossovers, and President Jimmy Carter's election all contributed to country's new status. Suddenly a singer did not have to be ashamed of a Southern drawl. There were fewer jokes about country being for folks with IQs below 100. Folk and folk rock stars had begun using many excellent country instrumentalists as sidemen in the late 1960s, and the commercial success just seconded the artistic approval. Yet women country singers presented a mixed picture. There remained the old barefoot-and-pregnant image of country women singers pining for their man. Indeed, Tammy Wynette was still singing "Stand by Your Man" while accusing her husband, country star George Jones, of physical abuse. Yet country music also had a good supply of gritty female singers, such as Loretta Lynn, who sang hard straight songs about poverty. Lynn even recorded a song about contraception, "The Pill," that was banned from Boston radio. On the other hand, Lynn's sister, Crystal Gayle, carved a very successful career singing typical country pining-for-my-man songs. But then Jeanie Riley had a big country hit with "Harper Valley PTA," which satirized middle-class morality. Finally, no matter what kind of music they sang, the country female vocalists were often tough-minded and independent businesswomen. Tammy Wynette, Loretta Lynn, and Dolly Parton were all strong women role models who warmed feminist hearts. Thus, if country bashing continued after 1980, it was not coming from feminists.

Another trend that confused the feminist search for popular musical heroines was the demise of the singer-songwriter mystique that had started with folk writers such as Bob Dylan and Joni Mitchell in the 1960s. By the late seventies, pop music no longer cared who wrote the song, but only what it sounded like. Alternative music in general and feminist music in particular continued to cherish music that came from personal experience and was sung by the writer. Very personal songs by women such as Dory Previn, who was somewhere between a popular singer and a cult singer in the early 1970s, were very clearly alternative music by the end of the decade. As Joni Mitchell's work became more personal and inventive during the 1970s, her popularity too markedly declined. By the 1980s, to make a stir you just could not have a good song, you had to have a whole new trendy image or style.

Cyndi Lauper and Madonna were two good examples of what it took to become a female musical superstar in the 1980s. Their clothes and general manner were more important than their music, yet these two were ironically very different in both their clothes and philosophy. In 1984, Cyndi Lauper topped the charts with her personal anthem, "Girls Just Want to Have Fun." She was quickly embraced by many feminists, most notably the editors of *Ms.* magazine. Her instant celebrity was capped with a *Newsweek* magazine cover picture on March 4, 1985. *Ms.* asked whether the song, written by a man, Robert Hazard, was "just another superficial and patronizing ditty designed to put us in our bubble-headed place"? *Ms.* not only gave Lauper the benefit of doubt, they gave her an achievement award, along with feminist singer Holly Near. *Ms.* noted that "if Helen Reddy's recording of 'I Am Woman' was about anger and a new collective pride, 'Girls Just Want to Have Fun' " was "about a newer defiant joy and the celebration of our strength." *Ms.* also suggested that "feminists couldn't have invented a more suitable pop hero." The reasons were very sketchy. "Her ditzy style" reminded *Ms.* of Gracie Allen; her clothes style was a cross "between tag-sale kitsch and finger-painted Dada." For *Ms.*, the bottom line was "the girl had chops." Among her other feminist credentials, Lauper had declared that her personal heroes included "John Lennon and Gloria Steinem." *Ms.* also noted that Lauper included and thus honored her mother in all her videos (because "she is very talented and she never really had a chance to show that because of circumstances").[40]

If it is hard to fully understand why *Ms.* venerated Lauper, it is not difficult to fathom why they were not high on the other big new female rock star of 1985—Madonna. Whereas Cyndi Lauper was just quirky, Madonna (real name Madonna Louise Ciccone) was quirkily sexy. At age twenty-six in 1985, Madonna did not at all suggest virginal youth, despite her second big hit record, *Like a Virgin*. She represented a mature woman who had been around the block. Yet parents might be more amenable to having their daughters dress like Madonna than Lauper. To model yourself after Lauper, orange-colored hair and a distaff punk look was essential; to style yourself after Madonna, one went for prefeminist Marilyn Monroe sexuality, with a stress on flimsy, lacy clothes that bared the midriff as much as possible. On one record, she mocked virginity; on the next, she exaggerated sex and longing; on a third, she painted herself as a material gold digger. No matter, she was all hype—a nonstop public relations tour guide for her career. She was in charge of her life and sassily independent of men, but she hardly convinced feminists she was Wonder Woman. Madonna was beyond left, right, and feminism. She hit feminist complaints head-on, but as usual talked in circles. For example, in 1985 *Time* magazine quoted her on feminists:

To call me an anti-feminist is ludicrous. Some people have said that I'm setting women back 30 years. Well, I think in the '50s, women weren't ashamed of their bodies. I think they luxuriated in their sexuality and being strong in their femininity. I think that is better than hiding it and saying, "I'm strong, I'm just like a man." Women aren't like men. They can do things that men can't do.[41]

One thing women rockers could do in the 1980s was turn music videos into the sexiest mass entertainment since burlesque. Unlike burlesque, sexy videos rejected nudity (which would not pass the censors anyway) and opted for suggestiveness in clothes, image, and style. Double-entendre lyrics also contributed. Rock music videos often combined the slickness of television ads with the energy of go-go dancing. They were topless dancing in full dress. Madonna's "Like a Virgin" video, for example, has her dressed in a full-length wedding dress, but half the time she is writhing and moaning in it, while stretched out on a bed. Yet music videos were not a complete swamp for feminism. Like most new media, music videos offered diverse possibilities. For example, Tina Turner's videos stressed her strength, optimism, and independence with such songs as "Better Be Good to Me" and "What's Love Got to Do with It." Turner was now in her forties and her message may have been lost on teenagers, but surely older women picked up on it.

Feminists had a tough time competing with Madonna for the allegiance of the young. Madonna said sexiness is okay again. She said she was natural. After all, she didn't "shave the side of " her head or dye her "hair pink." She argued that kids had been brainwashed to believe that it was not "right to want to dress up and be feminine," because if they did, men would not "respect them." But for Madonna, being sexy meant also being a "brazen, aggressive" woman. She felt that she was "just expressing sexual desire and not really caring what people think about it."[42]

If Madonna was not a clear symbol of sexism, most rock lyrics were and feminists used them skillfully. As a general rule, the older the lyrics, the more blatantly sexist they were. Women's liberation had reformed most aging rockers by 1980. Bob Dylan, Rod Stewart, and the Rolling Stones, for example, were a mere shadow of their sexist selves after a decade of feminist attacks. The really sexist music thereafter came from rock groups which appealed to very young teenagers—so-called teenyboppers. The bubblegum-rock groups, such as Kiss and Queen, spun out sexist hits far more offensive than older rock. Queen's 1978 hit "Fat Bottomed Girls" was a graphic example. Feminists were slow to discover and attack this new category of sexist music because they largely followed classic rock. However, since Queen and Kiss affected kids at a very impressionable age, they were now probably more dangerous than Mick Jagger.

Feminist critics focused on classic rock music because it permeated youth culture. The phrase "oldies but baddies" summed up their general assessment. They generally found rock lyrics a wasteland devoid of positive female images, yet it was a fruitful area to expose negative images. Women holding a torch for that special man has a long musical history, and rock furnished its own classics in that genre. For example, there were Gladys Knight's "Midnight Train to Georgia," Sammi Smith's "Help Me Make It Through the Night," and Janis Joplin's "Piece of My Heart." Irritating macho male views of women appeared in songs such as "Good Hearted Woman" by Waylon Jennings and Willie Nelson, the Rolling Stones's "Honky Tonk Woman," and Glen Campbell's "Everyday Housewife." There were traditional, passive female complaint songs such as Linda Ronstadt's "When Will I Be Loved," Janis Joplin's "Down on Me," and Janis Ian's "Society's Child." Feminists usually ignored the many male torch songs (especially common in country music) that portray men hopelessly in love with women who rejected them. Instead, they generally fastened on the few songs that featured strong, sassy independent women. For example, feminists hailed songs such as Carly Simon's "You're So Vain" and Nancy Sinatra's "How Does That Grab You Darlin" and "These Boots Are Made for Walking." The problem, however, was not the exceptional song that proved the rule, but the average songs that shaped youthful images and attitudes. For every sassy "You're So Vain" song, there were a dozen passive "Angel of the Morning" type songs. On the other hand, for every male torch song, there were a dozen macho brag songs such as Jim Croce's "I've Got a Song" and "Big Bad Leroy Brown." Feminist music critics had the same general complaint as the Rolling Stones. With rock lyrics women "couldn't get no satisfaction."[43]

Beyond the lyrics, male rock was ironically sexy in traditional feminine ways. Male rockers, such as Mick Jagger and his imitators, minced around the stage, giving come-hither looks and sexy pouts, teasing women en masse. To label Madonna a female Mick Jagger was the height of irony. Clearly, Jagger was a male Madonna if not a male burlesque queen. Rock alone allowed men to be more female without becoming less macho. Male athletes, businessmen, and politicians would all be decimated by any hint of femininity. Conventional wisdom argued that although women were increasingly able to look and act like men, males were unable to take on female attributes. For example, women could wear slacks, carry briefcases, and smoke Marlboro cigarettes, but men could not wear dresses, carry purses, or smoke Eve cigarettes. This suggested that male attributes had higher status and that women benefited by copying them. But the reverse was not true, because women's ways and styles were considered inferior. If that was true of the social world, it was not true in the rock world.

Women rockers had to pattern themselves after male rockers imitating females, but turning on women. This had to be sexually confusing. For example, female rocker Patti Smith noted:

I'm lucky. Most girls related to, like, say, the Beatles or the Stones because sexually they aroused them, they moved them as guys. Those guys, after they finished moving me as guys, they moved me as artists, and so I was able to transcend that little sexual giggle and relate to those people on a more brainiac level and steal from them. . . . But most girls don't know who to turn to, to develop themselves.[44]

Feminists too had a difficult time relating to male rock. They had grown up on it and always identified it with rebellion. To see it suddenly as male dominated or woman hating was overreaction. Men did dominate popular music, but why not? Men dominated almost all big business, and popular music was one of the biggest businesses. Yet men could not dominate art anymore than women could. Artists were genderless, which gave women the opportunity to create feminist music, no matter how small the audience. Yet feminist music became politicized. It was judged not by standards of art, but by its sentiments. It did not have to be "politically correct," which was essentially as meaningless then as now, but it had to be prowoman. Because women were a very diverse group, prowoman music had considerable artistic space. The problem was that art was no longer being judged as art. Most feminists could not separate art from feminism. For them, any song that demeaned women could not be great art. It might be the Rolling Stones or it might be Wagner. Of course, the reverse is also true. Some prowoman music is not great art, but rather corny and simplistic like a lot of topical music written by men.

Feminists who tried to use popular music as a countercultural tool always defeated themselves when they ignored the popular. Just as sexist rock had captured them, it continued to capture the young. People like art because it makes them feel good. One can appreciate a song for its art without endorsing its sentiment. Artful sexist songs are no problem when they are surrounded by equally artful feminist songs. Indeed, the contrast is often instructive. Whenever feminists insisted on a pure world of women-oriented music, they lost both their credibility with the young and their liberating image.

Feminists often forgot that singers have to sing about a world they never made. A sexist song could be as effective a learning tool as a feminist song when used as a negative example. Also, women who did not project as feminists were not taken seriously, even when they made fine feminist role models. Madonna is perhaps the best example. Feminists blamed men but Madonna used them. Feminists talked about not letting men dominate you, but Madonna practiced it. Madonna may have manipulated men in traditional feminine ways, but she did it in a quite modern and forthright way that excited young women, as well as men. That Madonna left most older feminists cold illustrated a major problem of countercultural change. While changing the next generation through cultural factors, you may find that you no longer have much in common with that younger generation. The culture you use has an effect on the young, but perhaps not as much effect as new cultural factors you cannot control. Feminists were depressed by Madonna in the same way that suffragists were depressed by the flappers of the Jazz Age. Feminists had struggled to liberate women, but Madonna's style of freedom was not exactly what they had in mind. But Madonna is as surely a partial product of women's liberation, as flappers were a product of the suffrage movement.

Aging feminists often forgot that countercultural music had less to do with the music and more to do with the young. Their own music made them feel better, but might well be irrelevant to the young. Feminist songs spoke to older women and promoted sisterhood among adults, but often ignored younger women. Feminism had to encourage different kinds of feminist sensibility and feminist artists to capture the young. Mass consciousness raising was misleading. There were several mass audiences: They were divided by class, ethnic background, race, region, and age. Women, of course, were in all of these. Reaching them through music was far more complicated than it had seemed back in the 1960s, when music was so effectively used with live feminist audiences. Some other, less diverse, and more pervasive media, such as cinema, television, and advertising, offered better opportunities and different problems in the countercultural struggle.

4

Mass Consciousness Raising: Liberating the Media

FILM

Cinema lacked both popular music's diversity and artistic access. Alternative feminist films were expensive to make and difficult to distribute. They were usually seen only at feminist film festivals by those already convinced of their merit. To get to the masses, feminist film producers had to convince big studios or investors to back projects that would make a profit. Because cinema is largely entertainment, straight message films had little chance. Yet cinema, like other media, had to respond to women's liberation. After 1970, studios slowly but steadily added more talented women directors, such as Elaine May and Penny Marshall, and screenwriters, such as Joan Didion and Nora Ephron. In the wake of the post–1960 films that dealt with social issues, came a host of new women actresses playing realistic roles. Ellen Burstyn, Faye Dunaway, and the midcareer Jane Fonda are good examples. Also, as cinema increasingly exploited sexual themes, women's issues were often stressed inadvertently. For example, the 1969 film *Bob & Carol & Ted & Alice* used intercouple sexual swinging to titillate audiences, but also shed light on marriage roles and furnished Dyan Cannon with an unusual role that showed substantial character growth.

The real battleground for feminists interested in film were the images of women in past and present films. Throughout the 20th century, Americans had been in love with the movies. Bigger-than-life screen images had affected every facet of American culture from clothing styles to sex. The movies grabbed Americans young and never let go. Before television and even radio, cinema was America's national culture, and films never lost their position to the newer media. Radio was pale compared with cinema, and television eventually became largely a theater for film viewing. The invention of video film players capped the triumph of cinema culture. Americans might listen to more radio and see more television relative to film viewing, but cinema won the influence contest throughout this century.

The film roles women played in 20th-century America were a comprehensive clinic on women's social position. Feminist film critics quickly saw the opportunity and the most effective method. Criticizing the many vapid, demeaning, and stereotypical roles that women played dramatized the position of women and made an argument for change. More diverse and realistic female film roles not only would provide justice, they could positively shape the next generation by providing good role models. The strategy was simple and promising. The problem was agreeing on which roles and stereotypes were harmful and which were positive. Another question was which past stereotypes were frozen in time and irrelevant to contemporary conditions and which were still a drag on progress. A key problem was the general adulation of actors and actresses. They, after all, did not control their roles. Criticism of their roles became for some fans attacks on their idols and not simply attacks on the stereotypes their roles helped fasten. Thus, criticism of Marilyn Monroe's dumb blond roles were seen as attacks on the sainted, tragic Marilyn, herself. Critiques of John Wayne's macho roles attacked an American institution, not just a man.

The two most influential early books of feminist film criticism were Marjorie Rosen's *Popcorn Venus: Women, Movies, and the American Dream* published in 1973[1] and Molly Haskell's *From Reverence to Rape: The Treatment of Women in the Movies*, published in 1974.[2] These were fitting answers to film books with such titles as *Man and the Movies*. Haskell's book was better written and more subtle, but Rosen's book was far more comprehensive and had a better feel for the commercial side of cinema. The two became the pathbreaking models for feminist film criticism and helped break the role stereotypes they cataloged.

The most important and numerous female film stereotypes involved sex. The one cinema constant was its increasing preoccupation with sex as a way to keep the audience interested. Although Hollywood had to back down periodically when they overstepped contemporary good taste or were suddenly blamed for social problems, the direction has always been toward more frank film sexuality. Before the 1960s, women film stars were clearly divided between good, wholesome girls and bad, sultry, sexy girls. Neither type was called woman. This virgin-whore dichotomy had a long Hollywood history.

In the silent film era (1900–1930), the virgin was best represented by film stars such as Mary Pickford and Lillian Gish. Mary Pickford eventually became America's sweetheart, known to all as "Little Mary," although at first her fans did not know her name. Studios such as Biograph avoided building up name identification to avoid the star syndrome, which could mean higher salaries for stars. For years, Pickford was known only as the Biograph girl, yet her fans made her the personification of feminine sweetness. Pickford's movie success helped make girlishness sexy. Soon thousands of adult women wanted to look like little girls—sweet and innocent. Lillian Gish transferred Pickford's chaste innocent image to urban film fare. Gish represented adult female innocence in the wicked city. Whereas Pickford's characteristic role was in *Polyanna* (1911), Gish hit her stride in D. W. Griffith's *Broken Blossoms* (1919) as a London street waif, victimized by a brutal bully. Whether glad or sad, the film virgin remained chaste. Pickford became so identified with these roles that although she was a fine actress, she could never play anything but girlish innocent parts. Her fans felt betrayed by anything less. Gish was luckier and branched out into a variety of character roles through a long career that carried through the 1980s.

Films did not at first offer whore roles to women, but sex entered films quickly. At first, there were sexy exotic dancers patterned after Little Egypt, the belly dancer who shocked the 1893 Columbian Exposition in Chicago by dancing with a bare midriff. Little Egypt had a score of imitators on stage and screen. Sex at the office also became a favorite of screenwriters before World War I. These office hanky-panky films soon merged into general triangle films, with a man caught between a wife and mistress. Titles such as *Who's in the Bedroom?* and *The Maid's Guest* suggest the plot.

The sexy romance film was only one genre among others such as westerns, comedies, classics, and mysteries, but it was perhaps the most generally popular. The star system had emerged by 1914, and now a major film was defined by casting popular movie stars. A "B" film used unknown actors. The women stars (known and unknown) were increasingly sexy. Hollywood merged the exotic dancer with the sexpot by 1916, to create the vamp—a woman who ate men alive. On the silent screen, stars such as Nita Naldi and Theda Bara played the roles to perfection. Now these femme fatales look like early comic renditions of Elvira or Vampirella, but then they were taken more seriously. Indeed, during World War I a woman's group convinced New York theaters not to screen Theda Bara films while innocent young American soldiers were in town to board ships to Europe.[3]

The 1920s brought the sexual revolution and flappers. The flapper woman often looked like a little girl with her lean athletic look and rolled-up stockings, but she acted more like a man-eating vamp. Short hair added to the boyish or girlish look, but the makeup that was added sent a different message. The face now exuded rouge, mascara, and supposedly sexy femininity. H. L. Mencken acidly noted that mascara did not make women glamorous, it made them look "diabetic." Yet makeup became an everyday standard in the twenties as women copied the stars. Before World War I, only actresses and prostitutes wore makeup. Movies made cosmetics universal. If women could not all be movie stars, they could all look more like them.

The new Jazz Age stars were flapper types that exuded sex appeal. Among the most popular were Clara Bow, Gloria Swanson, and Joan Crawford. Besides sexiness, the flappers were known for intellectual shallowness and kookiness. They personified flakiness four decades before the word was invented. They starred in little remembered films such as *Rag Doll*, *Ladies of the Night*, *The Joy Girl*, and *Ladies of Pleasure*. The early 1920s film industry throve on sexy movies, but were rocked by Hollywood sex scandals involving top stars, such as the Fatty Arbuckle rape-murder trial. In 1922, Hollywood fought off demands for national censorship by setting up its own office to regulate morality in films. The office was headed by Will Hays, once Woodrow Wilson's postmaster general.

The result was films that hid sex and sexy-costumed women in morally acceptable story vehicles. Suddenly female film stars constantly undressed on screen to take a bath or just change clothes, rather than disrobe for sex. Also, exotic, skimpy pagan costumes and suggestive dances were often hidden within biblical spectaculars such as *Ben Hur* and *The Ten Commandments*. Cecil B. De Mille was the grand master of all these production strategies. He switched from urban bed-and-bath films in the early 1920s to biblical films in the late 1920s—just to provide vehicles for sexy women. The twenties continued to be a time when women in film were generally seen in various states of glamor and undress but were generally not really heard.

The perfection of sound films in the 1930s theoretically allowed everyone to be heard. Along with the depression, "talkies" encouraged serious acting and serious films. The change from silent films was almost immediate. In 1930, Hollywood produced over three hundred talkies and almost two hundred silent films. The next year only two silent films were released—Chaplin's *City Lights* and a jungle picture, *Tabu*.[4] Talkies favored a whole range of new approaches from musicals to horror films, but women stars especially benefited from the new complex acting and comedy roles that sound brought in its wake. Stars such as Bette Davis, Marie Dressler, Irene Dunne, and Greer Garson gave new meaning to the word actress.

There were also less edifying and more traditional glamour girls, but even these were usually more interesting and complex in 1930s films. Moreover, the new sexy film stars often dominated men. Marlene Dietrich was a femme fatale that men literally died for. Greta Garbo, Hedy Lamarr, and Vivien Leigh played similar roles, although Garbo had much greater range. Even the sex goddesses, such as Jean Harlow and Mae West, had a complex, distinctive flair. Harlow is sometimes called the Marilyn Monroe of the 1930s, but Monroe was really the Harlow of the 1950s. Harlow was platinum blond, funny, and constantly suggestive without being lurid or ridiculous. Mae West had a similar personae, but lacked Harlow's vulnerability. Mae was always in command and never apologized. She took men as she found them and left them as she pleased. Whether clowning with W. C. Fields or bantering with leading men, such as Robert Taylor, she was always cynical, aggressive, and independent.[5]

There were many 1930s female film roles that pleased feminists after 1960, but caused little stir in the thirties. Even 1930s gangster molls were seen as closet feminists by 1960s critics. In one 1930s scene with gangster Edward G. Robinson, Barbara Stanwyck is told: "You're my girl." She replies: "I'm my Mother's girl." The one thirties genre that frustrates contemporary feminists most are the female career films which often starred Katharine Hepburn and Rosalind Russell. These films opened with a hard-driving career woman ignoring men in general and her male co-star in particular. Early in the film she is dressed chastely in a woman's suit and throwing out devil-may-care one liners about hypocritical men, but surely (and not particularly slowly), as the film moves on, she falls for the charming, if somewhat oafish, leading man—Cary Grant or Spencer Tracy, for example. By films' end, the heroine is wearing sexy nightgowns and has made a difficult decision to give up her career for wedded bliss. Contemporary feminists suggest that these films asked the right questions, but gave the wrong answer: A career woman could only be fulfilled and feminized by a man's love and a traditional marriage.

Nevertheless, the thirties were famous for strong female roles, from Greer Garson as Madam Curie in the Hollywood biography to Jane Darwell's Ma Joad in director John Ford's *The Grapes of Wrath*. No shrinking violets, these women held center stage and were riveting individuals. There were few generic roles for women, except perhaps in musicals and formula westerns. Here, a showgirl was interchangeable as were the western saloon girl or schoolmarm. Not surprisingly, women reaped the rewards of their strength in public affection. For the first time female screen stars surpassed their male counterparts in popularity. In 1914, when United Artists became the first film company founded by movie stars, only one artist in the quartet

was a woman—-Mary Pickford. The three male stars were Douglas Fair-
banks, Charlie Chaplin, and director D. W. Griffith. However, in the 1930s
women screen idols turned the tables. Of the top ten stars in 1932, five were
women, and the top three were Marie Dressler, Janet Gaynor, and Joan
Crawford. Women held their own throughout the thirties with popular stars
such as Mae West, Shirley Temple, and Ginger Rogers. Indeed, a woman
held the top popularity spot for six of the years from 1933 to 1939.[6]
    The war years, however, proved disastrous. In 1940, only two women
were among the ten most popular stars—Bette Davis and Judy Garland.
Men held this eight-to-two margin through 1944. The war highlighted macho values and sacrifices. Women became support troops in cinema as well
as in real life. Yet female film stars continued to set clothing and hair styles
for women, even if their roles no longer had the social voltage of their thirties films. In the 1930s, sexy blond stars such as Harlow, West, and Marlene
Dietrich reversed the old formula which made dark-haired women darkly
sexual and blonde women chaste and virginal. The question, "Do blondes
really have more fun?" only makes sense after 1930. In the forties, film stars
such as Rita Hayworth, Lizabeth Scott, and Veronica Lake made long hair
appear sexy. Increasingly, in the aftermath of war it was the man's job to
perform well on screen and the woman's job to look well. But a woman no
longer need be stridently sexy to look well. After 1945, Greer Garson, Irene
Dunne, and later Deborah Kerr played beautiful ladies on a pedestal. In the
1950s, Doris Day, Julie Andrews, Debbie Reynolds, and Sandra Dee all
managed to look sexy and wholesome at the same time, before real cinema
sex was possible. Doris Day, June Allyson, and later Eva Marie Saint often
played wives and mothers who looked like fashion models, but were
strangely sexless, standing amidst their shiny kitchen appliances and surrounded by children.[7] Indeed, in the 1950s as historian Daniel Boorstin observed, the undeveloped third world view of American women was Doris
Day standing in a new Westinghouse electric kitchen.
    Perhaps the women's liberation generation also saw American film
women as Doris Day. The young feminists grew up in the 1950s, and their
film heroines, such as plucky, earnest Eva Marie Saint in *On the Waterfront*,
were few and far between. Much more pervasive were the beach bunny movies, the *Tammy and the Bachelor*—type films, Marilyn Monroe's ditzy blond
role in *The Seven Year Itch*, and *The Girl Can't Help It*, starring buxom
Jayne Mansfield. These roles, from Debbie Reynold's naive Tammy to
Mansfield's sexy rocker, were all essentially dumb-bunny roles. Film images
of women in the fifties were one unstated reason for women's liberation.
    This is indirectly suggested by Brandon French's perceptive study of
1950s films, *On the Verge of Revolt: Women in American Films of the 1950s*.

She argued that fifties films did not merely illustrate the subservience and domesticity that Betty Friedan described, they also reflected women's anger in subtle ways. French analyzed films such as *Some Like It Hot* and *Picnic* which are filled with typical stereotypes.[8] *Picnic* featured Kim Novak as a beautiful prom queen type, who her intellectual but jealous sister suggests was so dumb they had to burn the school down to get her out. *Picnic* also included Rosalind Russell playing a self-described "old maid school teacher" who ends up begging a man to marry her. Yet Russell's aging teacher is feisty throughout most of the film, and Novak's character does turn down marriage with a wealthy man she does not love to marry an engaging drifter played by William Holden. And the younger sister after a brief try at matching her sister's glamour decides to take advantage of a college scholarship and become a novelist. Yet there is also Novak's bitter mother complaining about her husband leaving her and urging her daughter to sacrifice love for security. French stresses the ambivalence of these films. She sees Novak's character as caught between the traditional rewards of domesticity and the heady feeling of independence.

French finds women's rebellion accelerating steadily throughout the decade. Before 1952, women in film were largely ambivalent about their traditional roles. From that point through 1956, films stressed love-starved women. *Picnic* would be a good example. Late in the decade, films such as *Some Like It Hot* starring Marilyn Monroe were using subtle, but clear, androgynous comedy to attack sexist roles. In a chapter titled, "Brides of Christ," French also places two nun films—*Heaven Knows Mr. Allison* with Deborah Kerr and *The Nun's Story* with Audrey Hepburn—in this category. These films feature very aggressive and independent women disguised in a nun's habit. A less-disguised, independent-woman-role model in a similar film was Katharine Hepburn's portrayal of the brave missionary in *The African Queen*.

Some other films that French categorizes are *The Quiet Man*, *Shane*, and *The Country Girl* early in the decade and *Marty* and *All That Heaven Allows* from the later period. These are enough to remind us that amidst the sexist comedies and musicals of the fifties were films that honestly grappled with male-female relationships. French persuasively illustrated the rebellious underside of several films dealing with women, but she probably overestimated their importance within the spectrum of cinema and popular culture. Even films that she picked out often had an overwhelming macho atmosphere that she usually overlooked.[9] For example, in *Picnic* William Holden completely charms and dominates all women of all ages with his macho ways. Mrs. Potts, Kim Novak's elderly next-door neighbor, articulates Holden's charisma best. She notes that Holden stamped around in his boots like "he was still outdoors." He shook them all up. Suddenly, "there was a man in the house again" and it "felt good."

The Quiet Man and *Shane* are also filled with machismo. John Wayne only proves himself to the Irish community by riding, brawling, and properly dominating his wife in *The Quiet Man*. Maureen O'Hara plays a feisty Irish bride here to Wayne's pacifist American ex-prizefighter, but O'Hara is the background, not the central issue. *Shane* is an even more overwhelming paean to righteous violence. Like *High Noon*, another 1950s western, it might also be a Cold War parable that shows there are some threats that a man cannot walk away from or settle peacefully. Women are in the background, urging peace, but men are in the foreground, venting macho rage and righteousness to earn peace. The plot and decisions are more complex than those that you find in later macho films such as *Rambo*, but the result is similar.

The 1960s cinema pioneered open sexuality and youth-oriented films. *The Graduate*, *Easy Rider*, and *Midnight Cowboy* are good examples. This trend continued throughout the 1970s and 1980s, but feminist critics became disenchanted with both genres early. They started looking for "woman's films." Primarily, these were films that portrayed women realistically facing common feminist-identified problems, hopefully with strength and character. Feminists also complained about the increasing number of blockbuster male-buddy films, which dwarfed the few strong woman films, both in number and popularity. Besides *Easy Rider* and *Midnight Cowboy*, good examples of buddy films are *The Sting*, *Butch Cassidy and the Sundance Kid*, *The French Connection*, and *Dirty Harry*. The female roles in such films supplied strictly romantic backgrounds as in old style westerns. The women had to be there if for no other reason than to prove the male buddies were not homosexual. Indeed, film critic Leslie Fielder called this male film bonding cultural homosexuality.

In part, the dominance of male screen idols was a carryover from World War II. Women film stars never regained their relative popularity in the postwar period. From 1944 to 1960, a male film star was voted most popular Hollywood star every year until Doris Day broke the cycle in 1960. Moreover, from 1948 to 1958 the top-ten star list (with at least one tie that brought the number to eleven) featured nine male stars and only two women stars. In 1948, for example, Bing Crosby was number one and Betty Grable and Ingrid Bergman were numbers two and ten, respectively. By 1951, John Wayne was number one, and Betty Grable and Doris Day were three and nine on the list. In 1956, William Holden held number one, with Marilyn Monroe and Kim Novak coming in eight and nine. The low point for women came in 1957, when the top ten list contained all male stars, and the top four were Rock Hudson, John Wayne, Pat Boone, and Elvis Presley.

Women did better as box office draws in the 1960s. Indeed, a woman star held the top spot in every year from 1960 through 1964 in the persons of Doris Day (1960 plus 1962 thru 1964) and Elizabeth Taylor in 1961. However, the top ten score for all the years 1961 through 1965 was three women and seven men. From 1967 to 1971, top women stars dropped another notch or two. Although Julie Andrews was number one in 1967, Elizabeth Taylor was the only other female star on the list. In 1968, Andrews and Taylor remained the only woman on the list—tied at number nine. In 1971, as John Wayne took number one honors, Ali McGraw was the lone woman at number eight.[10]

Julie Burchill noted in the introduction to her 1986 book *Girls on Film* that Americans were "encouraged to worship men in life, love, bed, war and politics," and were "only encouraged to worship girls on film." But she ruefully continued:

Recently, not even this heaven-haven has been available: Cimino, Scorcese and Coppola and the rest of the Boys Town Mafia would prefer us to sit in the darkened mezzanine gasping at the touching relationship between man and man. In these boy-meets-boy blockbusters there can be no room for the kind of girl who made the cinema great. We have progressed from the days of the women's film. Yet the thirst to see the films of the goddesses . . . grows more unquenchable every year. They were the stuff that dreams are made of.[11]

The 1960s and 1970s were indeed a general cultural wasteland for strong woman roles. Whereas male stars generally played strong, confident, and successful heroes, many of the big women stars played basket cases. Good examples are Anne Bancroft in *The Graduate*, Joanne Woodward in *Rachel, Rachel*, and Shirley McLaine in *The Apartment*. To find suitable film-role models, feminists had to become increasingly selective. Even strong women roles often portrayed neurotic, maladjusted women with multiple hang-ups, for example, Jane Fonda in *Klute* and Elizabeth Taylor in *Who's Afraid of Virginia Woolf*.

The ambivalence of female screen images during the 1950s and 1960s likely colored Marjorie Rosen's views. In 1973, in *Popcorn Venus* she argued that whereas films encouraged feminism by providing fresh insights on women's roles, cinematic images of women often reinforced traditional roles and attitudes. Rosen looked at films and roles in their own times, but her contemporary feminist views determined what she looked for. She did not often like what she found. According to Rosen, then as now the film industry was run by men for profit. Films had to reflect society to be credible and thus profitable, but any benefits to women were accidental by-products.

Molly Haskell in her 1974 book *From Reverence to Rape* comes to similar conclusions, although she is less interested in society and more interested in cinema. However, Haskell argued that the 1950s and 1960s were a particularly bad time for women film stars, because many Hollywood moguls and directors were homosexuals or woman haters. They saw women as inconsequential trinkets to decorate their films.

Haskell points out that the industry codes in the 1920s and again in the 1930s that outlawed blatant sexuality, accidentally helped women. If women could not be overtly sexual, the vacuum was filled by making them more complicated, ambitious seekers and achievers. Thus the brainless flapper images of the 1920s and the sassy Mae West roles of the 1930s were replaced by Kate Hepburn's sassy, almost asexual, career-woman roles.

If times had changed for the worse after 1945 for film women, many of the stereotypical roles had remained constant. For example, virtuous lady roles of the past as played by Mary Pickford, Lillian Gish, Janet Gaynor, and Shirley Temple had very similar counterparts in roles played by June Allyson, Doris Day, Sandra Dee, and Debbie Reynolds. Earlier sexpots such as Theda Bara, Clara Bow, Jean Harlow, and Marlene Dietrich had mirror images in the more contemporary sex queens, such as Ava Gardner, Marilyn Monroe, and Raquel Welch. Showgirls such as Ruby Keeler, Alice Fay, and Ginger Rogers were replaced by Ann Miller, Cyd Charisse, and Mitzi Gaynor. The serious emotive actresses such as Bette Davis, Katharine Hepburn, and Barbara Stanwyck were replaced by stars such as Meryl Streep, Barbara Hershey, and Glen Close. Comic stars such as Joan Blondell and Judy Holliday have modern facsimiles such as Goldie Hawn and Cher. Like the Joan Crawfords, Kate Hepburns, and Bette Davises of the past, many contemporary women stars, such as Barbra Streisand and Jessica Lange, move easily through many genres.[12]

The stars or stereotypes have not changed as much as the films. Before 1960, the film was usually a vehicle for a star. Increasingly since 1960, the star is fitted into the film. There are more social-problem films, more action films, and more spectacular special-effects films. This has not made the stars bit players, but it has diminished their importance. Yet the late 1970s and early 1980s saw a small but steady stream of strong woman roles. Good examples are *Norma Rae*, *Gloria*, *An Unmarried Woman*, and *Julia*. However, for every gun-toting Gloria there were at least two films such as *Pretty Baby* and *The Blue Lagoon*, both of which featured a sexy teenager, Brooke Shields.

The 1980s also brought a film genre that particularly bothered feminist critics—a genre Molly Haskell said was best described as "male weepies." In a 1983 essay, "Lights, Camera, Daddy!" she denigrated films that show men "discovering how good they are at loving their children." Her examples were *Kramer vs. Kramer, Author! Author!, Ordinary People, The Great Santini, On Golden Pond, The Champ*, and *Table for Five*. Haskell jibed that with the "juicily androgynous roles" in these movies, actors such as "Al Pacino, Dustin Hoffman and Jon Voight" could "compete for the Mother of the Year Award." The men in these movies do so well as fathers that Haskell quipped: "Mothers may soon become obsolete."

Haskell found these new films more dangerous to women than the old negative mother stereotypes. Past Hollywood mothers could never "get it quite right." They were "either too remiss or too self sacrificing." Yet at least the flawed mother was there and learning. In the new father films, mothers were banished. Haskell thought these new films were the product of "a new breed of producers, directors, and screenwriters," most of whom had "been divorced at least once." They harbored the guilt of "divorced (or workaholic) Fathers" who valued their own happiness "over that of their children." This led them to right their own past sins in films "by making Dad over" as in *Tribute* and *On Golden Pond*. The complaint theme of these films was that being a "male parent was a full-time job."[13]

Haskell felt that in most of these films what began "as a stopgap measure" when mom made her exit, ended "as a paean to the emotional and domestic virtuosity of the male." In fact, the fathers learn little more than how to make French toast and how much wash detergent to use. Haskell argues that these films often allow father and son to "regress into an ideal world of all-male permissiveness." As father and son "form a mutual admiration society," men find the hero worship their wives used to provide in their children's eyes. Simply by taking on child rearing, men in these films gave parenting a status and dignity it never had when women did it. Haskell calls this "the men-upgrade-the neighborhood" but "women ruin-the-property-values" phenomenon. Haskell concluded that although women are told that they can "have it all, the message of these movies is that" they cannot "have much of anything." She noted: "The Mother is dead. Long live the Mother. And his name is . . . fill in the blank with your favorite bankable male star."[14]

The irony is that most male parent films are produced for women audiences. Haskell suggested that instead of crying over doting film fathers, women should be "laughing these male Mothers off the screen." Yet her complaints throughout harbor obvious contradictions. Feminist critics constantly called for female roles and images that cast women into professions and situations that men dominate, but that women could and do fill. When men attempt the same, they are usually attacked for invading female turf or playing it for laughs.

Indeed, in the 1980s there was a concerted effort to redo common plots and even actual classic movies with a feminine twist. The classic film, *Portrait of Dorian Gray*, was remade on television with a woman playing Dorian. Another television movie reworked the 1946 film classic, *It's a Wonderful Life*, with Marlo Thomas playing Jimmy Stewart's role and Cloris Leachman playing the originally male angel. Also Mary Tyler Moore debuted on Broadway in 1980, playing the original male character in *Whose Life Is It Anyway?*

In a *Time* essay, Roger Rosenblatt satirically complained that this trifling with classic male film roles had gone far enough. He rhetorically asked whether we would soon see *The Sisters Karamazov*, *Twelve Angry Ladies*, *Mrs. Roberts* or *Young Girl with a Coronet*. If so, he forecast that soon after would come a *Moby Dick* remake with Victoria Principal as Captain Alice and the "ubiquitous Meryl Streep as the passionate yet complex crew." Rosenblatt complained that in male-female role reversals the message is "when a man assumes the role of a woman, or when a woman assumes a role formerly occupied by a man," it is "always males who gain from the newly acquired virtues."

Rosenblatt suggested that long before Alan Alda played sensitive roles, Henry Fonda and Jimmy Stewart often played men with "the desirable female attributes of gentleness, forbearance, and sensitivity." They supposedly developed these virtues from "therapeutic and enobling" associations with women. Although womanly qualities made cinematic men better, it was less clear that masculine qualities improved movie women, Rosenblatt charged. But because turnaround is fair play, he looked forward to films such as *Monsieur Bovary*, *Dick Eyre*, and *Coal Miner's Son-in-Law*. The real danger, according to Rosenblatt, was that this sort of "wishful revisionism" might be applied to the real world. He warned that this century has taught us that "the fair sex, given the opportunities of the unfair, behave no better." For example, Indira Ghandi had the "habit of revoking civil liberties from time to time," and for good reason, Margaret Thatcher's enemies called her "Attila the Hen." Rosenblatt concluded that since the "future belongs to women," men had a right to the past.[15]

Women need not look to role reversals for signs of progress in the 1980s. Each year had several noteworthy movies with strong feminine role models: Faye Dunaway in *Network*, Sally Field in *Places in the Heart*, Jane Fonda in *The China Syndrome*, Meryl Streep in *Sophie's Choice*, Holly Hunter in *Broadcast News*, and Meryl Streep again in *Out of Africa*. Indeed, some actresses are quite typecast as strong women. Stars such as Faye Dunaway, Jane Fonda, Glenda Jackson, and Sally Field have long made a career of playing very strong feminine roles. More recently, such cinema stars as Barbra Streisand, Cher, Madonna, and Holly Hunter have followed their example. The 1990s have thus also provided strong feminine roles, but the younger women stars are not as typecast or consistent. Meg Ryan plays strong in one film, *Courage under Fire* and then mostly dependent in another, *When a Man Loves a Woman*. Julia Roberts plays both strong and weak in films such as *Pretty Woman* and *Sleeping with the Enemy*. Geena Davis and Sandra Bullock often played similarly ambivalent roles. Exceptions were Susan Sarandon (in *White Palace, Thelma and Louise*, and *Dead Man Walking*) and Sigourney Weaver (*Alien* and *Working Girl*) who played consistently strong roles. Unlike popular music, films must work under more rigid tests of reality. Unless film reflects actual social conditions, it lacks credibility. And when it treats the past, there is considerable danger that contemporary youth, who usually suffer from historical amnesia, will not understand. Youth tends to react more to the characters than the context. When a young person sees a Sally Field film one week and a Madonna film the next, there is little continuity. The messages are so mixed that for youth cinema often remains just an entertainment bazaar. With the increasing number of eight and twelve screen theaters, you pay your money and take your choice. This week you choose a comedy, next week a horror film, and the week after romantic fluff.

Yet there is always cinema magic. There is always that one film and character that keenly affects the individual for a month, a year, or a lifetime. As the number of films portraying suitable women role models increase, feminists can still hope that they can lose cinema battles, but win the war. Yet probably the individual film triumphs are a case of losing the war but winning some important battles. Films such as *Silkwood*, starring Meryl Streep as a brave, resourceful nuclear whistleblower, and *Silence of the Lambs*, starring Jodie Foster as a bright, brave FBI agent break stereotypes and provide powerful role models, though they lack a unified feminist perspective. Demi Moore's plucky *G. I. Jane* is another good example of a film that rasies more questions than it answers about women in the military, but provides an excellent role model.

For every *Silkwood* or *G. I. Jane*, there are a dozen teenage films that indirectly tell young women that the biggest problems are looking good and having a guy. Those who are affected most by films—youth—are least likely to see many of the serious films. Also, the new freedom to express sexuality in films has not only brought a steady procession of sexploitation films in all traditional genres, including teenage films, but has increased pornographic films. With the video revolution, one need not travel to San Francisco to see pornographic classics such as *Deep Throat*. Local video stores have a full stock of hard and soft porn films. Through video, this generation can also find easier exposure to the earlier sexist escape films of the late 1960s such as *Barbarella* or *Valley of the Dolls*.

On the other hand, the lack of women screenwriters and directors is slowly undergoing amelioration. Screenwriter Elaine May has been joined by Nora Ephron. Penny Marshall, Barbra Streisand, and even young Jodie Foster have become successful directors. And there are a number of bright young actresses who may permanently move into directing, such as Sigourney Weaver, Shelley Duvall, Holly Hunter, and Meryl Streep. Moreover, directors such as Jane Campion are near the top of their profession, and serious women's film festivals play for appreciative feminist audiences.

Hollywood still is uneasy with creative change, as reflected by the formula remakes with 2 and 3 after the original title. And then there are the new wave of film remakes such as *The Parent Trap* and *Dial M for Murder*. A director such as Campion can have an occasional mass market film such as *The Piano*, but Campion-style commercial successes will be few and far between. And how many teenagers will see such films or view films from women's film festivals? There has also been a new tide of male, macho buddy films and male mobster films. Julie Burchill complained in 1986 that films used to have titles such as *Gilda, Jezabel, Roberta, and Claudia*. At worst, there were mixed titles such as *Pat and Mike* or *Samson and Delilah*. Instead, contemporary films had titles such as *Willie and Phil, Melvin and Howard*, and *Thunderbolt and Lightfoot*. Burchill derisively suggested that if they remade *Gone with the Wind*, it would be called *Rhett and Ashley*.[16]

The women pals that Molly Haskell called for in *From Reverence to Rape* were a long time coming. Haskell recalled that screen women of the 1920s, 1930s, 1940s, and even 1950s supported each other—albeit in traditional ways. But in the 1960s and 1970s, she found the "camaraderie" and "the much-vaunted mutual support among women" missing. Haskell felt that modern commercial cinema had a monolithic sexism worse than "the old days of Hollywood." Finally in 1991 America got *Thelma and Louise*, starring Susan Sarandon and Geena Davis as the feminist easy riders of the 1990s. Of course, feminists could have celebrated a decade earlier with the film *Nine to Five*, starring Lily Tomlin, Jane Fonda, and Dolly Parton as a trio of office girls who find womanhood by kidnapping their male office manager, played by Dabney Coleman. However, this was clear satire and comedy and any lessons were muted.

Another 1991 film, *The Prince of Tides*, warmed feminist hearts. It starred Barbra Streisand as a New York psychiatrist who heals a troubled Nick Nolte. It capped a five-year period that annually provided at least two important films that portrayed woman as feisty role models. *Thelma and Louise* may have been the raunchy icing on the cake, but it was really only the tip of the iceberg. Feisty women films of the period 1986 to 1991 included *The Witches of Eastwick*, starring Cher, Michelle Pfeiffer, and Susan Sarandon; *The War of the Roses*, and *V. I. Warshawski* starring Kathleen Turner; and *The Fabulous Baker Boys* with Michelle Pfeiffer. Turner, Pfeiffer, and Cher were now regularly playing women who could take men or leave them alone. Turner was a gunslinging detective in *V. I. Warshawski* and a mafia hit woman in *Prizzi's Honor*. Sarandon had already prefaced her *Thelma and Louise* role in *White Palace* (1990) by playing an older woman who walked out on a younger man, played by James Spader.

On balance, images of women in film have been improving. That is the good news for feminist counterculturalists. The bad news is that on balance it likely has very little effect when surrounded by the many contemporary sexist images and the much larger number of past sexist movie roles. The new sexuality in films also has ambivalent effects on images of women and likewise on feminist critics. At the same time, it frees women to enjoy sex more openly, and it makes them more clearly sexual prey for men. It has precisely the same give and take effects of the sexual revolution itself and is really only a reflection of that change.

Pornography on the other hand is simpler to assess. The new pornography since the 1960s depicts even kinky sex as healthy as opposed to the old pornography which presented it as an appealing type of sin. Also, the new pornography as represented by the early classic porn films such as *Deep Throat* starring Linda Lovelace and *Behind the Green Door* starring Marilyn Chambers were directed at middle-class professionals instead of dirty old men. Many couples saw these films together at public theaters. At first, the porn films were chic and daring, but most pornography has its own self-destruct mode as film fare. It quickly becomes boring. The dialogue is usually inane, and thus, most porn films are not sexy. For most viewers, porn becomes comic and its availability has taken much of its taboo appeal away. It is now the province of schoolboys and a few older addicts. Pornographic films are hardly a mass media. Mainstream films are still the quintessential American mass media of this century. They speak so powerfully that they can often overcome pervasive long-standing images. Thus, *Serpico* completely reshaped the way many Americans thought about the police. *Three Days of the Condor* changed many Americans views about the CIA. *J.F.K.* made many people rethink the Kennedy assassination. Films have always changed American views of women. Feminists who believe in countercultural change must work on and with cinema, not because it is the only game in town, but because it remains the most powerful media yet devised.

TELEVISION

Television was well established by the time women's liberation appeared in the 1960s. Television was invented in the 1920s and became both technically and commercially feasible by 1941; however, because of World War II, its commercial appearance was delayed until 1948. Between 1948 and 1952, one of every three Americans bought TV sets at an average cost of $300. By 1952, there were 109 commercial stations broadcasting nationally. Television merged some important aspects of radio and cinema, but also added unique possibilities and genres.[17] Although the most consistently popular TV fare has been Hollywood movies or made-for-television films, these just made homes into private movie theaters. Television's most unique features are its pervasiveness and its variety. The cable revolution has just enhanced an always present trend. Also, because television invites family viewing, it has been more conservative than film in portraying sexuality and sensitive social issues. The gap between film and television in these areas has closed recently, but not entirely disappeared.

At first, television simply transferred radio programs to the new media. Thus, TV offered variety shows, quiz shows, dramas, comedy, westerns, music, talk shows, and news. It also offered feature films, but because Hollywood would not cooperate at first, television could only gain the rights to very old, dated films—often B movies. As television mushroomed in the 1950s, the program format became set. The number of stations increased from 357 in 1954 to 501 by 1960. Television set owners jumped from 26 million in 1954 to 45 million by 1960. Also NBC started color broadcasting in 1954, when its RCA color sets sold for $1,000.[18]

By the late 1950s television had a program mix that has changed amazingly little. In May 1959, New York television presented "six children's shows, five cartoons, eight situation comedies, eleven movies, four talk shows, two musical programs, five comedy-dramas and thirteen audience-participation shows." A decade later, in 1969, the mix was essentially the same with "a small increase in the percentage of situation comedies and talk shows." By 1990, there were even more talk shows, more movies and more sports, but without cable specialty channels, the mix would be reasonably close.[19]

The genres that feminist television critics have centered on most are the game shows and soap operas (shown largely in daytime) and the prime-time situation comedies. There has also been more recent interest in women as newscasters and talk show hosts. Feminists generally complain that as the family oriented media, television portrays women in very traditional roles.

The older shows and images are clearly more sexist. Reruns mean that even more outdated images continue to find their way into homes.

Even in contemporary shows, women are often relegated to specific roles. Whereas almost as many women as men star in situation comedies, about twice as many men as women star in television dramas, and there are almost no women starring in adventure shows. A 1977 study by Judith Lemon suggested that women were generally dominated by men in prime-time TV shows. Although Lemon found that class (as evidenced by occupation) was more influential than sex in dominance, men were generally cast in dominating occupations. She found less dominance of women in situation comedies and much more in crime dramas.[20] Twenty years later, there is very little evidence to change Lemon's conclusions.

Daytime television presented a mixed picture. Soap operas generally treated women much more equally, because they were produced specifically for women. However, women in soap operas are universally victims. Yet they often look good because so many of the male stars are such shallow cads. Soap opera heroines are very much like the *Cosmopolitan* magazine reader. She has beauty problems, marital problems, sexual problems, weight problems, and more. The show revolves around her facing the slings and arrows of an outrageous script. Of course, the idea is to make housewives watching the show feel better, because their problems pale by comparison even though women in soap operas are no longer usually housewives—they are now more often lawyers, doctors, and businessmen. However, we seldom see them doing professional work. Instead, they are plagued by divorce and sexual affairs and thus dominated by personal relationships and problems. The hidden message to housewife viewers is that being a professional woman is no bed of roses, which hardly warms feminist hearts. Meanwhile, soap opera male characters are usually versions of the *Playboy* male—completely wrapped up in self. Strangely, they too, are not seen doing professional work. Rather, they are always wrestling with personal problems—usually with women. This creates a rough equality between men and women professionals on soap operas and presents more sympathetic females and less sympathetic males.

If soap opera had some advantages for female images, daytime game shows were disastrous. The game show host has invariably been a confident, wise-cracking male who knows all the answers to life, as well as to his game questions. The contestants have been predominantly female and invariably flaky. They compete for cash and prizes in a festival of greed, with the cool, detached male host poking gentle fun at them. With the sexual revolution of the 1960s came racier daytime game shows such as *The Dating Game* and *The Newlywed Game* for younger housewives. These new genres had the typical male host, but he poked fun at both male and female contestants, but because the host was male, most of the joking was from a male point of view.

The worst thing about daytime television for feminist critics was its dim view of American housewives. It assumed that the typical housewife was interested only in simple games of greed and soap opera suffering. Not until the *Donohue Show* in the late 1970s did the daytime talk shows get much past cooking and children. Donohue took on complicated political issues and had a spectrum of guests which included William Buckley, Ralph Nader, and Gloria Steinem. However, by 1990 Donohue too had surrendered to the daytime syndrome. Except for an occasional program on politics, Donohue went for titillating domestic subjects to compete with similar topics on *The Oprah Winfrey Show* and that of Geraldo Rivera. The constant rerun of old sentimental sitcoms on daytime television also reinforced the general notion that those who watched television in the daytime had IQs below 100.

Women did better on prime time, but had trouble looking strong. They often out-thought men on situation comedies, or at least they had the last word. However, early on they tended to play helpless victims on crime-drama shows, and on most adventure shows they were nonexistent or weak. Even in comedy shows women were not usually able to compete with men physically, unless they had special powers. Good examples are the genie in *I Dream of Jeannie*, the witch in *Bewitched*, and the nun in *The Flying Nun*. Television adventure shows also gave us *Wonder Woman*, *The Bionic Woman*, and Batgirl in the *Batman* series. Men, however, could be very physical in westerns and crime shows without special powers.

There were a few exceptions to male crime dominance. Angie Dickinson pioneered a strong role in *Policewoman* in the 1970s, and this was followed by even stronger, more realistic female police roles in the 1980s with the *Cagney and Lacey* series. *Charlie's Angels*, a mid-1970s hit, had stressed the sexiness of Farah Fawcett and Jaclyn Smith more than their detective prowess. Yet, the three angels gave each other sisterly support and supported themselves by carrying guns, and using a variety of shrewd ploys. Susan St. James on *McMillan and Wife* was far less effective as Rock Hudson's co-star. She generally got him into trouble with stereotypical feminine approaches.[21]

Westerns offered very few possibilities to women. Even television westerns suffered from the Butch Cassidy–Sundance Kid syndrome. Series from *The Rifleman* and *Have Gun, Will Travel* to *Gunsmoke* and *Bat Masterson* featured either male buddies or loners. The one noteworthy exception was Amanda Blake's rendition of Kitty, the saloon owner on *Gunsmoke*.

She was usually a resourceful confidante of Sheriff Matt Dillon (James Arness). She did not have as many lines as Dillon's male sidekick, Chester (Dennis Weaver), but she was much brighter. Yet on balance, women played the same role in television westerns that they played in Hollywood westerns. Women were somebody the male star could protect and be tender with so he could show his tender side. When women or children were not available, the western star was kind to his horse, making women in westerns glorified horses.

A big problem with female images in situation comedies was that women lacked clear occupations. The female stars in comedy series, such as Doris Day, Lucille Ball, and Valerie Harper, never worked very seriously at anything. Harper, unlike Lucy and Archie Bunker's wife, Jean Stapleton, was ostensibly a window dresser, even though she spent all her time trying to get married. Maude, played by Beatrice Lillie on the show of the same name, did almost nothing outside the home. She simply wisecracked while at home. Mary Tyler Moore played a television producer on *The Mary Tyler Moore Show*, but she was constantly delegated domestic chores at work. She called her boss, played by Ed Asner, Mr. Grant, but all her male coworkers with supposedly equal status called him Lou. Program after program found Moore making coffee, cleaning up, and generally playing mommy to grown men. As popular as she was with women, Moore was hardly a model of the liberated woman. Comedic women such as Cher and Carol Burnett did offer sassy role models, but they did not play roles, they played themselves.

Men took some juicy roles away from women in the 1960s and 1970s. *Mr. Novak* portrayed a high school teacher who statistically should have been Ms. Novak. *Room 222* later used a black male teacher, and the *Welcome Back Kotter* series featured a white male teacher. *Room 222* also had as supporting stars, a white male principal, a young inexperienced female teacher, and a woman school counselor. Nevertheless, the show focused on problems between the black male teacher and his class.

There were no female physicians to challenge *Marcus Welby Ben Casey*, or *Dr. Kildare*. Decades later, *Dr. Quinn Medicine Woman* features a woman doctor, but places her on the 19th-century American frontier, where any medical skills were scarce and welcome. Nor were there star female lawyers to compete with *Perry Mason* or *Ironside*, both played by Raymond Burr. There were shows that placed a woman in a potent group, such as *The Mod Squad* and *The Storefront Lawyers*. However, the spectrum often seemed odd or forced. *Mad* magazine satirized the biracial *Mod Squad* as "The Odd Squad"—one black, one white, and one blonde.

The only traditional place for a woman was a family series such as *The Waltons* or *Little House on the Prairie*. There was obviously no substitute for a mother when focusing on a nuclear family, then or now, yet Edith Bunker, as played by Maureen Stapleton on *All in the Family,* was largely seen as a disaster by feminists. Men on family comedy series were often as lame-brained as Edith Bunker: Archie Bunker was a good example. But they did not reinforce an image of the stupid house-husband. In part, they were funny because they were anomalies—men with little to do, but sit around the house and gripe.

The other side of the coin for women was that family responsibilities often complicated their roles. Betty Friedan once asked Norman Felton, an MGM executive producer, why *Mr. Novak* could not be a woman teacher. He explained:

If you have a woman lead in a television series, she has to be either married or unmarried. If she's unmarried, what's wrong with her? After all, it's housewives we're appealing to and marriage is their whole life. If she's married, what's her husband doing in the background? He must not be very effective. He should be making the decisions. For drama there has to be action, conflict. . . . For a woman to make decisions, to triumph over anything, would be unpleasant, dominant, masculine. After all, most women are housewives, at home with children; most women are dominated by men, and they would react against a woman who succeeded at anything.[22]

In situation comedies, women housewives often triumphed over children or husbands, but because it was comic, the audience did not take it seriously and just laughed at or with the housewife. Friedan believed that by centering on housewife images in the 1950s and 1960s, television encouraged young, impressionable girls to settle for being housewives. Friedan charged that the TV image suggested there was "no need" for a woman "to work or study in school." All she had to do was "get that boy to marry" her, and he would take care of the woman's life. The images said: "Do anything you can to hook a man . . . because you can't be a person yourself." Yet, by marrying you could "be a housewife at 18" and get all those gifts you see on television on *Queen for a Day* as wedding presents. Friedan saw many of the "new teenage housewives—the growth-stunted young mothers who quit school to marry" as "female Frankenstein monsters," created by television. She felt that television badly needed to provide "some heroines" as "images of real women to help girls and women take themselves seriously."[23] Friedan has been identified with the older, more conservative women's liberation wing, because of her stress on procedural rights and founding of N.O.W. However, Friedan should get much more credit as one of the first countercultural activists, because of her consistent stress on negative images.

Friedan had called for new heroic female images in 1965. They never really appeared in quantity and quality until the late 1980s—twenty years later. In 1989, *Newsweek* even talked about the "feminization of television." It centered on Roseanne Barr's portrayal of a feisty blue collar wife on *Roseanne* and Candice Bergen's portrayal of a sophisticated newswoman on *Murphy Brown*. However, the large number of new shows with almost all female casts were more important. These shows included *Heart Beat* (about women in medicine), *A Different World* (about women college students), *China Beach* (about military nurses in Vietnam), *Nightingales* (about nursing students), *Designing Women* (about businesswomen), and *Golden Girls* (about retired women).[24]

In addition, there were many recent and new situation comedies and feature shows that supplied female heroines or at least focused on women's problems. These shows included *Day by Day, Who's the Boss, Dynasty, Falcon Crest, Kate and Allie, A Fine Romance*, and *227*. In a class by itself was the very popular, *Murder She Wrote*, starring Angela Lansbury as a sort of modern, female Sherlock Holmes.

Not all the shows were seen as feminist triumphs. For example, some California nurses protested that *Nightingales* presented a false and negative image of nurses. They saw *Nightingales* as a "kind of 'Charlie's Angels' with bedpans." Yet, no matter how poor, tasteless, or indirectly sexist some of the shows were, the important point was their use of women who actually worked at their chosen profession. However, Cherie Rankin, who served in Vietnam as a Red Cross worker, still fumed about the sexy nurses serving in Vietnam on the *China Beach* show. She angrily noted: "Most of the women on the show are preoccupied with men rather than their jobs." Rankin felt that the actresses were "bimbos or hookers, always dressed in seductive clothes." She described them as "a GI's fantasy." Indeed, *Newsweek* described them as "Beach" bunnies.[25]

Nightingales and *China Beach* were created by men, although *Murphy Brown* (about a newswoman) and *Heart Beat* (about women doctors who run their own clinic) were written and produced by women. Their heroines are much more hardheaded about their professional life and hardhearted about the men in their life.

Roseanne Barr's show also changed the family situation comedy. The early 1980s had pioneered family shows such as *Family Ties* and *The Cosby Show*. Wives such as Mrs. Claire Huxtable played perfect superwomen, who juggled motherhood and career with few problems or complaints. They were about as representative of mothers as Bill Cosby's character was of obstetricians. Roseanne, however, had constant problems juggling anything, and she took out her problems directly on her husband and children.

Roseanne had not read Dr. Spock. She was the vengeful antidote to Mrs. Cleaver and Harriet Nelson. She did not want to understand her kids. She was totally self-centered and wanted everybody to understand her.

Murphy Brown was uniquely unmotherly. She seldom dealt with children or handled the simplest domestic chores. More importantly, she was proud of it, or at least guiltless. Even when she later became an unwed single mother, the show rather ignored her infant. Brown's professional life was everything for her, and the show made sure viewers knew how well she was doing by constant name-dropping. She met and ate with celebrity world figures, such as Walter Cronkite and Henry Kissinger, while even ex-President Nixon called her for a date. Her energy was limitless. In one episode, Brown attempted to integrate a men only journalists club by first lying down in front of Morely Safer's auto and then extorting her way in. After failing to gain membership, she philosophically asked why someone over forty still had to push "her way into everything." Of course, her pushiness was the show's point and focus.[26] It was likely her flagrant feminism that got Vice President Dan Quayle on her case, when she became an unmarried single mother. He clearly would not have criticized a traditional woman for sacrificing her time and career for a child, whether or not she was married.

Women writers, directors, and producers are still trying to push their way into television. In 1989, male TV writers earned an estimated one third more than women writers. Yet, while women made up only 8 percent of the television directors, they received 24 percent of the awards. This does not seem odd, because only the best women creative talents push their way through. If women are scarce in the trenches, they are completely absent in the boardrooms. Network presidents, vice presidents, and even local station managers are almost always male. In the early days of women's liberation, studio newsmen often asked feminists if America was ready for a woman president. Often the studio show had both a woman producer and camera person. The answer should have been: America will be ready for a woman president when this station is ready for a woman station manager.

If women failed to integrate television management, they did move toward parity in newscasting. In 1968, Marya Mannes complained about the lack of women newscasters as role models. She noted:

Walter, Chet, David, Eric, Frank, Ed—wonderful guys, superb professionals, and we know them better than anybody else in the world, except for our husbands. For they come into the room every night and tell us what the score is and where the action is, and we don't care if they're handsome or homely, or 40 or 50 or 60, because they have authority, they have presence, they have experience and reason because they are men.[27]

Mannes complained that except for an occasional field reporter, such as Pauline Frederick who covered the United Nations for *NBC Nightly News*, women were absent from television as commentators. Mannes noted that pretty women were allowed to inform us about the weather or tell us what the president's wife was wearing, but not to read the news, which is all that most male anchors did. The result was "that the only national television female of real authority" was "Julia Child," the French Chef who taught cooking.[28]

Women slowly but surely broke into network and local newscasting. In 1976, Barbara Walters became the first network news anchor when she signed a five-year contract to co-anchor *ABC Evening News* with Harry Reasoner. Reasoner soon left in protest, but Walters had broken the gender barrier. In the 1980s, women began to co-anchor local news shows everywhere. At the national level, field reporters, such as Connie Chung and Sally Quinn, took on more interpretive, high-profile news roles. At the same time, Jane Pauley of the NBC *Today* show and Barbara Walters established themselves as two of the best interviewers around. Pauley specialized in entertainment figures; Walters was known for her no-holds-barred political interviews with world leaders, but was also good with show-business celebrities.

By 1990, the male stranglehold on news and talk shows had been clearly dented, if not completely broken. Cokie Roberts sat in with George Will and Sam Donaldson to discuss politics on *The David Brinkley Show* and became co-host in 1996 after Brinkley retired. Also, Oprah Winfrey and Sally Jesse Raphael had followed Joan Rivers into the increasingly popular sex-celebrity talk show genre. They were followed by movie star Rosie O'Donnell in 1995. They were the female equivalent of male movie star talk hosts, George Hamilton and Charles Grodin—but the women were much more popular.

Women newscasters were caught in a peculiar bind. They were expected to look sexy, which meant they had to be fairly young, yet expertise in newscasting came with age. Almost anyone could read news script from the teleprompter, but it took wisdom to comment. This problem has never been resolved. There are no examples of elderly newswomen to match Walter Cronkite's career or the ongoing career of David Brinkley, even though on average women live longer than men. There are no female equivalents of sixtyish newscasters such as Ted Koppel and Dan Rather. Barbara Walters still does specials, but she is no longer an anchor or regular newscaster. Murphy Brown is a television image without a real-life counterpart. The career of newswoman Cokie Roberts encourages some feminists, but she is younger than almost all her male colleagues. She also has been somewhat reinvented with more stylish hair and dress, a strategy the nerdish George Will (her ABC colleague) never found necessary for success.

In general, the television image of women seems to have made enormous gains, because it started so far back. The plastic women on early sitcoms, who seldom stepped out of the kitchen except to wave good-bye to their off-to-work husbands, left no where to go but up. Whereas the housewife image remained strong on game shows and soap operas in the 1970s, the next generation of women in situation comedies at least were interesting, and for the first time, like Mary Tyler Moore's character, they were often single. If Mary Tyler Moore's Mary Richards was not aggressive, she was independent and fairly happy. This told millions of women that long term or short term they could be single and still be happy. Yet as women's liberation picked up steam in the 1970s, television never supplied any clearly feminist models. Instead, the 1970s were famous for "jiggle" sex as one female star after another from *Charlie's Angels* to Suzanne Somers on *Three's Company* stripped down as far as censors would allow and then shook it for the audience. The era of video-bimbo saturation ended in the 1980s, but the sexy woman remains a dominant image in television as in film.

Since 1950, television has been the dominant American media. The average home watches television six hours a day, and the average high school graduate has spent more time watching television than in classrooms. Television became our electronic babysitter early on. As such, it shaped children at an early impressionable age. There is a tendency for some cultural critics to ignore it, because so much television content is obviously imbecilic. Yet feminists dare not ignore low-quality programming. Television works by pattern and repetition. The thing many people and especially children like about television is that they see what they expect.

Television programming is not very adventurous. It picks up trends from other media and culture in general. Just as fashions tend to spring up on both coasts in America and work their way inward, television takes its cues from cinema and general trends. In part, this explains why feminism had such little immediate impact on television, compared with music and film. The feminist charges that television presented distorted and unfair images of women came early and have continued. Reform has been slow and complicated. Clearly, the largest audience for the most sexist shows, such as game shows, soap operas, and traditional situation comedies, has been composed of women. Feminists are not likely to dislodge these shows as long as ratings hold up. They have to create a new audience for shows with better images, and these new shows have to be entertaining before they can be anything else. Liberating the mass media comes down to liberating the audience.

ADVERTISING

If there is anything more pervasive than television, it is advertising. Television itself is fueled with constant ads, and people are further bombarded by ads on radio, billboards, and in magazines. Advertising connects mass media and business. Without it, media such as television and magazines would be tailored for those willing and able to pay for it. Advertising allows media producers to collect viewers by offering content with large mass appeal. The producer then sells the audience to business advertisers. Commercials are the price radio and television audiences pay for free programming; print ads are the price subscribers pay for magazines and newspapers.

Advertising creates a community of both commercial consumers and mass cultural consumers. Americans share both the advertised products and the entertainments that sell them. Advertising is uninterested in the content effects of television shows or magazine articles, unless they make prospective customers mad at the advertiser. Content is used simply to build the largest possible audience. Yet advertising has an increasingly sophisticated content of its own. Advertising directors and producers spend much more money per minute on creating television ads than on producing programs, and the ads themselves have unintended content effects. In the process of convincing people what to buy, they must convince them what kind of man, woman, or child they want to be, or at least what image they choose for themselves.

Images of women had long been used to sell products through advertising. In the 19th century, illustrations of glamorous women were used both in America and Europe to sell products such as cigars and patent medicines. The sexual sell inherent in cigar-girl labels was extended to the countless new products that males bought in 20th-century America. The first thirty years of this century were the golden age of American illustration. Illustrators such as Maxfield Parrish, Harrison Fisher, and Coles Phillips were masters of the sexual sell. They constantly mixed products and beautiful women in the ads they produced. Photographs largely replaced illustrated advertising after 1950, but sexual sell with beautiful female models remained a constant. After World War II, advertising tended to use housewife ad-models much more than in the past. The end of the war brought a flood of new marriages and children, and motherhood was a common ideal. Moreover, advertisers estimated that women purchased almost 75 percent of what their families bought.

In her pathbreaking 1963 book *The Feminine Mystique*, Betty Friedan laid much of the blame for the mystique on Madison Avenue ad-men. She saw the constant pitch to, and images of, housewives as part of a general business plot to keep women out of the job market and in the supermarket as mere consumers. Friedan claimed that an advertising researcher told her that "properly manipulated . . . American housewives" could "be given the sense of identity, purpose, creativity, the self-realization, even the sexual joy they lack—by the buying of things."[29]

Friedan quotes a survey by an appliance maker in 1945 that divides American housewives into three types—the "true housewife," the "career woman or would be career woman," and the "balanced homemaker." The survey of forty-five hundred homemakers concluded that the problem with selling appliances to the true housewife was her reluctance to accept new devices that might make her skills less valuable. The career women were a much tougher market because they did "not believe that a woman's place is primarily in the home." The balanced homemaker was the ideal consumer because she had some "outside interests" or had held a job before home-making. She readily accepted new devices, yet was practical enough "not to expect them to do the impossible." The study's final conclusion was that be-cause the balanced homemaker had the greatest consumer potential, busi-ness should make "women aware of the desirability of belonging to this group." Industry should "educate them through advertising that it is possi-ble to have outside interests and become alert to wider intellectual influ-ences without becoming a career woman." The underlying message was clear: "The art of good homemaking" should be the goal of every woman.[30]

Friedan's conspiracy theory aside, business had a clear incentive to culti-vate and encourage housewives—America's chief consumers. Friedan noted that it was not easy for advertisers "to give American women that feeling of achievement, and yet keep housework their main purpose in life." Anything that prepared them for new experiences, such as "education, inde-pendence, and individuality" had to be neutralized or "channeled back to the home."

By the mid-1950s, Friedan suggested that advertising surveys showed that career women "who reacted to domestic slavery with indignation" were largely gone. They were replaced by "less worldly" women whose PTA ac-tivity furnished outside contacts and who found their "femininity and indi-vidualism" in housework. Yet advertising consultants warned that suburban housewives were developing "individual standards." They were less likely to try to "keep up with the Joneses." Advertisers had to appeal to her per-sonal zest for life, by "adding more enjoyment . . . new experiences . . . and lessons in living." Thus, a manufacturer of a cleaning appliance was advised to advertise with the slogan: "House cleaning should be fun."

Friedan noted that another report urged advertisers to gain sales by mak-ing the housewife feel she was a specialist who used "specialized products for specialized tasks." Another way of raising her stature was to teach her "tricks of the trade" unknown to others. The report continued: "Help her to justify her menial task by building up her role as the protector of the family. . . . Emphasize her kingpin role in the family . . . help her be an expert rather than a menial worker . . . make housework a matter of knowledge and skill, rather than a matter of brawn and dull unremitting effort."[31]

According to advertising writers, new products not only decreased work, but engaged housewives "in the world of scientific development." Besides making her more professional, a new appliance "increased a woman's feeling of economic security and luxury, just as a new automobile" did "for a man."

Friedan felt that advertisers also discovered a new teenage market in the 1950s. They found that young wives who married right after high school were insecure and easier to sell. They generally believed they could become middle class without work or study simply by purchasing certain goods. One advertising report noted:

Forty-nine percent of the new brides are teenagers, and more girls marry at the age of eighteen than at any other age. . . . This . . . yields a larger number . . . on the threshold of their own . . . decision making in purchases. But the most important fact is. . . . Marriage today is not only the culmination of a romantic attachment, more consciously . . . it is also a decision to create a partnership in establishing a comfortable home, equipped with a great number of desirable products.

The report advised concentrating on the younger teenagers because the young would "want what the others want, even if their mothers don't." Advertisers saw teens as "the big market of the future" and argued that "word-of-mouth advertising, along with group pressure" was not only a potent influence, "but in the absence of tradition, a most necessary one."[32]

For the older housewives, the key sell strategy was creativity, not peer pressure. Sewing in suburbia was sold as creative achievement in dress, rather than work or a way to save money on clothes. Friedan marveled at how perceptively advertisers had analyzed the psyche of housewives and how shrewdly they had manipulated psychological needs. Thus, department stores made themselves interesting places for housewives to visit, and they filled a housewife's need to get out in the world. Similarly, bargains filled a need for achievement. For the affluent, price sensitivity was not financial. A bargain did not mean getting something you could not otherwise afford. It meant that the woman was "doing a good job as a housewife." Just as stores were the extended schools for housewives, advertisements were the textbooks.

Friedan gave advertising researchers credit for discovering "the reality of the housewife's life and needs," as opposed to sociologists and psychologists still behind the "Freudian veil." Advertisers knew that housewives had complex needs that home, husband, and children left unfulfilled. Friedan did not claim advertising manipulators had created the feminine mystique, but she did label them its most powerful perpetrators. They flattered American housewives, diverted their guilt, and partially filled their "growing sense of emptiness."[33]

What bothered Friedan most was the campaign for young girls. She noted:

The real crime, no matter how profitable . . . is the callous and growing acceptance of the manipulator's advice "to get them young"—the television commercials that children sing or recite even before they learn to read, "Look, Sally, Look," the big beautiful ads that magazines deliberatively designed to turn teenage girls into housewife buyers of things before they grow up to be women.

Friedan believed that through advertising, America "sacrificed little girls" to the feminine mystique just as primitive cultures "sacrificed little girls to its tribal gods." She pointed out that ads often said, "Never underestimate the power of a woman." But advertising constantly underestimated that power by segregating it in the home.[34]

With the rise of women's liberation in the 1960s came increased scrutiny of advertisements both on television and in the print media. Ironically ads became even more sexist in the late 1960s and early 1970s. The sixties also brought the sexual revolution and a generally freer climate for any artistic expression. Advertisements became less inhibited across the board. Ads that courted women as housewives did not disappear, but they suddenly seemed prosaic compared with the new sexual sell ads, especially those pitched to the young. The result was total war between advertisers and feminist media critics. Feminists complained that ads either portrayed them as housewives, sexual objects, or grannies. Sexual-object ads were generally defined as ad images that presented sexy women for male contemplation. The range of sexist ads was much wider, and also included ads showing women as childlike, secondary to men, or helpmates to men.

The feminist invasion of the *Ladies Home Journal* editorial offices in 1969 and the confrontation with editor John Mack Carter was a good example of feminist complaints. The invaders charged that the *Journal* was a sexist magazine with sexist ads, largely because most of the editors, including chief editor Carter, were men. When Carter asked what they meant by sexist ads, the women gave examples from the current *Journal*. One ad was a

Jell-O ad that pumped a new dessert by suggesting it could be made to celebrate a husband's promotion even if the wife did not understand her husband's new job. A woman protester told Carter that the ad really said that even if a woman was too dumb to understand what an assistant vice president did, she could still make this Jell-O dessert because it was simple, like her. As other examples, the feminists picked on an ad for Secret Antiperspirant for a woman's "special feelings" and a cosmetic ad that said "put on a happy face tonight." Carter asked what was wrong with the cosmetic ad. He was told that cosmetic ads encouraged women to paint themselves as children did on Halloween and to make themselves glamorous at all times and to be ashamed of their natural appearance.[35] This confrontation convinced Carter to offer feminists a small section of a future *Journal*. The result was a nine-page section in the August 1970 issue that included eight feminist articles with titles such as "Should This Marriage Be Saved?" (a take off on their regular feature, "Can This Marriage Be Saved?") and "How Appearance Divides Women."

Lucy Komisar's 1970 article "The Image of Woman in Advertising" reflected most of the new feminist criticism of ads. For example, she covered a December 1969 protest at New York's Macy's department store, against the image of women in the Mattel Toys ads. Mattel had recently run an ad in *Life* magazine which noted: "Because girls dream about being a ballerina, Mattel makes Dancerina . . . a pink confection in a silken blouse and ruffled tutu. . . . Wishing you were older is part of growing up. . . . Barbie, a young fashion model, and her friends do the 'in' things girls should do—talk about new places to visit, new clothes to wear and new friends to meet." Another part of the ad declared: "Because boys were born to build and learn, Mattel makes Togol [a block building set]." The illustration also shows a boy playing with scientific toys and the ad proclaimed: "Because boys are curious about things big and small, Mattel makes Super-Eyes, a telescope that boys can have in one ingenious set of optically engineered lenses and scopes . . . that . . . create dozens of viewing devices—all for science or all for fun."[36]

Komisar reported that the protesters at Macy's carried signs such as "Mattel Limits Little Girls' Dreams" and "Girls Were Also Born to Build and Learn." Komisar argued that stereotyping boys and girls by their interests had clear negative effects on women. The girl who wanted to be a dancer or model and was "imbued with the importance of how she looks and what she wears" would more likely become "a thirty-year-old Barbie Doll." Komisar felt advertisers saw women as "a combination sex object and wife and mother who" fulfilled herself "by looking beautiful and alluring for boy friends and lovers and cooking, cleaning, washing, or polishing for her husband and family." The female-ad stereotype was generally submissive, "subservient to men," and "not very bright." Ads about working women were likely to show women as stewardesses or secretaries. A woman's job, in any event, was less important than looking good for the man in her life. Komisar gave an example from a Parker Pen ad: "You might as well give her a gorgeous pen to keep her checkbook unbalanced with. A sleek and shining pen will make her feel prettier. Which is more important to any girl than solving mathematical mysteries." For Komisar, this adult woman's interests had not advanced much from her Barbie days. In short, Komisar depicted the American ad woman as totally involved in the "quest for the holy male." Clearly, most ads in the 1970s and 1980s told women how to look sexy or how to take care of their family.[37]

There have always been at least four distinct types of women that ads go after. The distinctions are basically age groups. First, there is the young woman, obsessed with cosmetics and clothes and even willing to buy tooth-paste that promises to make her sexier. Second, there is the married mom who is a full-time homemaker. She is focused on making better meals and having a cleaner, germ-free home. She seeks a cleaner wash; sparkling glasses; lower calorie, but delicious cakes; and miraculously waxed floors. Her daughter, the young fox, seeks only smoother skin, bouncier hair, and sexy clothes. The third type is the older grandmother figure. She suffers from the infirmities of age and is constantly looking for softer toilet paper and better denture adhesive. The fourth type is generally missing in ads. She is the career woman who works out of the home. It is assumed she will buy beauty products just like young women and household products, too, but she does not have an individual image, because she is not an identifiable market. The first three types of women are often portrayed as stupid because of their narrow obsessions.

Men (especially fat husbands) are also often portrayed as stupid, but there are many positive ad images of men to balance the negative ones. The young sexy women are vapid models with a constant generic smile. The housewives are either sentimental and womanly robots or crude, blue-collar types with a whining voice like a buzz saw. The grannies are generally old and out of it, as if in the first stages of Alzheimer's disease. Working women in general, and professional women in particular, simply did not appear in ads before the late 1970s. When professional women did appear, it was still often a pitch for beauty or household products. Thus, a woman lawyer, sci-entist, or engineer would supposedly be bright enough to recognize a supe-rior lipstick or brand of orange juice.

Whether a beauty queen or homemaker, women in ads generally pleased men by looking good and performing well. The perfect man had power, knowledge, and money. The perfect woman in ads had the cleanest house and the best meals around, but also the brightest hair, smoothest skin, and she was absolutely odorless, unless she was wearing the latest expensive perfume. Moreover, women in ads were constantly instructed on what to buy by an authoritative male voice reading the television ad copy. Often men appeared in the ads as instructors. Thus, although Virginia Slim cigarette ads told women they had come a long way, most other ads suggested that they had not. Ads of the 1970s suggested that they needed a man from Glad to show them how to wrap sandwiches and the Tydee Bowl Man to motor around in their toilet bowls while dispensing cleaning instructions. Also, the names of new cleaning products were increasingly macho in the 1960s and 1970s. Bold, Drive, Ajax, and Hero were good subtle examples; Mr. Clean and Big Wally were more overt signs.[38]

Ads that demeaned women were everywhere. While selling alligator purses, an ad noted: "An alligator is like a woman, the wise man said, the best are soft, supple, and non-belligerent." To sell cigarettes, Silva Thins suggested: "Cigarettes are like women, the best ones are thin and rich."[39] In selling cigarettes and purses, advertisers were defining women. Airline ads were particularly suggestive in advertising their stewardesses with sexy phrases or poses. An American ad for Spain's Iberia Airlines showed a blond stewardess with the ad line: "This nice little blonde from Barcelona will romance you all the way to Spain." American Airlines featured a shapely stewardess curled up in an airline seat in a sexy pose and giving a come-hither look. The caption read: "Think of her as your Mother." National Airlines ran an ad featuring a beautiful stewardess with the ad line: "I'm Cheryl, Fly Me, Fly National." Feminists actually complained to the Federal Trade Commission that the National ad was misleading, because National stewardesses did not really fly their planes.

The National "fly me" ad also made the 1972 N.O.W. list of the year's three worst ads. The other top two offenders were the Olivetti Girl ads, which sold typewriters by calling secretaries girls, and the Geritol television ad. The Geritol wife took Geritol brand vitamins and supposedly was the best of the best—an efficient homemaker and a beautiful wife. But her only reward was her husband's laconic comment: "My wife, I guess I'll keep her." Another ad that bothered the N.O.W. media watchers was a Weyenberg shoe ad that showed a nude woman lying next to a man's shoe. The ad line read: "Keep her where she belongs." Weyenberg defended protests with this official statement: "Weyenberg is taking the first positive stand for masculinity . . . against the influences of the women's liberation movement." Weyenberg also noted that it was "appealing to men who" rejected "effeminate and women's liberation appeals." N.O.W. responded by giving Weyenberg's ad its "Keep Her in Her Place Award."[40]

N.O.W. also gave awards to ads with positive images of women. In 1972, Pampers received their first "Positive Image of Women Award" for its ad showing a cute girl toddler with a diaper. The ad caption noted: "The future President of the United States deserves a drier bottom." Feminists in New York City also awarded Breakthrough Advertising Awards in August 1971 and again in August 1972 for ads "depicting a more enlightened image of women." A Breakthrough Award was given to Band-Aid in 1971 for depicting girls in roles as active as boys. Additional Breakthrough Awards were given to White Label Scotch and Arrid Deodorant for ads depicting women in professional roles. However, the same group gave "Barefoot and Pregnant" and "Old Hat Awards" for sexist ads. In 1971, "Old Hat" awards were derisively given to Brillo cleansing pads, Mattel Toys, Skinny Dip Cologne, and ironically to Virginia Slims ads (for distorting images of women's liberation with their "You've Come a Long Way Baby" ads). Indeed, the only clear message Virginia Slims ads gave was that women could now smoke and get their equal share of lung cancer.[41]

Many sexist ads were doubly ironic. A Fem-Iron ad showed a woman at a typewriter who brags: "Unlike my mother who never worked, I'm putting my husband through school, so he can be a great architect." A Clairol ad rebelled against youth when the male announcer intoned: "You're not getting older, you're getting better." The ludicrous irony evidently escaped most women, or market researchers would have cut the ad. Women were getting better not older, but they had to dye their hair so they would not appear older, even if older was better.

The sexy ads got steadily more suggestive through the early 1970s. A National Car Rental ad showed a female auto rental representative sitting in a chair with disheveled clothes and hair. The headline read: "Take Advantage of Us." An After Six tuxedo ad showed a wedding couple and the caption: "Other products hint at sex, we guarantee it." An ad for Kayser lingerie showed a scantily clad woman with a curtain behind her and the headline: "You owe it to your audience."[42]

Sexual sell ads had a long history. Although the new sexier ads got a lot of attention, feminists probably centered more on ads that denigrated what women did. For example, an IBM ad showed a businessman and his female secretary. The ad line noted: "If she makes a mistake, she types right over it. If her boss makes a revision, she types right over it." The suggestion that women secretaries make errors, but male bosses only make revisions was likely to infuriate women. Feminists have struck back periodically with turnaround ads. For example, an ad run in jest shows a male dressed in a business suit pulling up his pants to show his legs. The caption reads: "Hire him, he has great legs." Feminists have also struck back at ads by pasting labels on them that read: "This ad exploits women" or "This ad insults women." In some cases similar sentiments were spray painted on billboard ads by angry feminists. One famous billboard ad originally showed a Ferrari sports car and noted: "If a beautiful woman was a car she would be a Ferrari." Someone painted over the caption: "If this Lady was a sports car, she would run men down."

Advertising does not often create negative images of women, but it does often reinforce those images by constant repetition. Moreover, male advertising executives often carry stereotypical negative images of women into their jobs. It is difficult to know how objective their surveys are, but the profile of the housewife has been overwhelmingly negative. Thus, in 1970 Lucy Kosimar noted that a survey of housewives, done by Haug Associates of Los Angeles and printed in *Ad Age*, gave the following profile:

She likes to watch television and she does not enjoy reading a great deal. She is most easily reached through television and the simple down-to-earth magazines. She finds her satisfaction within a rather small world and the center of this world is her home. She has little interest or skill to explore, to probe into things for herself. . . . She tends to have a negative or anti-conceptual way of thinking. Mental activity is arduous for her. . . . And she tends to experience discomfort and confusion when faced with ambiguity or too many alternatives. . . . She is a person who wants to have things she can believe in, rather than things she has to think about.[43]

The real question is if this really describes the average housewife, did American advertising help make her a self-fulfilling prophecy with its simple-minded sell strategies? In 1971, Alice Courtney and Sarah Lockeretz published a study based on analyzing 729 ads in *Life*, *Look*, *Newsweek*, *The New Yorker*, *Saturday Review*, *Time*, *U.S. News and World Report*, and *Reader's Digest* during the week of April 18, 1970. The analysis sorted ads by product and the number and sexes of all adults and their occupations and activities. Ads with children or teenagers were not analyzed. Thus, the study focused on 312 ads containing 397 adult men and 278 adult women. Their study noted that although in 1970, 33 percent of full-time workers were women, only 12 percent of the 1970 ads showed women workers. When entertainers were excluded, the percentage dropped to 7 percent for ads depicting working women, compared with 45 percent of the ads showing working men. Of those women shown working, not one was in a professional role. On the basis of their study, the researchers found that the attitudes advertisers held regarding housewives were (1) a woman's place is in the home; (2) women do not make important decisions or do important things; (3) women are dependent and need men's protection; and (4) men regard women primarily as sexual objects—they are not interested in women as people.[44] Ironically, these conclusions were so broad and subjective, given the limited data, that the profiles of advertisers' views of housewives are as sketchy as the advertisers own studies of housewives.

Images of women in advertising made some small, but clear, gains in the late 1970s and 1980s that paralleled image gains in film and television, but the total effect was likely negligible. More professional women were pictured in ads, albeit often pushing household and beauty products. Also although the more demeaning and insulting ads were pushed out, sexual sell ads are still rampant and more subtle than ever. Relatively few working women are portrayed. Voice-overs on ads are still predominantly male. Although ads are now more likely to acknowledge that the housewife also works outside the home, they center on the housewife role anyway. Advertising remains a wasteland for women after thirty years of feminist criticism. Thus, the twenty-five to thirty-five year-old analysis of pioneer countercultural critics such as Betty Friedan and Lucy Komisar, are still fresh. They are a grim historical reminder of countercultural failure and neglect.

It is hard to argue with successful advertising. With a lot of money at stake, ad executives take very few chances and market test their ads relentlessly. If sexist ads sell, they feel they are justified. Also, because women are the largest group of buyers, they clearly can reject ad campaigns if they wish. They could even boycott products pushed in sexist ad campaigns, although there are very few examples of successful boycotting of any products on either a political or feminist basis.

The bright side of sexist ads is their role as perennial feminist consciousness raisers. The humiliating ads can constantly remind women that they have a long way to go. What more could feminists ask for than a constant nagging reminder that women are not taken seriously or treated fairly. If sexist advertising really disappears, feminists might have to reintroduce it as a key element of countercultural consciousness raising.

Perhaps the most effective consciousness raisers were women who operated as living countercultural models. The most effective counterculturists were not usually feminists, but charismatic women who exemplified the changes feminists called for. Many youths saw feminists as relevant, but preachy. Aggressive, successful, charismatic women promoted feminist ideals by subtle and almost subliminal example. Even when clearly feminist women, such as Gloria Steinem, were similarly successful, it was usually because of their personal charisma rather than their feminist ideas and credentials.

5

Feminist Heroines: Countercultural Models

Perhaps the most important elements of the feminist counterculture were the countercultural heroines. Their lives and lifestyles instructed and inspired a new breed of women in the 1960s and after. Each role model was a living counterculture, and their separate journeys dramatically illustrated countercultural change. The era of women's liberation was a treacherous time for both heroes and heroines. The 1960s and 1970s shook up culture, as well as society and politics. Indeed, the cultural terrain moved even more quickly and further than social foundations. In a time of cynicism and despair, young people had difficulty finding suitable heroes in the traditional fields of politics, business, and sports. Their new heroes were increasingly activists and entertainers (especially musicians and singers). Since American women had never found heroines in politics and business, and precious few in sports, the change seemed less revolutionary. Women entertainers had always been viewed frivolously, and women activists had usually been ladylike. Thus, the new female heroines were more revolutionary in their way than Bob Dylan or Abbie Hoffman. These women were all cultural artists, whether they painted or composed. What they did and how they lived were more important than what they said. They were models of life and not exponents of ideology. In short, they were countercultural heroines. Among the many heroines this era produced, three have been chosen to represent the spectrum—Janis Joplin, Joan Baez, and Gloria Steinem. Only one, Steinem, was a card-carrying feminist, but all three were important feminist role models.

More time is spent analyzing Joplin, because her role as a credible model is less obvious and her cultural effect more subtle. Neither Baez nor Joplin were particularly identified with the women's movement. Indeed, both women criticized women's liberation at various times. But heroines do not need groups. The loner is usually even more heroic. Gloria Steinem seems the exception here—a clear feminist insider. For many she was Ms. Liberation—the madonna of women's liberation as surely as Joan Baez was the madonna of folk music. Steinem was hardly the typical feminist leader. She was strikingly attractive, yet often private and withdrawn. She was sometimes called the great stone face. Steinem was always more a life model than a motivator or organizer.

Especially since 1920, America witnessed the decline of real heroes and the rise of mere celebrities. Historian Daniel Boorstin defined the modern celebrity as someone "known for his well-knowness." Unlike the hero who is famous for his deeds, the celebrity is famous for his fame. Whereas the hero's reputation grows over the years, the passage of time destroys the celebrity. The hero had, by definition, "stood the test of time." As Boorstin put it: "The hero created himself; the celebrity is created by the media. The hero was a big man; the celebrity is a big name." Celebrities did not achieve fame by accomplishing great deeds. Rather fame enveloped them because of their press agent's skill and society's constant need for new instant cultural heroes.[1]

Perhaps the classic celebrities are entertainment figures. Movie stars such as Marilyn Monroe, James Dean, Robert Redford, and Meryl Streep all fit Boorstin's definition and so do pop singers such as Bruce Springsteen, Michael Jackson, and Madonna. Yet one can be both a celebrity and a hero or heroine.

David Harris, an organizer of draft resistance in the 1960s, compared heroes with idols, instead of posing heroes against celebrities. This helped explain the peculiar type of cultural heroes entertainers often became in the 1960s and 1970s. Harris saw heroes and idols as the two primary public figures. The idol "existed beyond the people" and provided a vicarious life. The idol demonstrated what people could not attain, and thus they worshiped him or her as a "negation of themselves." Marilyn Monroe, for example, was worshiped by fans who knew they could never be Marilyn Monroe. A hero, on the other hand was "an available model" who demonstrated what people could do and be. Harris viewed the hero as only the "embodiment" of human potential. He was likely thinking of his own role and that of other political organizers, yet his ideas surely apply to some role models in the entertainment world as well.[2] They certainly applied to Janis Joplin, Joan Baez, and Gloria Steinem. This trio were not three who made a revolution, but rather three who were made by the revolution and then disseminated the new ideas with their lifestyle.

One factor that helped make entertainers heroic was the increasing pressure on all artists to at least be socially relevant, if not politically active. Traditionally, artists worked in splendid isolation—apart from social norms—so they were free to see what the masses could not. In the 19th century, Henry Thoreau might combine his life with his art and work out his ideas in the woods or Harriet Beecher Stowe might write for a political purpose, but these were exceptions. The 1930s depression brought a proletarian vogue among artists who suddenly discovered social injustice, but thirties artists, such as John Steinbeck and Edward Hopper, only reflected social ills. They were not models for change or heroes in any direct way. Many still think artistic detachment is functional. Without it, they argue, artists would lose that special ability to see and feel what the political hacks and social grinds could not. For example, some feel that blacks and Jews sometimes saw more about American society, because they were often outcasts operating outside conventional social boundaries. Even Canadians see themselves as detached observers of America.

Today, fewer critics argue the merits of artistic detachment. Personal experience and passion is increasingly more valued in artists and entertainers alike. Each election finds more entertainers taking sides. Each year finds more stars doing benefits for the environment, AIDS research, the poor, or other causes. For both artists and entertainers, it was no longer acceptable to fiddle while Rome burned. You had to be at least a volunteer fireperson. Since the 1960s, the worst charge leveled against popular artists were that they copped out. Traditionally, copping out meant prostituting your talent for fame or fortune; however, now copping out is almost indistinguishable from sitting out.

One interesting explanation of artistic activism and the new importance of cultural role models comes from extending Marshall McLuhan's subtle, confusing media philosophy. If, as McLuhan insisted, the medium is the message, then a person's life may teach us as much as his or her ideas. McLuhan aside, we increasingly center more on the artist's lifestyle than art or ideas. And if McLuhan is correct in seeing the artist as a distant early warning system,who senses the new social reality long before the masses, then almost anything the artist experiences or experiments with may merit consideration.

Even artists and entertainers who lack interest in politics can have radical social effects. People such as Janis Joplin and Andy Warhol, the pop artist, are both part of what historian Christopher Lasch called the new radicalism—a radicalism that merged power and art, attempted to raise an underground consciousness, exalted individual direct action, and sought to identify with society's downtrodden.[3] Radicals are generally seen as subversive, and this tends to bolster their heroic image. Countercultural approaches are by definition subversive, and art itself springs from subversive origins. If artists saw the world as others did, they would not create art.

Janis Joplin, Joan Baez, and Gloria Steinem were all cultural subversives. They were good examples of the new radicalism in the individual ways they mixed culture, lifestyle, and power. As different as they were in personality, background, education, and purpose, they had similar cultural effects. They all served as important countercultural models. Each was a unique, if unlikely, feminist heroine. Baez and Joplin were not technically feminists, yet they had important cultural connections to feminism and were both admired by many feminists. Joplin was seldom directly involved in political or social change, but she was often involved in cultural change. Of the three, Baez had the most international and universal perspective. She traveled to all corners of the world and became increasingly cosmopolitan. Steinem was the pure feminist in mind and spirit, but she hardly represented the typical feminist either in personality or lifestyle. Joplin and Baez were singers and Steinem was a writer. Joan Baez became a songwriter in midcareer and wrote two autobiographical books. All three women were artistically creative, yet their most important creation was the persona that made them models for other women.

JANIS JOPLIN AND THE NEW FEMINISM

Janis Joplin was born January 19, 1943, in Port Arthur, Texas, during World War II. In October 1970, at age twenty-seven, she died of a heroin overdose while the Vietnamese War still raged. Although Janis was clearly of the angry sixties generation, her malaise, unlike that of some rock-culture stars, seemed unrelated to national dissension or world strife. Joplin's former lover, rock singer Country Joe McDonald, for example, felt that because really grasping the total reality of Vietnam would probably drive him insane, he intended to "take drugs . . . turn up the music very loud" and "build a fantasy world where everything's beautiful."[4] However, Janis's move toward a drugged personal world was clearly linked to a long, drawn-out struggle within her psyche. Joplin was killed by a far more subtle war than Vietnam—the war between the sexes. Ironically, she was a victim of sexism within a sexual revolution that she helped fuel. This is but one of many contradictions in her rise as a rock superstar, but perhaps the most important irony was her role as a feminist symbol in a male dominated, sexist, rock culture.

At first glance, it seems odd to describe the rock world as sexist. Rock, after all, was an integral ingredient of a youth culture that championed unisexual clothing and sexual freedom, while revolting against conformist middle-class values. Yet rock lyrics almost universally stereotyped women as sexual objects, and rock music was almost entirely written and performed by male musicians. Similarly, female, rock-oriented disc jockeys were almost nonexistent. Rock festivals, however, would be impossible without a plentiful supply of "groovy chicks." There is one primary difference between the "groovy chick" and the more traditional "American Sweetheart." The "groovy chick" is a willing sexual partner who seldom fails to perform in the lyrics of rock songs.[5] Likewise, the stage patter of rock performers was obviously geared to males. Comments were invariably addressed to "you and your chick." Janis Joplin was an anomaly—a groovy chick who was performing and rapping with the audience rather than passively enjoying the scene.

There was little in Joplin's background to suggest that she would become either a feminist symbol or a rock superstar. Her hometown, Port Arthur, was an oil refinery center with a population of sixty thousand, located in Texas's southeastern corner. Houston lay one hundred miles away and Louisiana was just across the river. Port Arthur had a mixed population of native Texans, Louisiana Cajuns, Mexican-American immigrants, and African Americans from around the country—all drawn by the good union refinery jobs. When NBC-TV's *First Tuesday* show did a feature on Janis in February 1971, they simply described Port Arthur as "drab." On balance, Port Arthur was a typical Texas boomtown—the Southern Baptists dominated religion; the Democratic Party held most political power; and oil companies held the economic power. Not surprisingly, NBC found that the average citizen was proud of Port Arthur, hostile to the federal government, and suspicious of the "Eastern" media.

Janis's parents were not particularly average Port Arthur residents. Her mother, Dorothy, moved to Port Arthur from Amarillo at age twenty-two, and, after a one-year courtship, married Seth Joplin in 1936. Dorothy had a high school education and usually worked as a businesswoman; Seth held an engineering degree from Texas A & M University and had worked for Texaco Corporation ever since coming to Port Arthur. The Joplins had three children all told, including another daughter, Laura, and a son, Michael. Janis, however, was the firstborn.[6] As the first born, she basked in parental attention as a baby and by most accounts was a happy, normal child. Seth Joplin was a resourceful and active father. Janis often later referred to him as "a secret intellectual," who only had one other person in Port Arthur to whom he could talk. Traditionally, American feminists have had strong intellectual relationships with their fathers, and Janis seemed to enjoy such a paternal bond during her formative years. In a July 1970 interview, Janis reminisced about her father's influence and noted:

My father was like a secret intellectual, a book reader, a talker, a thinker. He was very important to me, because he made me think. He's the reason I am like I am, I guess. . . . The biggest thing in our house was when you learnt to write your name, you got to go and get a library card. He wouldn't get us a TV, he wouldn't allow a TV in the house.[7]

Despite the simple, just-folks verbal style that Janis cultivated, she was surprisingly intelligent and well read—especially in the area of classic American fiction. As a child, she was a quick learner and creative student. As a teenager, she showed a flair for writing and a more substantial talent for painting. Unfortunately, adolescence brought physical problems that haunted Janis throughout her life. Her childish good looks dissolved into a general heaviness, complicated by an extremely bad case of facial acne. Thereafter, Janis would be preoccupied by the fear that she was not attractive to men. As a high school junior, she solved her relationship with boys by becoming an equal member of a gang of four hell-raising males. For the first of many times, she tried to just be one of the boys. In the process, she picked up a reputation for Bohemian toughness and was ostracized by most of her classmates. Janis was relieved to graduate in 1960, and she immediately enrolled at Lamar Tech University, a state school, in nearby Beaumont. After an unhappy year at Lamar, she traveled to the West Coast, and in Los Angeles and San Francisco, the moody freshman became a world-weary hippie almost overnight.

Back in Texas in 1962, she tried to impress her old friends with her hip ways, first in Port Arthur and then at the University of Texas at Austin, where she enrolled in the summer of 1962. She had occasionally sung at coffeehouses in Beaumont and Houston earlier in 1962, but in Austin, she sang regularly, both at the student union and a bar named Threadgill's. She was drinking harder now and had become a favorite with the Austin postbeatnik crowd that centered around an apartment complex called "The Ghetto."

Janis's happiness abruptly ended in January 1964, when a thoughtless joke officially named her "Ugliest Man on Campus" in a contest. Janis then wrote her parents an emotional letter about the cruelty of the Austin campus and told them that she would have to leave. Shortly thereafter, Joplin and a male friend hitchhiked to San Francisco. Janis would return to Port Arthur and Austin in 1965 before going to San Francisco for good in 1966. However, Texas was never home for Joplin after 1963. Looking back in 1970, Janis felt that in Texas she had been "a beatnik" and "weirdo," and she observed: "Texas is OK if you want to settle down and do your own thing quietly, but it's not for outrageous people, and I was always outrageous. I got treated very badly in Texas. They don't treat beatniks too good in Texas."[8]

Her father agreed that she was out of place in Texas. After her death, he acknowledged that Janis "had a pretty rough time of it in high school," because "she insisted on dressing and acting differently and they hated her for it." Seth felt Janis was "one of the first revolutionary youths" in Port Arthur, and was unable to relate to her peers.[9] Later, a successful Janis would often gloat over her Bohemian image. For example, on a poster of herself she once wrote: "Guess what, I might be the first hippie pinup girl."[10]

After 1974, Joplin gained increasing acceptance in San Francisco, New York, and other centers of rock culture. Her crude, natural manner and dress now fit in perfectly with the new lifestyles. Unfortunately, drugs were part of these lifestyles, and Joplin took to them quickly and passionately. From barbiturates to speed to heroin to liquor and back to heroin, Janis never got free of the downward spiral. Some rock stars used drugs to live the life, but Janis increasingly used drugs to ease the pain of life.

When Joplin returned to San Francisco in 1966 to team up with a rock band called Big Brother and the Holding Company, she was an instant success at the Monterey Pop Festival. Two gold record albums later, she was a nationwide sensation and a symbol for gutsy singing and living. Her public image was symbolized by the tentative title of her second album, *Sex, Dope, and Cheap Thrills*, subsequently censored down to *Cheap Thrills*. During the next four years, Janis broke up with Big Brother, formed her own Full Tilt Boogie Band, and put out another album, *Kozmic Blues*. However, her success was always based on the image established during her first triumph at Monterey. From festival to festival and concert to concert, her legend grew while her body and voice deteriorated. Yet her voice was not of primary importance. Janis expressed feeling rather than lyrics; she communicated anxiety rather than art. She was never much of a vocalist, but she had considerable influence as a hip model for youth—especially young women.

At the same time, both Joplin's life and lifestyle lent themselves to the new feminism in America. Indeed, Janis's path to stardom exactly paralleled the rise of the women's liberation movement. The same year Janis got her start at Monterey (1966), radical college women began streaming out of SDS and forming their own feminist groups and Betty Friedan founded

N.O.W. Joplin was largely oblivious to the feminist movement, but she served as an unconscious feminist symbol for younger women. Janis's most universal influence came through her popularization of naturalistic dress and hairstyles. Then, as now, millions of young women dressed in ostentatious poverty in uniforms of blue jeans and work shirts. But their hair and makeup often came directly from *Vogue*. Moreover, on dates, jeans were usually discarded in favor of pantie girdles and dresses. Joplin hardly originated the natural look that she picked up in San Francisco, but she did spread it nationwide. Janis liberated millions of young girls from lipstick and girdles, while she pioneered the braless look and wild, loose, individual clothes combinations. Also, Joplin's long, brown, lack-luster hair helped free some women from an exaggerated brush, wash, set, color, and spray syndrome that still grips America through long hair and short. She brought new confidence to girls who had always worn their locks short because they had "bad" hair and their clothes long because they had "bad" figures. With the new, diverse, natural styles, many women who could never be beautiful in classic ways radiated a unique personal charm. The Joplin look was well fitted to the rock scene. You would not dress otherwise when going to a concert or festival. As Lillian Roxon observed about rock festival dress: "If you didn't look like Janis when you got there, you sure as hell looked like her by the time you left." For Roxon, and for countless others, Joplin "personified the new woman—blunt, straightforward, honest, unfettered, impatient and brave."[11] Joplin was hardly unfettered or brave. Rather, she was hung-up and frightened, but her legend was always more important than her life.

Although Joplin's clothing did not often suggest that she was sexually liberated, her manner usually did. Dress styles aside, the popularly defined, sexy woman must be the pursued and not the pursuer. Joplin was clearly liberated, both in her bandstand patter and private life. She reserved the right to be the hunter as well as the hunted. Janis had the courage to decline to dress sexily on the one hand, yet to act sexually aggressive on the other.

Not surprisingly, Janis's concert performances generated sexuality. Thus, after listening to her album *Cheap Thrills*, Al Aronowitz, a *Life* reviewer, suggested that, like Mae West, Joplin "could be the greatest lady who ever worked the streets." Aronowitz felt that Janis's singing made you feel she was "calling out to you from the second-story window of a bordello, inviting you up."[12] Within her sexual style, however, were the typical contradictions of the sexual revolution. Janis reflected the feminist desire to be equal to men, yet uniquely feminine, to be sexually liberated yet captive to true love, and wildly sexually fulfilled in the process. Joplin could not satisfy her own sexual longings, but when on stage she held out the promise to others. In the midst of her success, Joplin lamented: "On stage I make love to twenty-five thousand people, then I go home alone."[13] The more Janis gave her audiences, the less she seemed to get for herself. From the start, she became a victim of her performing image. Country Joe McDonald felt that Janis often wanted to be just another person offstage, but that others saw her as a conventional sex symbol. According to McDonald, people wanted her to be "feminine and dainty," and when she could not comply, they treated her like one of the guys.[14]

Janis's lesbian activities may have been part and parcel of her refusal to be sexy in traditional ways. Her homosexuality has been exaggerated by lesbian feminists who often suggest that her problems stemmed from not admitting her lesbianism. However, Janis's possible bisexuality had also been ignored by many rock writers who feared it would destroy her sexy image. Because Joplin was bisexual, her lesbianism was more likely just part of her determination to get as much love or sex as she could—sexual orientation aside. Yet, Diane Gravenites, a close friend of Joplin, noted that Janis "was more comfortable, more 'herself' . . . in the presence of women. She was less on the rack of self-deprecation, less prone to play buffoon, and because she was less driven to sexual priority, was less ridden with anxiety."[15] Possibly Joplin's ostentatious heterosexual behavior was a compensation for her bisexuality. In any case, as an aggressive bisexual, she appealed to all sides of the feminist camp.

In one sense, Joplin was a fake. Blues singers were traditionally black and poor. A blues superstar was thus a contradiction in terms. Steve Katz, a blues guitarist, felt that although Joplin was "a good primitive blues singer," she was no longer credible since because "you're making $10,000 a night," you could not "come on hard luck and trouble."[16] But Janis knew suffering, and to the charge that she could not sing realistic blues, she aptly replied: "You know why we're stuck with the myth that only black people have soul? Because white people don't let themselves feel things. Man, you and any housewife have all sorts of pain and joy. You'd have soul if you'd give into it."[17]

Just as the black blues had furnished equipment for living for generations of poverty-stricken blacks, Janis's blues eased her personal suffering. The pain her songs reflected also fit in with one new philosophy of contemporary feminism. The "anti-brain-washing" position of the Redstockings, a New York radical feminist group, stressed standing up for women who were down and not blaming women for their oppression. The antibrainwashing mode tended to glorify women as victims. The more marks of suffering you could show, the more credible your struggle with sexism and consequently the more support you deserved from your sisters. Clearly, Janis's music glorified suffering.

Joplin's music also proclaimed a primitive joy at times. In dozens of ways, Janis made it clear that she would live for today. She was not going to save her voice, cut down her drinking, or pass by a sexual partner in hopes of happier, healthier tomorrows. Janis had decided that philosophically tomorrow never comes. Her most characteristic song perhaps was "Get It While You Can." This hedonistic stress complimented the impatient mood of youth, but it also struck a responsive feminist chord. Women were constantly urged to put off personal pleasure for a more suitable time. Young girls were told to save themselves for their husbands. Wives were supposed to sacrifice immediate pleasures for their children. Even grandmothers had responsibilities to daughters and grandchildren. Joplin insisted that you were number one and that the present was everything. Feminists, too, increasingly stressed their own primacy, and the slogan "Liberation Now" stressed now almost as much as liberation.

In the final analysis, Joplin made women feel better, but hardly altered their problems. Her songs of complaint suggested things to identify with rather than goals to work toward. Moreover, her attempts to reconcile femininity with sexual aggressiveness and professional success with personal happiness were so personal and intense as to exclude the possibility of applying many lessons. Joplin's solutions were always sensory, anti-intellectual and short-sighted. For Janis, "being an intellectual" created "a lot of questions and no answers." You could "fill up your life with ideas and still go home lonely." The only things that really mattered to Joplin were "feelings" and the music that helped release and reflect them.[18] Janis felt that she had to sacrifice for her music. She could not "quit to become someone's old lady," because even though being dedicated to one man was "beautiful," it could not touch "hitting the stage at full-tilt boogie."[19] A man could be a rock star, do gigs, and "know that he was going to get laid that night," as Janis put it, but a woman had to sacrifice love to be a rock singer.[20] Janis's philosophy was compensatory. She was going to get drunk, get laid, and, in the lyrics of her friend, songwriter Kris Kristofferson, "let the devil take tomorrow." Her simple creed brought back visions of the ancient Greek ideal of a short but glorious life. It was, after all, quite romantic to live fast, die young, and have a good-looking corpse.

Joplin's music raised the right questions, but suggested no answers. Her songs offered solace, but not wisdom. As feminist educator Florence Howe aptly put it, popular songs tell women "to love being a sex object," but they need songs that show them how to "love being a woman."[21] Joplin told us about the pain of being a woman and how to live with the pain and compensate for it. It remained for other voices to teach women how to prevent or avoid that pain. Janis adapted the black blues tradition to the needs of an affluent, but culturally rootless, youth culture. As Myra Friedman wisely suggested, Joplin was a verbal minstrel. Instead of using blackface, she sang with a black voice.[22] Yet it was clearly a confused generation of white Americans that she spoke to. Her uninhibited style and flamboyant escape from the oppressive and outdated conventions of a small Texas city acted out the conscious desires of thousands of American teenagers. Joplin's music provided them with a vicarious escape from middle-class America. In the words of Mimi Farina's memorial ballad for Janis ("In the Quiet Morning"), Joplin was, indeed, "the great Southwest unbound."[23]

JOAN BAEZ: THE SINGER AS ACTIVIST

Baez was an unlikely cultural heroine. Born in Staten Island, New York, in 1941, she was one of three sisters. Her father a Mexican-born physicist, and her mother, of Scotch-English ancestry, met at Drew University in Madison, New Jersey. The family moved around the country while Dr. Baez built a career as a physics researcher and scientific consultant. Her family's strong religious background—especially her mother's—could explain Joan's moral fervor. Her maternal grandfather was an Episcopalian minister, and her paternal grandfather was a Catholic who became a Methodist clergyman. More importantly, her parents were serious converts to the Quaker faith, although Joan became religiously nonaligned. Joan attended high school in Palo Alto, California, near Stanford University and then moved to Boston with her family in 1959. She enrolled at Boston College, but dropped out after a month. She liked college towns and college atmosphere and had grown up in college communities such as Palo Alto and Ithaca, New York, near Cornell University, but she could not handle the dull repetitive part of general education. Looking back, in 1967, she felt that college was just another way for parents "to hang on to their children." She could understand putting up with "the trivia of college" to enter some profession, but not because "your parents or society says you should."[24]

Joan felt she rebelled so strongly against education because her father's academic position pressured her to be a "student-type." Joan had moved to the left of her father on nonviolence, and seemed pleased that although he "was peace-marching long before" Joan, her radical swing left him "looking and acting . . . fairly moderate."[25] Almost immediately, she was attracted to the civil rights movement. While still in high school, she had heard Martin Luther King Jr. speak at her church, and she remained a strong supporter of King. Joan also had personally experienced racism growing up in Redlands, California. Although Dr. Baez had professional standing, Joan was not accepted by whites because she was dark and part Mexican, and the

Mexican-American community rejected her because she could not speak Spanish. Later, when the Baez family moved to Clarence Center, New York, a town of eight hundred people, Joan felt that "as far as they knew we were niggers."[26]

As a college dropout in the Boston area, she turned to singing at the new folk coffeehouses around Harvard and Boston College. She had sung at high school events and taught herself guitar, and, by now, her largely untrained voice was already striking enough to make her a local folk star. The folk boom was just beginning, and Baez picked up songs and techniques from local folksingers such as Ric Von Schmidt. She also met national folk star, Bob Gibson, while she performed as a guest singer at a Chicago folk club, The Gate of Horn. That summer, Gibson introduced her at the 1959 Newport Folk Festival, and they sang a duet. As the sensation of Newport, she had recording contract offers from Columbia Records, the industry giant and future home of superstar, Bob Dylan, and Vanguard Records, a small producer of classical records that was interested in folk music. Characteristically, she chose Vanguard because they seemed more interested in music than money, and that company retained her loyalty for twelve years. Joan's first record was released in 1960. She also began one of many national concert tours, concentrating mostly on college campuses. Joan Baez was suddenly America's premier folksinger and she was all of twenty years of age.[27]

Slowly but surely, the young queen of folk music turned into a national symbol for activism and pacifism and a heroine of the left. The 1960s were particularly hard for American heroes—even John Kennedy had his memory badly tarnished by the results of his foreign policy in Vietnam. Thus, it is noteworthy that Joan Baez's intellectual image soared during a period of general cynicism. Her rise was helped by good timing, for Joan rather grew up with the decade. In 1960, she was a largely unknown nineteen-year-old singer with a gifted soprano voice and a way with Anglo-American folk songs. As political events grew darker in 1963 and after, she gradually became an activist, both in civil rights and universal nonviolence. In 1964, she symbolically demonstrated her pacifist stance by refusing to pay that portion of her income tax (60 percent) designated for defense spending. The next year, she funded an Institute for the Study of Nonviolence, headquartered in her hometown—Carmel, California.[28]

Baez's early criticisms of the nation-state were often vague, but the steadily accelerating Vietnam War documented many of her points. Joan was frankly and consistently radical in an age of polarization and pacifist in an era of increasing violence. She also spoke from a universal perspective, at a time when many Americans and Europeans were vomiting on Cold War nationalism. Above all, there was her singing, which compensated for her early, relative intellectual shallowness and inarticulateness. Throughout the 1960s, her crystal-clear voice soared through the soprano register, high above the political struggles. Always the most artful, distinct singer in the folk field, Joan shifted her repertory from ancient balladry to protest songs to Bob Dylan's prose songs, to country-and-western, and finally to a mixture that included her own compositions. Baez albums always sold well until the late 1970s, but except for her first two folk albums, they were never best-sellers. As she became more political, this relative lack of commercial success helped protect her credibility. As the child of a decade of agitation, her attitudes and lifestyle evolved so smoothly that she seemed not to have changed at all. Baez blended into the protest tradition, into activism, into pacifism, into a publicized marriage to David Harris (a famous draft resister who chose jail over the draft), into motherhood, and, finally, into a national symbol for nonviolent activism.

Many folksingers, besides Baez, actively supported civil rights. For example, when she attended the famous "March on Washington" rally in August 1963, Bob Dylan, Peter, Paul, and Mary, and others performed with her. Yet none of these risked personal harm as Joan had when she escorted a small black girl to her integrated school through a hostile crowd in Birmingham, Alabama, earlier that year. Nor did other protest singers tend to physically take part in student campaigns or demonstrations against the Vietnam War. Joan was often a physical demonstrator. In December 1964, at the University of California's Berkeley campus, Joan helped draw a large rally crowd to protest the school's ban on specific campus political activities. She then marched into the university's administration building, at the head of one thousand undergraduates who occupied the building for fifteen hours.

On June 8, 1965, Joan sang at an Emergency Rally Against the Vietnam War in Madison Square Garden in New York City. But before performing, she told the crowd, "This is mainly to the young people here, but really to everybody. . . . You must listen to your heart and do what it dictates. . . . If you feel that to. . .go to war is wrong, you have to say no to the draft. And if young ladies think it is wrong to kill . . . you can say yes to the young men who say no to the draft."[29] Joan made this point more graphically with her sisters Pauline and Mimi. The next year a poster came out showing the three Baez sisters sitting on a couch, looking straight out at the audience. The caption read: "Girls Say Yes to Boys Who Say No." Proceeds from poster sales went to the draft resistance, but Joan later acknowledged that the poster had "unwittingly" alienated "the women's movement, while raising bucks for a cause" she "held dear." Feminists obviously rejected suggestions that women bribe men with sexual favors, no matter how good the cause.[30] In August 1965, Joan joined 1,000 anti-Vietnam demonstrators in picketing the White House. She later commented: "I don't think the President gives a damn."[31] Although it would be almost three years before she met her husband, David Harris, marriage to a draft resistor seemed almost inevitable.

After continuing her antiwar and civil rights activities in 1966, Baez made her first concert tour abroad, when she visited Japan in January 1967. However, at her Tokyo concert, which was later shown on Japanese television, the Japanese translator admitted that he left out all of Baez's political remarks at the urging of a man who identified himself as a CIA agent. Thus, when Joan explained the song, "What Have They Done to the Rain" (about atomic fallout), the translator stated only that "the show was being televised." When she interpreted her subtle antiwar song, "Saigon Bride," he said only: "This is a song about the Vietnam War." And when Joan told the audience she had refused to pay her taxes as a protest against the Vietnam War, the translator said only: "Taxes are high in the United States." On balance, Joan's trip was not a political success. She said she came to Japan "first as a human being, second as a pacifist, and third as a folksinger." However, the Japanese tended to accept her primarily as a folksinger, only secondarily as a human being, and hardly at all as a pacifist.[32]

Back in the United States, Joan became more aggressive. She was arrested in Oakland, California, in October 1967 for blocking the Armed Forces Induction Center and served a ten-day prison sentence. Two months later she served a month for the same offense. Her mother, then fifty-four years old, accompanied her both times, or, as Joan put it, "My Mother's been to jail with me twice now. We did civil disobedience together."[33] During her October sit-in, Joan first met David Harris. In a rather unique courtship, Harris visited Joan during her second jail term, and they agreed to tour colleges and selected cities to speak for draft resistance. Joan would usually give a concert, and then David and she would speak about the resistance. In the middle of their tour, in March 1968, they were married. On May 29, 1968, Harris, then twenty-two years old and a former Stanford University student body president, was sentenced to three years in prison for refusing induction into the armed forces. To avoid media coverage, the government finally took him into custody July 16, 1969—the day the Apollo 11 moon shot started. In December 1969, Joan gave birth to their son, Gabriel, and after a few months, she continued to travel around the country singing and espousing her nonviolent philosophy, while her husband served his sentence.[34]

The shock of David's incarceration produced a new Joan Baez. Most people noticed that she cut her long hair (once a distinct trademark), but her mental change was far more striking. The uncertain, often petulant, folksinger suddenly became a more confident, aggressive, extemporaneous speaker. Her appearances on national television talk shows underscored the change. As a guest on the *Alan Burke Show* in 1967, Baez had been browbeaten and put on the defensive by the generally shallow Burke. The following year, when she and David appeared on *The Les Crane Show*, Joan sang songs, but let David do most of the talking. However, a year later, on *The Dick Cavett Show*, a month after David's imprisonment, she completely confounded Cavett's attempt at witty superficiality with a moving and articulate explanation of her pacifist philosophy. Joan so outpointed the usually glib, if not profound, Cavett that the next day Howard K. Smith was moved to use the commentary portion of his nightly ABC news show to respond to Baez's arguments. Smith called Joan "one of our high income revolutionaries," and dismissed her as an idealist who naively believed that revolution would bring perfection out of ruins. Smith contended that America was a middle-class country which abhorred revolution and that the path to progress was one of slow "precinct work" in elections and legislation.[35]

In getting Smith's attention and criticism, Baez had leaped ahead of many feminist women critics who centered on women's issues. Television newsmen such as Smith largely ignored women's issues. They said in effect: You are a woman, so do day care or abortion or equal pay. Leave war, politics, and serious things to men. Baez refused to be limited. There was also a noticeable change in Baez's concert appearances. She insisted that tickets to her performances could cost no more than $2, and she developed a more commanding stage presence. In September 1970, for example, she demonstrated her new confidence at a concert in Sopot, Poland. After singing "Blowin in the Wind," and a Beatles's song, she explained why David was in prison (through a translator) and then sang one of her own compositions, which she dedicated to the young Poles who she felt were in the same position as American youths—"hitchhiking but with no place to go." Afterward at a press conference, when asked about America's "sickness," she showed her universal focus by replying: "America is not the sickest but the biggest. If Poland was as big as America, she might be just as destructive." The translator omitted the last part of her answer.[36]

Back home she was now considered more dangerous by authorities. On February 3, 1971, Miami, Florida, officials refused to allow her to give a college-sponsored concert in the city's Marine Stadium, arguing that her appearance might present a "problem of crowd control."[37] Yet she was never a direct political threat. People were generally unwilling to hear her speak unless she also sang. During her February 1971 tour, for example, she drew seven-thousand people to a paid concert, but only four hundred showed up for a free political talk.[38]

David Harris was paroled on March 15, 1971, after serving twenty months of his three-year sentence. Meanwhile, Joan had been in good form on talk shows. Upon her return to *The Dick Cavett Show*, the somewhat chastened host introduced her as "the leading lady of American folk music." Despite this respectful introduction, Baez's manner was very condescending. She obviously resented Cavett's mild attempts at levity and treated him as a somewhat backward child. The conversation centered on prisons and Joan observed that incarceration was educative. Because bank robbers came out of prison better bank robbers, she argued: "If you go into prison a pacifist, you come out a better pacifist." Cavett later noted that prisons were bad, but asked Joan what society should do with serious criminals, like murderers. She replied: "If you talk about serious murderers, they are not in our jails, they are running nations." A month later, Baez faced a generally hostile audience on the *David Frost Show*, although Frost himself was sympathetic. Here she adopted a lecture stance and noted that even though people were afraid of chaos if they did not have government, our government was chaotic. She argued that Americans were "disciplined to the point where" they could not even think, and thus were insulated from "the Cambodian Mother whose child has been burned." Joan's solution was to work outside the system to build a society that did not "corrupt people." She felt it was impossible to reform the system itself. When asked to sing a song that reflected her present mood, she sang, "Heaven Help Us All."[39]

Critics could point out that Baez still came up with simplistic, one-dimensional answers, but there was a new, strangely effective power in her verbal arguments. The often shy folksinger had suddenly become a rather charismatic agitator. Looking back, it is ironic that Bob Dylan, who had become perhaps the most reclusive of the pop singers, had criticized Baez for her passiveness and lack of relevance. In 1962, Dylan chided: "It ain't nothin' just to walk around and sing . . . you have to step out a little, right? Take Joanie man, she's still singing about Mary Hamilton. I mean where's that at? She's walked around on picket lines, she's got all kinds of feeling, so why ain't she steppin' out?"[40]

Although by 1965 Dylan had completely rejected activism or even relevance and had literally dropped out physically, Joan did indeed step out. Other serious and gifted folksingers, such as Judy Collins, sang Malvina Reynold's song, "It Isn't Nice," about how it was not nice "to block the doorways" and "go to jail." However, Baez actually sat in the doorways and went to jail. While other former topical singers turned to catchy top-ten ballads and cashed in on television guest appearances, Joan put out an average of one record per year, sang college-circuit concerts, and invested most of her money in pacifist causes such as her own institute. In an era when credibility became the magic word, it is not hard to understand why Joan Baez's star was steadily rising.

Joan's personal philosophy of nonviolence had become increasingly sophisticated. Her two major influences were Ira Sandperl, a veteran of West Coast pacifist crusades, and David Harris, her husband. In 1964, Joan asked Sandperl to tutor her on the philosophy of nonviolence, and the lessons turned into The Institute for the Study of Nonviolence. David Harris's influence on Baez had largely been one of emphasis. His philosophy (set forth in his book, *Goliath*) was hazy, but he styled himself an organizer rather than a preacher, and Joan's new aggressiveness can be traced to her husband's vigorous brand of organized pacifism.[41] Joan probably summed up her outlook in the following passage from her autobiographical book, *Daybreak:*

The problem isn't Communism. The problem is consensus. There's a consensus out that it's OK to kill when your government decides who to kill. If you kill inside the country you get in trouble. If you kill outside the country, right time, right season, latest enemy, you get a medal. There are about 130 nation-states, and each of them thinks it's a swell idea to bump off all the rest because he is more important. The pacifist thinks there is only one tribe. Three billion members. They come first. We think killing any member of the family is a dumb idea. We think there are more decent and intelligent ways of settling differences. And man had better start investigating these other possibilities because if he doesn't, then by mistake or by design, he will probably kill off the whole damn race.[42]

At various times, Baez stressed that music alone was not enough for her. In 1970, she observed that if she did not stand up for life in deed as well as in song, all those beautiful sounds were "irrelevant to the only real question of this century: How do we stop men from murdering each other."[43] Nevertheless, for millions of Americans she was her music. Divorced from her songs, she seemed incomplete. For Joan personally, the music was both hope and catharsis. "To sing," Joan wrote, "is to love and to affirm, to fly and soar, to coast into the hearts of the people who listen, to tell them that life is to live, that love is there, that nothing is a promise, but that beauty exists, and must be hunted for and found."[44]

Yet, if her songs did give her wings, it was not apparent at her concerts. Baez's singing had a solemnity, independent of her material and quickly transferred to the audience. People did not sway to her music, and hand clapping would seem ludicrous. The fragile nature of her lyrics encouraged people to protect them with a hushed silence. Her later concerts were considerably looser because of the larger, less intimate audiences and her new outgoing style. The earlier concerts were rather mystical. I first heard Baez perform in November 1962, at the University of Illinois. Dressed in a plain skirt and blouse, she walked onto the stage of an auditorium filled with fifteen-hundred students, sat down on a stool, and without a word started playing. After some forty minutes of songs, punctuated only by brief introductions and the dedication of one song to Pete Seeger, she walked off at intermission without any indication she was returning. The second half of her program was a copy of the first. She ended her concert with one encore and a simple, "thank you, goodnight." Yet, few faulted her lack of showmanship. Baez's voice seemed completely independent of the frail figure on the stage. At one point, she quietly commanded the audience: "Sing this one with me"; and the assembly sang along in whispered voices as if they were in church. It is easy to understand her magnetic effect at Woodstock in August 1969, when at 2:00 A.M., she stood, noticeably pregnant, singing to a dreamy sea of flower children.

Over time Baez's voice lost some of its youthful magic. Yet periodically, her voice broke through—all the stronger in contrast. Balance has been the strong point of Joan's albums. She never sang one type of song, and even her hard-core protest songs were seldom tedious. Thus, though many of her songs featured strong women models, no one ever regarded her as simply a woman singer. This balance enhanced her overall credibility. Nevertheless, Joan always had critics. In regard to her early albums, *Little Sandy Review*, headquarters for "folkier than thou" criticism, conceded that Baez was "perhaps the most thrilling young voice of our time," but sadly concluded that her vocal gifts were "too rich and too grandiose to carry the simplicity of the humble folk song." When a traditional singer, like Woody Guthrie or Leadbelly, sang a folk song, the *LSR* reviewers argued, it described "the basic nature of his land and people." Baez, however, could only describe herself, for in "molding a song to her own powerful personality," she destroyed it. Joan did not lack defenders. After reviewing Baez's first album, the *LSR* reviewers noted that her many fervent fans had requested that they "quit picking on Joan" and "go back to beating" their "grandmothers with old Library of Congress albums."[45] Likewise, Baez's 1969 dual album of Bob Dylan songs, *Any Day Now*, was panned by Dylanologist Alan Weberman, because "Joanie's sweet soprano voice" could not express the heavy contemptuous sarcasm of many of Dylan's songs.[46]

Ironically, as Baez has increased the scope and control of her music, her musical identity has become less important. Once she was a pacifist folksinger, now she is seen as a folksinger pacifist. However, most Americans saw Joan as a celebrity. Her celebrity status was evidenced by the regular appearance of her name in the "People" sections of *Newsweek* and *Time* and in daily syndicated gossip columns. It was further evidenced by the balloting for the Playboy Jazz & Pop Hall of Fame. In a 1972 poll, Joan placed thirteenth right behind rock-star Frank Zappa and ahead of singer Barbra Streisand. Daniel Boorstin defined a celebrity as "a person who is known for his well-knowness," not for his or her deeds.[47] Yet Baez was not a classic celebrity. She was not suddenly created by the media's need for instant cultural heroes. It was her deeds rather than her image that had changed over the years. Baez's celebrity status made her beliefs and actions newsworthy, but her political activism usually threatened her professional career.

Moreover, Joan felt celebrities have a responsibility. In 1967, when Bob Dylan was at the height of his popularity, and Baez's career was somewhat in eclipse, Joan noted:

The kids idealize Dylan more than me. For that reason I think he should help them more, not play up to their negative feelings. What they want to hear is that nothing matters; and in a way that's what his newer songs tell them. I say just the opposite; I believe everything matters, and you have to take a stand.[48]

Unlike Dylan and other rock stars, Baez had neither the attitudes nor lifestyle to endear her to either the feminist or general counterculture. True, she condoned premarital sex and advocated trial marriage (and had practiced both by age twenty), but she urged discipline and commitment and was rather puritanical about drugs. In 1968, she admitted a "total dislike" for liquor and cigarettes, as well as marijuana or other drugs. "I get high as a cloud on one sleeping pill," Joan observed, "if that's what it means to get high; and it's not a whole lot different from what I feel like on a fall day in New England, or listening to the Faure Requiem."[49] Moreover, Baez steadily drew criticism from the young New Left for her negative attitude toward various black power movements. She also drew fire from women's liberation groups for her consistent refusal to organize around gender issues. Joan's position was based on the belief that people should concentrate on what they have in common rather than what sets them apart. She felt that power ultimately subverts and corrupts those who gain it. Thus, for Baez, even Martin Luther King Jr.'s nonviolent movement was faulty, because it sought narrow changes by pressuring government. Joan's hero was Gandhi who never asked for power, but "assumed that the power was the people's" and brought change by asking the people, rather than government, to act.[50]

Not surprisingly, Baez was often attacked from the Right. For example, in 1966 David Noebel, a fundamentalist minister, charged that Joan's institute was a marxist-oriented front that trained "muscle-bound toughs" for group disruptions. Noebel also noted that in 1962 the two biggest donors to the United Nations were Nelson Rockefeller and Joan Baez (who gave $1,361.60); and that Joan's father held "down one of the highest paid jobs in the UNESCO Secretariat."[51] More importantly, in 1967 cartoonist Al Capp introduced a character into his "Li'l Abner" strip named "Joanie Phoanie." Miss Phoanie was a long-haired folksinger who collected $10,000 a concert, refused to pay taxes, and spent most of her spare time organizing sordid, anti-American demonstrations. Joan's defenders pointed out that Capp had made his fortune distorting and maligning the image of Appalachian whites, so his treatment of Baez was a logical extension of his work.[52]

Largely because of the controversy that always surrounded her, Baez was a cultural hero of youth throughout the 1960s. Earlier, however, she was only a model of style. Thus, in 1962 *Time* suggested how to look like a female "folknik": "It is not absolutely essential to have hair hanging to the waist—but it helps. Other aids: no lipstick, flat shoes, a guitar."[53] *Time* really described how to look like Joan Baez. By the late 1960s, a cursory glance at any group of teenage girls (or perhaps boys also) quickly indicated that the style Baez picked up in the Bohemian corners of Harvard, and later helped popularize, had become a classic countercultural look. Even today, many youths seeking an offbeat image continue to wear their hair long and dress in ostentatious poverty. Yet Joan does not cherish her part in the style revolution, because her message was never explicitly in her lifestyle. As early as 1961, Baez felt that she had "a lot to say," but added: "I don't know how to say it so I just sing it."[54] Later, no doubt, she felt that it was not enough to sing it or say it, so she did it.

Baez has come a long way intellectually, but her answers to social problems often remain naive, hopeful, and vague (or as social scientists would say, without empirical foundation). Joan clearly realized this much more in her later maturity. She has admitted that she cannot explain her "innermost convictions." For her, it was enough to say: "A tree is known by its fruits. People see how I manage myself, and maybe from that they can see what I'm about."[55] Perhaps Joan Baez was a fake—the brainchild of a brilliant public relations man—a pseudoprotest singer who chose to become commercial by being noncommercial. Perhaps her activities were really sublimations for personal conflicts that she only dimly perceived. Perhaps her vision of a nonviolent world was based on untenable assumptions about human nature. In any case, I read the record of her life as indicating that she came by her convictions honestly—indeed, that her beliefs were rationally shaped by her odyssey through the turbulent 1960s.

Baez was clearly cast in the heroine's role. In 1971, for example, in Antioch College's annual poll of their freshmen to determine what prominent persons of recent history the students most admired, Joan Baez placed eleventh—right behind John Kennedy. Women's liberation notwithstanding, she was the first woman on the list. Gandhi ranked first and Martin Luther

King Jr. second; others among the top ten were Malcolm X, Albert Schweit-zer, Ralph Nader, Cesar Chavez, and Pablo Picasso.[56] Baez was indeed in august company. However, perhaps her strong showing was not too surpris-ing. Increasingly, Joan appeared wherever the action was. Marching in the streets, on television talk shows, in daily news dispatches, or singing the ti-tle song in a movie about Sacco and Vanzetti, she seemed a natural symbol of conscientious activism.

Perhaps in no other era could a female pacifist have become a cultural hero, or could a folksinger become a symbol for American youth. Like Joan of Arc, Baez inspired by example and symbolized innocence and purity. For many, Joan Baez fulfilled the perennial quest for an individual pure in heart who could not be bought. Although she has long since written off the 1964 Berkeley Free Speech Movement as an "unviolent" movement (ready to switch to violence to obtain its goals), as opposed to a truly "nonviolent" movement, her part in the Berkeley turmoil was a good example of her cha-risma. "Have love as you do this thing," Joan told a Berkeley mob, "and it will succeed." Later, *Time* magazine reported that one-thousand under-graduates had "stormed" the administration building "marching behind their Joan of Arc, who was wearing a jeweled crucifix." At first glance it seemed odd to compare the peaceful Baez to the warrior-maid of France but then Baez did insist on describing herself as a "nonviolent soldier." And on *The Les Crane Show,* she had admitted once instructing a crowd of protes-tors: "Be nonviolent or I'll kill you!" Many Americans saw her as "A Paci-fist St. Joan"—on a white horse, without armor, guitar (rather than lance) in hand—riding at the head of a nonviolent army.[57]

Baez was clearly too volatile and profane for sainthood, although she still has a saintly image. Her activism featured many saintly actions, yet her cha-otic private life was filled with the pettiness and mistakes that mark most people's lives. Considering the strains of balancing an activist's life with a professional singer's career and also trying to function as a wife and mother, that is hardly surprising. In her 1987 autobiography *And a Voice to Sing With,* Baez wrote frankly about her mistakes, vanity, paranoia, and petti-ness. She wisely was hard on herself and thus allowed less room for critics. The downside is that the book's often inane personal detail blunts the drama of some historic events in which she figured, but overall there is an amazing record of Baez's consistent growth, courage, and commitment. Very few sixties activists managed to hold on to their ideals and enthusiasm through the 1970s, 1980s, and 1990s. Even though her artistic career as a singer and composer declined as folk music was eclipsed by rock and country music, her composing and stage presence continued to improve. Continuing her activism and career under very adverse conditions was perhaps more heroic than her sixties activism in the national limelight. Ironically, Baez is more popular in Europe than in America. European youth are more political than contemporary American college students and also more favorably nostalgic about the 1960s. In Europe, Joan Baez is a link between past and present activism; in America, Joan is increasingly just vaguely reminiscent of the sixties.

Baez had often been seen as an enemy of feminism. In 1970, as women's liberation gathered steam and garnered media attention, Baez quickly wrote it off as one of several Left movements that sought to divide people instead of uniting them. She joked that "one of these days some of those feminists will bump me off in an alley." In her 1970 *Playboy* magazine interview, she felt uneasy about the women's "stuff" she had seen around Berkeley because they seemed to be saying, "I'm a woman. I demand my rights. I can be as good a soldier or a competitor as any man." On the other hand, she had heard some good things about "women's liberation activities—like cooperative nurseries" that allowed women "stuck in a house" to "get out." Baez said as a performer she had done the things most males do. Now, as a wife, she was trying to do more of the things women do, such as cook. But when *Playboy* asked whether she saw "a necessity for the liberation of women as people," Baez answered:

I see very, very clearly the need for women to free themselves of many things—having to wear brassieres and make-up and take all those pains to fit into a stereotypical pattern of how you're supposed to look in order to be a sex object. . . . And . . . the still prevalent concept . . . that the woman's place is in the home. Well it isn't or shouldn't be for many women. And even for those who refuse to accept that role, the jobs open to them are equally stereotyped and limited and they earn about half what a man does for the same work.[58]

Yet Baez felt it "boiled down to means and ends" and that if women used crazy means, the end result would not "be real."

By 1972, after two years of marriage Baez acknowledged that she understood women's liberation much better. Now even things such as who did the dishes had become political. She felt the real problem for women was getting trapped in roles. The solution was figuring out how you were "allowing yourself to be trapped." Joan's problem marriage forced her to conclude that women's liberation was "more her problem than" she wanted "to think."[59]

In March 1973, Baez made the news by frankly commenting on a lesbian incident in her life. She told a reporter that she was bisexual. However, this referred only to a year when she was twenty-one and had a woman lover. The lesbian experience had nothing to do with solidarity with women, yet some felt that Baez's sudden confession was an attempt to support both the women's and the gay movements.[60]

However, neither women's liberation nor the isolated lesbian affair was relevant to Baez's life or her effect as a role model. Both were incidental. Baez was a free spirit. Her personal life was a mass of contradictions. What made her heroic was her ability to mesh her activism and singing so consistently and stylishly despite personal problems, diminishing audiences, and changing times.

It all came together at the Live Aid Concert in Philadelphia in 1985. Joan Baez was "thrilled" to open the U.S. portion of the worldwide show. In her six minutes, she opened with two verses of "Amazing Grace" for the older people and several verses of "We Are the World," so that the young kids could sing along with a chorus they knew. But before singing, she opened Live Aid USA very characteristically.

Good morning, children of the Eighties! This is your Woodstock, and it's long overdue. And it's nice to know the money out of your pockets will go to feed hungry children. I can think of no more glorious way of starting our part of the day than by saying grace together, which means that we thank each of us . . . for the many blessings that we have in a world in which so many people have nothing. And when we say this grace, we also reach deep in our hearts and say that we will move a little from the comfort of our lives to understand their hurt and their discomfort. And that will make their lives richer and it will make our lives real. "Amazing Grace, how sweet the sound."[61]

Baez was suddenly back where she belonged, cementing the old and young together and looking at the world from an international, universal perspective. Clearly gender was irrelevant. The years melted and the old became younger and the young got older. That is an effect only a real countercultural heroine can have.

GLORIA STEINEM: THE FEMINIST AS PINUP

If Joan Baez was the activist folk music queen and Janis Joplin was the first hippie pinup, Gloria Steinem was surely the first feminist pinup. Long before Steinem became *Ms.* magazine's founding editor in 1972, and before she received critical acclaim for her continually perceptive feminist writing in the 1970s and 1980s, she was famous for her looks. Specifically, she was famous for destroying the public stereotype of feminists. Women liberationists were supposedly not interested in looking attractive, too lazy to beautify themselves, or just naturally not pretty. Feminists were often seen as women who could not compete for men under the traditional beauty rules of engagement, so they rejected the game for fear of failure. Steinem broke the rules as well as the stereotypes and played her own game. She was bright, beautiful, feisty, and not looking for long-term relationships with men. She dated men, but did not covet them.

Steinem does not seem to fit in with Joplin and Baez as either an offbeat heroine or a countercultural model. There seems little offbeat about Steinem from her carefully selected clothes and classic grooming to her education at a prestigious "Seven Sister" school—Smith College. Yet despite her obvious mainstream feminist credentials, Steinem's glamorous image and unique lifestyle make her an anomaly as a feminist. She is as offbeat a model for women as Joplin and Baez. Steinem's feminist allies never knew how to treat her glamorous image. They mostly edged around it. Thus, in 1971 Betty Friedan cattily complained: "There is a touch of sexism in all the attention Gloria's getting, plus society's desire for acceptable public figures." Friedan noted that the fact that Gloria is very pretty and chic "was nice for the movement, but if that's all she was, it wouldn't be enough." And then Friedan quickly added, that "fortunately" Gloria "was so much more."[62]

Steinem's heroic image had a Horatio Alger rags-to-riches quality. Unlike Joplin and Baez who were thoroughly middle class and comfortable, Steinem grew up in poverty. Gloria was not born in poverty. Her father, Leo Steinem, was a Jewish antique dealer and sometime summer resort owner and incidentally the son of a suffragette. Ruth, her mother, had worked as a newspaper journalist before marriage. The Steinems spent most winters moving around the country in a trailer and summers at Leo's modest Michigan resort. However, when Gloria was eleven, her parents divorced. She had been born in Toledo, but now she and her mother moved to an industrial slum area in East Toledo. Gloria later recalled that neighborhood girls there "all got married before they graduated because they were pregnant." Her Mother owned a shabby house, but had little income and they shared their home with rats.[63]

At age fifteen, Gloria went to Washington, D.C., and lived with her twenty-five-year-old sister, Suzanne. Here, Steinem suddenly became middle class and flourished. She did not earn very good grades in high school because of her poor study habits; however, she had exceptional scores on her College Board exams and she was accepted at Smith College in 1954. Her mother Ruth promptly sold her Toledo slum house for $8,000 to pay college expenses. Steinem throve at Smith and graduated with a magna cum laude degree in political science. There followed a year and a half fellowship in India for graduate study. The poverty Steinem witnessed in India turned her decidedly to the Left and fueled her activist zeal.[64]

Steinem went to New York City in 1958 looking for a television job as a political reporter. She later lowered her sights to magazine reporting, but could not find anything but research support jobs. She finally took a job with the National Student Association. Meanwhile, she completed several freelance articles for *Esquire*, and in 1961 she wrote her first signed, feature piece for that magazine about the contraceptive pill. The article—"The Moral Disarmament of Betty Coed" was nowhere near the quality of Steinem's later prose style, but it was perceptive about the pill's effect on male-female relationships. Steinem warned that the pill was dangerous because it might change women's roles without changing the way men reacted to these new female roles.[65]

Although her subsequent *Esquire* writing covered the political spectrum of issues, slowly but surely, Steinem began to specialize in women's issues. Her article on the pill led directly to an undercover assignment from *Show* magazine. Steinem became an undercover bunny at New York's Playboy Club. The result was a tongue-in-cheek two-part expose of the club and her first real notoriety. After 1964, she also began to freelance for the *New York Times Magazine*, *Look*, and women's magazines such as *Vogue* and *Redbook*. Her favorite topics were critical pieces on women's fashions such as "Crazy Legs" or profiles of women celebrities such as a Julie Andrews's piece for *Vogue*. She also did profiles of male celebrities that included African-American novelist James Baldwin; Rudi Genreich, designer of the topless bathing suit; and actor Paul Newman.[66]

By 1968, she was dating Hollywood director Mike Nichols, saxophonist Paul Desmond, and African-American Olympic decathlon star, Rafer Johnson. Her friends now included George McGovern and Norman Mailer. Also in 1968, she started political writing in earnest, with a column in *New York Magazine* she named "The City Politic." Her first political coup came quickly: a 1968 interview with Pat Nixon in which Mrs. Nixon proved rather hostile and outspoken.[67]

As the women's liberation movement blossomed after 1968, Steinem became more and more in demand on talk shows as a women's advocate and spokesperson. At this point, she was still more famous as a speaker than a writer. Her glamorous looks made her a natural for television shows. Her cool, elegant, low-keyed, yet angry speaking style made her a great rally speaker. By 1971, she had become the most visible and striking symbol of women's liberation. In July 1971, it was not surprising that she helped found the National Women's Political Caucus, along with Betty Friedan, Shirley Chisholm, Bella Abzug, and others.

Her fashion-model looks continued to gain as much attention as her feminist rhetoric. If the comic book heroine, Wonder Woman, was the jock or Amazon as femme fatale, surely Steinem was the feminist as vamp. In 1969, *Time* magazine had referred to Gloria as the "Thinking Man's Shrimpton," suggesting she was almost as striking as famous model, Jean Shrimpton. Feminists were ambivalent about Steinem's physical appeal, but they could use it to advantage. Antifeminists had a history of putting feminists down as unattractive. In the 19th century, enemies had suggested that feminists were really men in disguise, lacking only pants. Other hostile voices suggested that most 19th-century feminists were lean and bony. Even in the 1960s, an FBI report told agents monitoring feminist activists that women liberationists could often be identified by their frizzy hair.

Steinem brushed off any criticism that her looks got in the way of her work or that she was showboating. She complained: "If you don't want to be a sex object, you have to make yourself unattractive." But, Steinem insisted that she was "not going to walk around in Army boots and cut off" her hair. She felt there was no reason for women to "look like men."[68] Increasingly, her glamour was accepted by other feminists because Steinem went out of her way to support any woman—Right to Left, lesbian or heterosexual, Democrat or Republican. She had long proved you could be pretty and bright. It took longer to build trust by proving she could be beautiful as well as loyal to women.

Steinem's dispassionate and derogatory criticism of male racism and sexism often made her appear antimale, especially to more conservative feminists. Gloria did not trust men as a group, but she stressed that she could have friendships with individual men. Steinem agreed with Friedan that the women's movement offered something for men, too. In her classic essay, "What It Would Be Like if Women Win," Steinem suggested that men would be free to indulge a broad range of emotions once women were equal. Also, men would no longer have to be the lone breadwinners, if women were not trained to be parasites. Sex would no longer be a barter commodity, in which women traded sex for security. Women who had the opportunity to fulfill themselves through work would no longer have the desire to dominate or emasculate husbands. Once women were liberated, Steinem pointed to myriad new social and family arrangements that nobody could forecast. These futuristic developments included group marriage arrangements, communal living, and extended families. One important result of equality was more equal parenting. Men would have to become better fathers because women would not be doing as much mothering. Steinem talked about men and promised them social rewards, but she mostly talked only to women.[69]

Unlike Friedan and other more conservative feminists, Steinem's support for lesbians was complete and unwavering. She consistently warned that men tried to control women by identifying antimale behavior as lesbian. She argued that men fear women who could live without men, whether those women were lesbian or heterosexual. She looked forward to a day when all homosexuals enjoyed full legal and social rights, including the right to marry and pass on wealth. Steinem's support of lesbians was part and parcel of her wider call for total sisterhood. She wanted a women's movement that united women, rich and poor, black and white, old and young, blue collar and professional, single and married, as well as straight or gay.[70]

To help unite women, Steinem founded *Ms.* magazine in 1972, along with Elizabeth Harris. Steinem edited the magazine and Harris was the publisher. The magazine was clearly aimed at single, professional women as an alternative to the many women's magazines for housewives such as *Redbook* and *Ladies Home Journal* or magazines that concentrated on feminine glamour such as *Cosmopolitan* and *Vogue*. The early issues of *Ms.* constantly called for universal sisterhood, but clearly were geared toward rather well-educated, sophisticated women. Although the subscription costs were low and the articles covered issues such as day care and abortion, the level of writing targeted college-educated professional women, rather than the mass of women.

Ms. did bring together some academics who put together the first women's studies programs and activist veterans of the first women's liberation groups. It also published some underground classics of the late 1960s such as Judy Syfer's "I Want a Wife" and Jill Johnson's "The Return of the Amazon Mother."[71] *Ms.* also tried to be countercultural. It included articles on media and popular culture, and its monthly "no comment" section featured sexist comments, ads, and writings sent in by readers. *Ms.* wore its national politics on its sleeve or, more precisely, on its cover. Early covers featured George McGovern and Shirley Chisholm. However, *Ms.* did not ignore subtle cultural topics. The third issue, for example, featured a beauty queen cover and included an article on Sylvia Plath. *Ms.* really tried for comprehensiveness. It published non-sexist stories for children, how-to mechanics for women, and articles on specific women's health problems. It became a veritable reader's digest of feminism as it tried to navigate to the center of the women's movement.[72]

Alas, either the movement was too wide or *Ms.*, despite its efforts, was still too narrow. From the start, *Ms.* was attacked from the Left and Right and also by minority women. Minorities charged that *Ms.* catered to white, upper middle-class, professional women who lived in New York City. Conservative feminists complained about the frank articles on sexuality and strong support of homosexuality as a viable lifestyle. Left-wing criticism was more sustained and harsher. Several early leaders of radical feminism, such as Carol Hanisch and Kathie Sarachild, turned on *Ms.* as a liberal opportunist. Sarachild called *Ms.* the teamsters of the women's movement. In 1973, the old New York Redstockings group was reestablished, and they charged that Gloria Steinem had CIA ties through her work for the National Student Association in the early 1960s. They suggested that the CIA was using *Ms.* to destroy radical feminism.[73] Nevertheless, both *Ms.* and Steinem continued to approximate the center of the women's movement. The equally vicious attacks from both Left and Right seemed to confirm their centrist position. Steinem refused to respond to most attacks against her, including the far-fetched CIA charges, and this caused further speculation. Betty Friedan, always suspicious and jealous of Steinem's influence, called for Gloria to respond. Radical feminists such as the Redstockings group were correct in seeing *Ms.* as their enemy. *Ms.* clearly was reformist rather than radical. More importantly, it carried the banner for both cultural feminism and countercultural change, albeit increasingly haltingly.[74]

Perhaps *Ms.*'s biggest problem was finances, which meant advertising. In the 1970s, *Ms.* did not aggressively seek advertising, because much of it was sexist by the definition of *Ms.* writers. It did accept ads that tried to attract feminists with prowoman slogans and images. At best, these ads were unisexual; at worst, they sloganeered with feminist buzz words, such as "today's woman," on the same level as Virginia Slims ads. By the 1980s, Steinem and *Ms.* were more desperate for funds and less particular about advertising. Many *Ms.* ads now pushed cosmetics and yuppie consumer goods. Even some liquor and tobacco ads were accepted. Many ads urged women to look sexy in exactly the ways *Ms.* had criticized in its early years.

The new *Ms.* also became more of a coach and teacher for the individual professional woman than a voice for all women. Increasingly, *Ms.* published articles on how to dress for success, how to rise on the corporate ladder, how to invest your savings, and in general how to make it in a man's world. In 1982, a typical *Ms.* article was "The Feminization of Poverty"; by the late 1980s, the typical *Ms.* article told an affluent woman how to get as rich as men.[75] By its tenth anniversary in 1982, *Ms.* at least had a life of its own and was no longer seen as Steinem's magazine. Steinem served only as an elder stateswoman from the mid 1980s. She now spoke from on high, above the many divisions within the movement. When *Ms.* profiled the many famous (and often glamorous) women who were making their marks in the 1970s and 1980s, they simply underscored the mark that Steinem had made. Steinem was still the classic model for women who made it and looked good doing it.

There were many ironies in Steinem's lofty position within the movement. Like Betty Friedan, the eldest spokeswoman, Steinem was educated at Smith, a prestigious women's college. Yet these colleges had largely found women's liberation irrelevant in the 1960s and early 1970s. The large coed state universities in the Midwest and on the West Coast had been the real bastion of campus feminism. Most feminists found good looks irrelevant, if not harmful to women, yet Steinem's looks were an important aspect of her success. Critics complained that the media had picked Steinem as a leader because of her looks, but then the media often choose all national leaders on that basis. Men such as John Kennedy, John Lindsey, and Ronald Reagan had also benefited from good looks. Their faces were part of their fortune.

It was always odd to hear Steinem attack the pressure society put on women to be beautiful. In a 1978 interview, for example, Steinem argued that although young men, like women, had to be attractive too, that the "older and more powerful" a man got "the less important it" was. Yet older women were not considered as valuable. They were "more judged on" their "outsides than" their "insides." She ironically noted: "Just look at the magazine business. You always have to have someone on the cover like a Cosmo girl. It creates such insecurity if the only women you see are skinny white beautiful women. In fact, it even makes skinny white women insecure because you are never quite beautiful enough."[76]

Here Steinem the consummate skinny, beautiful white woman tells us in a moment of vulnerability that she is insecure about aging. The interviewer concluded with the mandatory question: "[H]ow about you? Have your so-called good looks helped you?" Steinem replied: "It's hard to tell. I never was considered an especially beautiful woman until the feminist movement came along. But you see, they thought all of us had army boots and grenades and I was a surprise."[77] Steinem was a constant surprise. Nobody ever forgot the surprise, because like some lucky movie stars she refused to age. Throughout the 1980s, she remained the cool, unflappable beauty with brains. Indeed, *Newsweek* had labeled her the "great stone face" because of her characteristic deadpan, which was more characteristically masculine.

Steinem's taste in men was equally surprising and piled irony on irony. Like many feminists, Steinem seemed supportive of men's rights to be sensitive and avoid stereotypical, brutish masculine behavior. One might have expected her to date sensitive intellectual men—say halfway between Mr. Rogers and Alan Alda. Instead, her dating taste ran to macho types with an exalted position in their fields. Steinem dated Henry Kissinger, for example, even while criticizing his foreign policy. She dated the African American Olympic star, Rafer Johnson, while admonishing men for constantly playing Tarzan to a female Jane. She also dated Paul Desmond, the jazz saxophonist, and a reputed macho womanizer. The search for the real Gloria Steinem always led in circles. The Steinem mystique, her influence as a role model, and her image as a heroine were all wrapped in a massive contradiction. Although Gloria Steinem looked like one of the girls, she usually acted like one of the guys. The long hair and sunglasses and general glamour changed the image of feminists as surely and completely as Israeli soldiers changed the image of the Jew. Steinem made it harder to see women as victims.

This trio of heroines—Joplin, Baez, and Steinem—may seem even more incongruous after exploring their backgrounds and careers. Their essential common strand was how uncommon they were in their separate fields and their ability to break common stereotypes about women. They influenced by words, deeds, and images. Their achievements put them in the spotlight and gave them the opportunity to be heroines and models, but only the responses of masses of men and women confirmed their role. As real heroines, they appealed both to men and women. Indeed, if their mystique was limited to half of American society, they could not appear very powerful. All three heroines made it in different ways, but each rose above their careers to represent something vital, contemporary, and uniquely American in themselves.

Joplin was the only big female star to merge popular music and the counterculture. She was the closest female equivalent of a Bob Dylan in terms of mass influence. She taught men and women that a talented woman with problem hair, pimples, and a weakness for food could make herself beautiful because of who she was and not just how she looked. She invented a new style and standard for feminine beauty. As a cultural rebel, she helped men and women to see themselves in new ways.

Joan Baez was, for a time, a leading popular music star also, but her heroism came not from her efforts to transform herself, but her struggle to transform society. Moreover, Baez forced men and women to think about the responsibilities and opportunities of popular artists and entertainers. Baez sacrificed her career for her ideas. She made it much more difficult for the celebrities that followed her to stand on the sidelines of social struggle. She is often identified with pacifism, but she should be primarily linked with artistic activism. Although Joan was at first the consummate folkie, she grew past mere style. Unlike Joplin, Baez was not a model for cultural change or personal fulfillment, but for conscience.

Gloria Steinem was the least complicated and perhaps the less deserving of the three heroines. Steinem did not have to struggle or give up anything.

By simply doing what she always wanted to do—write about important social problems—she became a classic heroine and countercultural model. Many feminist and nonfeminist women writers were as perceptive as Steinem, and several wrote better. However, Steinem's Hollywood looks put her on another level. She told women and men, without uttering a word, that beauty was irrelevant. She could take men or leave them, and mostly she left them. Her call for sisterhood was little different from that of many feminists, but her looks lent her unspoken message credibility. A woman fulfilled herself by finding her work attractive and not by being attractive to men.

Joplin, Baez, and Steinem constituted a living counterculture for their own generation and an historical legacy for the future, but they did not operate in a cultural vacuum. Their influence was enhanced by the multiplier effect of changing images of women in music, film, television, advertising, and other areas. Above all, they gained power as role models from the dynamism and climate of change the 1960s and early 1970s provided. It was a time when many individual women felt that they should change—that it was almost their duty to change. Women were on the make for suitable cultural models, and when they found them, they did not apply a feminist litmus test. The all inclusive "sisterhood" umbrella covered all; it was wide enough to make unique loners such as Joplin and Baez feminist role models.

By the late 1970s, the social terrain and climate had changed. The question was whether feminist heroines and the feminist counterculture could survive this sea change. Would new countercultural heroines arise to inspire the next generation? Could older heroines continue to work their countercultural magic on the young? As always, the next generation was the only real countercultural test.

CODA

The Next Generation: Countercultural Test

6

The New Romanticism: Feminism versus Heterosexual Bliss

The news about classic rock music had reached practically every feminist by the late 1970s. In between the "sha la las," and "sha na nas" vintage rock lyrics both brainwashed young women and sabotaged the image of all women. The music's hard-driving, macho sexuality encouraged male teenagers to wear leather jackets, treat women rough, and make it in the back seats of cars. The male idol was the potent stud, a "sixty minute man" who could "rock 'em and roll 'em all night long," and leave them in the morning. The women in these songs turned from angels of the "Teen Angel" or "Earth Angel" variety to "California Girls" with tans and gorgeous hair or "northern girls" who knew how to "keep their boyfriends warm at night." Even the innocent, well-mannered Beatles, Hermits, and Monkees, who in the early sixties rhapsodized about holding hands with Mrs. Brown's daughter, were soon interested in "spending the night" with everybody's daughter. As feminist Marion Meade put it: "there was only one place for a woman in the rock scene" and that was "between the sheets."[1] Fran Taylor, a rock critic, expressed the moral outrage best when she referred to the classic rock songs as "oldies but baddies."[2]

Supposedly a new day had arrived in the 1970s. True male chauvinists still dominated the music industry and monopolized the really heavy electronic vibrations. Yet, assertive female singers, such as Helen Reddy, Cher, and Bette Midler, had pushed their way to the top. Meanwhile, even more biting satiric women songwriters, such as Dory Previn and Holly Near, sold their recordings to the serious feminist fringe groups. Between feminist music quarterlies, women's music networks, and the aggressive female superstars, the recent musical scene had often been viewed as a triumph of women's liberation. *Ms.* magazine had featured cover stories about female singers from Bette Midler to Judy Collins. First Cher and later Madonna asserted their independence off and on television. Earlier Helen Reddy and later Bonnie Raitt hosted rock concerts and won Grammy Awards. More importantly, new songs by female singers had increasingly depicted more aggressive attitudes and women.

The trend was well illustrated by those songs recorded by female singers, which rose to the top of the national popular song charts. Of the approximately 540 number one, single records between 1940 and 1974, sixty-three were performed by solo female singers. The hits of the late forties included such trite numbers as "Manana" (by Peggy Lee in 1948), "Buttons and Bows" (Dinah Shore, 1948), "A Little Bird Told Me" (Evelyn Knight, 1949), "Tennessee Waltz" (Patti Page, 1950), and "If I Knew You Were Comin' I'd've Baked a Cake" (Eileen Barton, 1950). The 1950s and early 1960s did not offer particularly more sophisticated fare. These years saw hits such as "How Much Is That Doggie in the Window" (Patti Page, 1953), "Little Things Mean a Lot" (Kitty Kallen, 1954), "Tammy" (Debbie Reynolds, 1957), "This Ole House" (Rosemary Clooney, 1954), "Johnny Angel" (Shelley Fabares, 1962), "I Will Follow Him" (Peggy March, 1963), and "It's My Party and I'll Cry if I Want To" (Leslie Gore, 1963). In distinct contrast, the late 1960s and early 1970s featured such assertive hits as "These Boots Are Made for Walking" (Nancy Sinatra, 1966), "Me and Bobby McGee" (Janis Joplin, 1971), "I Am Woman (Helen Reddy, 1972), "You're So Vain" (Carly Simon, 1973), and "Killing Me Softly with His Song" (Roberta Flack, 1973).[3]

Clearly the 1970s hits reflected women's new confidence, awareness, and aggressiveness, but they had few counterparts in the 1980s. The 1970s songs were no doubt partially inspired by the burgeoning women's liberation movement. In any event, the music could be interpreted as a triumph of consciousness raising, and the new singing stars, such as Janis Joplin, Helen Reddy, and Carly Simon, were strong and sassy enough to make excellent movement role models. The singers lacked clear connections to women's liberation, but Joplin was sexually aggressive on stage and off, Simon airily proclaimed her sexual independence, and Reddy offered sisterly support in her concert patter. With sexist rock music increasingly muted and the new tougher female music on the rise, it appeared that the feminist struggle to reform popular music was well on the road to success.

However, new musical and media trends subverted those feminist gains. Replacing the crude, overt sexism of the recent past, there grew a subtle new romanticism, which was far more dangerous to feminist consciousness and goals. At first glance, this seemed more a neoromanticism based on the traditional boy-girl romance formulas of American popular culture. Thus, the new romanticism elevated women rather than putting them down with sexist slurs. It told women that they are happiest, at their best, and worth most as a man's mate. It told men that the most important thing in life is loving a woman. The new romanticism celebrates what I call heterosexual bliss. The songs directly and indirectly stress that for both men and women the ultimate fulfillment is the mature male-female romantic relationship.

This newer music should not be confused with the romantic hit parade tunes of the 1930s, 1940s, and 1950s, nor with the rock love songs of the 1960s. The recent songs were both more sexually explicit and more artful. The romantic ditties of the 1930s and 1940s were tin-pan-alley tunes that rarely got past the June-moon-spoon stage of lyrics. Musically, these songs generally sacrificed both mood and melody for currently popular singing styles. From the crooning Andrew Sisters of the 1930s to bland singers such as Dinah Shore and Vaughn Monroe in the 1940s, renditions of popular love songs remained low keyed and detached. In the 1950s, early rock songs provided musical passion and a big beat, but like the romantic ballads they replaced, rock lyrics were too crude and rhymy to be emotionally involving. Also, before 1965, the level of physical contact described in all genres of popular music remained limited to kissing and holding hands. Post–1965 rock was sexually explicit, but it rather dehumanized both men and women. Moreover, rock music usually was so loud that it was difficult to linger over the lyrics. The mood of rock was active, aggressive, antiestablishment, and almost by definition unromantic. In contrast, the new heterosexual bliss songs combined state-of-the-art melodies and arrangements with dramatic, credible lyric renditions by skilled ballad singers. The songs were often in the captivating Frank Sinatra style with great attention to voice inflection. Indeed, it is no accident that singers such as Paul Anka and Mac Davis wrote so often for Sinatra. The new songs created a personal, mystic, romantic vision within an increasingly plastic impersonal world. The new, frank lyrics clearly suggested that true emotional fulfillment both stems from and leads to physical love.

This joyous sexual fulfillment continues to be musically available to men and women on an equal basis. If anything, the ballads promise more to women than to men. Clearly, they do not view women as sexual objects, made to gratify men. However, putting women on the pedestal is only the other side of the sexist coin. Suggesting that women fulfill their longings with sex and romance leads just as surely to "the problem with no name" as suburban maternity. (It may also lead to maternity.) Men, who are usually more pressured into individual achievement and practical pursuits, need not fear that they will be carried away in a romantic haze. Vivian Gornick, a feminist writer, put the problem well in her 1969 essay, "The Next Great Moment in History Is Ours." While reading the biography of a 19th-century English woman caught in the vise of Victorian conventions, Gornick felt she was reading about many of the contemporary women she knew. It suddenly occurred to her that "100 years ago sexual submission was all for a woman and today sexual fulfillment is all for a woman and the two are one and the same."[4]

The music of heterosexual bliss supplies two related messages: An all-encompassing romantic relationship is the most important thing in life, and the destruction of such a relationship is the worst tragedy that can occur. The chief corollary of these axioms is that a really loving woman is all that keeps a man going. Thus, in the 1970s male superstars, such as Paul Anka, Mac Davis, and even Bob Dylan, started to sing about the joys of the nuclear family and the supportive woman. Anka now sang "there is nothing stronger than our love" and complained that he didn't "like to sleep alone." However, just a few years before Anka wrote the overtly sexist ballad, "She's a Lady," for the benefit of the strutting Tom Jones. Bob Dylan, too, reformed. Until 1973, Dylan was putting down most women as bitches or depicting them as accessories to brass beds. However, in the 1970s he often rhapsodized about his wife's supportive role in songs such as "Wedding Song," "Shelter from the Storm," and "Sara."[5] Mac Davis's music is a little harder to type, but the commonest thread is the romantic stress on heterosexual bliss. Songwriters Kris Kristofferson and John Denver were other powerful examples of the new romantic trend. Singers such as Michael Bolton and Lionel Ritchie are more contemporary examples. There are certainly other popular content areas in contemporary music, but the new romance songs continue as an increasingly important element. The more aggressive women singers such as Helen Reddy at first stood apart from the romantic trend, but new, more traditionally feminine singers increasingly sang songs of heterosexual bliss. For example, in the 1970s superstar Toni Tennille belted out the line, "Love will keep us together," over and over, while looking adoringly at her Captain. In her top ten hit, "Muskrat Love" even muskrats succumb to romance. The genre continued popular, with contemporary female singers such as Whitney Houston, Mariah Carey, Celine Dion and a host of new-style "young country" singers such as Shania

Twain and LeAnn Rimes and male country singers such as George Strait and Billy Joe Cyrus.

Coupled with the new musical stress on heterosexual bliss was the increased use of joyous couples in American advertising. Madison Avenue had long used sexual sell. This usually involved a gorgeous female model lovingly wrapping herself around a product, or wearing it, or standing next to it, while projecting come-hither glances at the viewer. Sexy male models were only rarely used to sell products. Yet suddenly in the mid-1970s, sexy men littered the advertising landscape. Ads selling products to women had barely hinted at a man's presence. The new ads commonly showed partially dressed men lounging around women models—usually in the bedroom. While selling cosmetics and lingerie, women models now ran fingers across hairy male chests, whispered into men's ears, and generally twined themselves around the increasingly compulsory male model. These men often functioned as Madison Avenue, cigar store Indians. For example, in 1970s lingerie ads for Vassarette bras, men dressed in bathrobes lurked in the background admiring their women's new underwear. Many other ads just showed romantic couples next to a product. Whatever the situation, sexual intensity, or desired effect, the message was the same. If men and women were not in an intimate situation with their opposite number, they were incomplete and unfulfilled, if not un-American.

In the 1980s and 1990s, the trend intensified. For years Marlboro Man ads were the most recognized male ad in America. In 1985, they were edged out by Calvin Klein underwear ads, featuring sexy male models. Another Klein ad that year pushed his Obsession cologne by showing three men and a woman all hazily nude and intertwined. Soloflex body-building ads pictured famous brawny athletes, such as heavyweight boxing champion Ken Norton and Olympic gymnast Mitch Gaylord, being touched by a female hand. The caption read: "A Hard Man Is Good to Find." A 1985 Hennessy Cognac ad showed a sexy woman in a bikini flirting with a man in a bathing suit. Not only did ads now show men as sexy as women, but ad plots often depicted women as sexual aggressors. A Foster Grant sunglasses television ad, for example, showed a woman flirting with a man on a plane. She takes his Foster Grant glasses and hides them. When he protests, she gives him her business card and whispers: "I'll be staying at the Savoy."[6]

Whether the heterosexual bliss syndrome was a response to women's liberation, it was an obvious threat to it. The new media stress on heterosexual bliss could effectively blunt the feminist attack without ever confronting or acknowledging it. Feminists try to expose the conditioning which suggests that woman's eventual goal is to be supportive of men as a glamorous loving wife and capable mother of his children. The new romanticism hazes over the problem of sexist conditioning by stressing an equality of love and need. However, this romantic equality fails to dent the problem of female dependency. It ignores the social and economic foundations upon which truly equal love must rest.

Most feminist social critics have not really recognized the new cultural threat. For example, moderate feminists, such as *Ms.* magazine and the N.O.W. media watchers, continued to look for direct sexist slurs. As the number of sexist offenders declined, the few that these feminists did turn up appeared even more striking and offensive. To take on the new romanticism of Paul Anka, Bob Dylan, Michael Bolton, and company would leave moderate feminists open to several charges. Some would see their contempt as hatred of men; others would claim that they were against heterosexual relationships; and still other would charge them with a total lack of human feeling. Attacks on heterosexual sell in advertising would bring the same charges. Indeed, the coupling of male and female models in ads can be viewed as a symbol of equality. Given these general conditions, feminist critics are not likely to confront the new romanticism. It is safer to ignore it and simply praise alternative media vehicles. There are, after all, a number of prowoman songs and ads to celebrate.

In the final analysis, many feminists probably badly underestimate the new romanticism's appeal. In many ways, it represents a mood whose time has come. The new romanticism may not only have been a response to women's liberation, but to the rapidly accelerating divorce rate, the increasingly aggressive gay movement, and the trend toward unisexual dress and lifestyles. Heterosexual bliss is a natural antidote to all these phenomena. Moreover, it is especially effective because it attacks them indirectly. Instead of attacking abortion, Paul Anka could sing about the woman "having his baby." As opposed to criticizing the gay revolution, Mac Davis sang about "one hell of a woman" for "one hell of a man." The heartache of marital breakup in Vicki Carr's "With Pen in Hand" or Mac Davis's "I Woke Up on Your Side of the Bed" obviously worked against divorce. Michael Bolton's rendition of "When a Man Loves a Woman" celebrated general romance. Likewise, the constant contemporary use of loving couples in ads has a wide spectrum prescriptive effect on all the new social trends threatening heterosexual bliss. Ads, too, have become more intense, more sexually explicit, and more skilled at reaching people on an emotional level. Much the same can be said for cinema and television and the multiplier effect of these media greatly enhances the power of each medium. More recent hit films, such as *Sleepless in Seattle*, *Up Close and Personal*, *The Bridges of Madison County*, *Titanic*, and *The Horse Whisperer* illustrate the continuing romantic trend.

Even through the heyday of women's liberation, romanticism was alive and well in print media such as romance novels, self-help guides for women, and above all women's magazines. Romance novels had the same syrupy approach throughout the period. Love not only conquered all, but love should conquer everybody. The unstated message was if you did not get enough love in your marriage or life you could make up the difference vicariously through exotic novels. The covers got racier, the cleavage deeper, and the actual sexual descriptions became more graphic in the wake of the 1960s sexual revolution, but the romantic message stayed the same: Men and women must live for love or live a decidedly lesser life. It mattered not whether you lived in 17th-century England or in contemporary Tahiti, men were men and women were still women. Or in the immortal words that heralded the screen version of Margaret Mitchell's romantic novel, *Gone with the Wind:* "Scarlet's Back and Rhett's Got Her."

The femininity guidebooks did play a new role. In the 1970s, they became, by indirection, works of antifeminist sentiment. One early volume that directly confronted women's liberation was Lucianne Goldberg and Jeannie Sakol's 1971 book, *Purr Baby Purr.* Sakol founded the Pussycat League in 1969 as an antidote to raging feminism. Their book suggested that women can "be feminine and liberated," but they emphasized the former. The book asserted that "the lamb chop is mightier than the karate chop," for even the strongest female must be seductive to mate. *Purr Baby Purr* noted:

Despite militant talk about raping men and keeping them on stud farms to be enjoyed at will, the Pussycat League notes that nature has arranged it so that man can invade women sexually even if she resists, but that no woman, not even the strongest woman in the world can have a man if he doesn't want to be had. Thus, a man bent on sex doesn't have to be seductive, but the woman bent on sex must make herself desirable, smell nice, talk sweetly, and in general make nice-nice. This necessary seductive quality makes women uniquely passive or uniquely seductive or both and colors women's personality.[7]

Most feminine guidebooks were much less vivid and depended less on sociobiology and more on religion and tradition for support. Although the guides talked about romance, the goal was quite practical and the strategy quite simple. A woman made a happy marriage, not a man. She accomplished this with a shrewd mixture of romance, guile, and servitude. The two clear, best-seller feminine guidebooks of the 1970s were Helen Andelin's *Fascinating Womanhood* (written in 1965) and Marabel Morgan's 1973 book *The Total Woman*. However, Tracy Tanner's much less successful 1976 book, *How to Find a Man and Make Him Keep You* summed up the goal more clearly. The raciest entry in this genre came by way of the sexual revolution and an author known only as J. This 1975 bestseller bore the simple title, *The Sensuous Woman*.[8]

While Marabel Morgan quoted the Bible and stressed religious tradition, J quoted works of sexology such as *The Joy of Sex* and stressed sexual technique. Both, however, sought to make men happy through romance. For example, *The Total Woman* urged women to make their husband the clear family leader to give him confidence and make him love you. But to keep romance in your marriage, Morgan even suggested that wives sometimes greet their returning husbands at the door dressed only in plastic wrap. Andelin's *Fascinating Womanhood* is more straitlaced, less overtly romantic, and more obsequious to men, and it stresses old-fashioned femininity, without plastic-wrap costumes. For example, Andelin advises women to express anger by "tossing their curls" and "stamping their feet," in a childlike way. According to Andelin, a really feminine woman "always welcomes" her man's "most tedious monologue," while disdaining masculine jobs or money management, because these often cause her to lose "her feminine sparkle and charm." Yet, if the strategy is nonthreatening obedience, for both Morgan and Andelin, the goal is romance. The unstated message warns that anything that threatens your man's family leadership kills romance and eventually kills your marriage. Women's liberation was not usually mentioned directly, but it obviously threatened some men.

Women's magazines promoted a new romanticism in more diverse ways. Some traditional women's magazines such as *McCall's* and the *Ladies Home Journal* made an effort to accommodate the new consciousness that women's liberation produced in younger housewives and working women. Yet they basically appealed to the stay-at-home mother and provided hints and support to help them make marriage and homemaking work. They never said that woman's place is in the home, but they acted like it was. They all suggested that women should be married, or if single, trying to find Mr. Right. By the 1980s, the new romanticism could be seen clearly in women's magazine article titles, such as "What Makes Men Marry" or "How to Find Mr. Right." In 1982, the *Ladies Home Journal* featured an article titled "How to Keep Him Loving You Year after Year," And in 1984, *Redbook* published "How to Please a Man."[9] These were magazine versions of *The Total Woman*. They suggested that it was a woman's responsibility to keep romance and thus the marriage alive. If it was failing, *she* had to find the problem and fix it, and the fix was usually a new romantic scheme to bring back the flame of passion. More complicated marital problems appeared in features such as the *Journal*'s "Can This Marriage Be Saved" column. Increasingly, in the 1980s the suggested solution for problem marriages was more romance.

The romance fiction of women's magazines was usually simplistic in plot and sentimental in style. Whereas the leading men's magazines such as *Esquire* and *Playboy* often featured famous fiction writers such as Gore Vidal and James Dickey, most women's magazine fiction writers were mere hacks. As feminist critic Ellen Barker suggested, most women's magazine fiction stories "culminate in a passionate union between the lovers." This kind of romance formula fed "the notion that a woman's single goal in life" was "to search for love with one partner." This relationship was to make a woman "eternally happy" and secure in the home and marriage they had created.[10]

One woman's magazine that uniquely enhanced the new romanticism was *Cosmopolitan*. In 1966, under the leadership of its new editor Helen Gurley Brown, *Cosmopolitan* changed from a magazine geared to married homemakers to one aimed at primarily single women. Brown was the author of *Sex and the Single Girl*, and she almost single-handedly made *Cosmpolitan* into a female counterpart to *Playboy*. Suddenly articles about what men liked in women replaced articles about what husbands liked. Indeed, by the middle 1970s *Cosmopolitan* was the largest selling women's magazine on college campuses, just as *Playboy* was the largest selling college men's magazine. Both magazines celebrated sex, but *Cosmopolitan* was more interested in romance. *Cosmopolitan* taught women all the tricks of the trade that made romantic relationships perfect.

Yet as Nora Ephron, who once wrote for *Cosmopolitan*, noted, there was a big difference between the *Cosmopolitan* girl and the *Playboy* man. According to Ephron:

There is one major difference between *Playboy* and *Cosmopolitan*. The *Playboy* man has no problems. The *Cosmopolitan* girl has thousands. She has menstrual cramps, pimples, budget squeeze and hateful roommates. She cannot meet a man. She cannot think of what to say when she meets one. She doesn't know how to take off her clothes to get into bed with him. She doesn't know how to find a psychiatrist.[11]

Thus, *Cosmopolitan*, despite its racy covers with plunging necklines and sexual instruction articles, was closer to the traditional woman's magazine than it appeared. It instructed uncosmopolitan single women instead of novice housewives. As Nora Ephron explained:

They just don't understand Helen Gurley Brown and *Cosmopolitan*. They don't understand that she knows something they don't. She knows about the secretaries, nurses, and clerks who live out there somewhere, miles from psychiatrists, plastic surgeons, and birth control clinics. Only 8% of *Cosmopolitan*'s readers are in New York City. The rest are stuck in the wilds, coping with their first sit-down dinners and their first orgasms. . . . These are the girls who buy *Cosmopolitan* and swallow such tidbits as: "Rub your thighs together when you walk. The squish-squish sound of nylon . . . has a frenzying effect."[12]

Helen Gurley Brown knew these women and understood their needs. Ephron believed that *Cosmopolitan* demonstrated "rather forcefully that over one million women" would pay sixty cents "not to read about politics or women's lib, but merely how to get a man." Ephron admitted that although she had not been single for years, she read *Cosmopolitan* monthly. She noted:

I see it lying on the newsstand and I'm suckered in. How to increase the size of your bust, the cover line says or thirteen new ways to feminine satisfaction. I buy it . . . looking forward to . . . a bigger bra size and a completely new kind of orgasm. Yes, I should know better. . . . But she gets me every time. . . . And there it is. Buy a padded bra, the article on bustlines tells me. Fake it the article on orgasm says. And I should be furious. But I'm not. Not at all. How can you be angry at someone who's got your number.[13]

As the new romantic trend increased, *Cosmopolitan* had even more women's numbers. It became both a cause and symptom of a romantic renaissance and the changing relationships between men and women. At first glance, the cleavage covers of *Cosmopolitan* suggest only sexuality, as did some of the lead cover articles on sexual proficiency. However, *Cosmopolitan* also featured a wide range of articles about fashion, men, grooming, and the lives and loves of celebrities. *Cosmopolitan* was a guide to the new intimacy and the new romanticism and not simply a road map of the new sexuality. Like the new romanticism, *Cosmopolitan* did not attack women's liberation, it ignored it. Helen Gurley Brown's message was that women could fulfill themselves as individuals through career, marriage, beauty, romance, and sex. The unstated message was group movements were irrelevant to women. By the 1980s, feminists could not really attack either *Cosmopolitan* or the traditional women's magazines without appearing to attack housewives, romance, or both. Intimacy and romance were the shields for a new consciousness among many woman who were dissatisfied with their lives. Women's liberation became a scapegoat for many of the new problems of women who were freed from traditional ties and roles.

By 1984, even Susan Brownmiller, famous for her 1975 best-selling polemic against rape *Against Our Will*, acknowledged the trend toward femininity and romance. Her 1984 book *Femininity* argued that the increased competition for men and jobs was making women revert to feminine wiles.[14] New York City had five hundred thousand more women than men and this figure included an estimated male homosexual population of four hundred thousand. Brownmiller felt that women reacted to this threat in prefeminist ways. They expected less from men and deferred to them more, while spending more time on making themselves seductive with clothes and cosmetics.

Other famous feisty feminists of the 1970s were also joining the romantic chorus. Germaine Greer, whose feisty book *The Female Eunuch* had argued for female aggressiveness, independence, and sexuality in 1970, wrote *Sex and Destiny* in 1984. Greer now believed women could only be happy by accepting their crucial roles as wives and mothers, dressing chastely, and expecting more from love than sex.[15] Betty Friedan, universally acknowledged as the literary mother of feminism, had beaten Greer to the punch with her 1981 book *The Second Stage*. Friedan's new views criticized feminists for going too far, too fast, and suggested that in the current "second stage" of feminism, women had to start with the family and build on stable, loving relationships. Friedan had come full circle.[16] In 1963, her pathbreaking book *The Feminine Mystique* had tried to liberate women from the family. Eighteen years later, Friedan urged women to get back to the family's loving arms. Erica Jong, a favorite feminist novelist ever since her blockbuster book *Fear of Flying*, joined the romantic revisionists in a 1989 *Ms.* article which illustrated a fear of lost intimacy. Jong felt that feminists her age now looked wistfully at the loving marriages of their parents, compared with their own empty "single parent families."[17] Between the lines of all this nostalgic, recanting, revisionism is the thinly veiled yearning for romance. The "is this all there is" complaint of 1963's feminine mystique suburban housewife had become the 1989 complaint of many successful career women and older feminist veterans. The feminist career women of the seventies had money, self-esteem, and prestige. They sometimes had children and often had divorces. However, romance was often missing or irrelevant. Growing old made both women and men nostalgic about family and children. When the hardest-driving male executive is on his deathbed, he does not regret not having made more money or played more golf. He wishes he had more children, had spent more time with them, or had a better marriage. In the 1980s, aging feminists often started similar soul searching.

There seemed to be an inverse relationship between the decline of sexual obsession and the rise of romance. As overt sexuality retreated from film and declined in practice, new modes of romance and courtship crept in. There was less pressure to have sex on adult first dates and more kind words about the value of marital faithfulness. Magazine articles were filled with articles about intimacy, commitment, and long-term relationships. There was less talk about sexual frustration and dysfunction and more stress on making relationships work. Couples wanted more babies and more meaning and more togetherness. In 1984, *Time* magazine announced that the Sexual Revolution was over. America had been experiencing a "me generation," but now it was going through a "we generation." Similarly, *Cosmopolitan* editor Helen Gurley Brown suddenly discovered that "sex with commitment" was "absolutely delicious," whereas sex with your date was "too casual and meaningless" to be "marvelous."[18] Although sexual activity among youth, from junior high through college, continued to increase, adults were becoming more sexually conservative. Clearly, the medical threats of first herpes and later AIDS tended to make knowledgeable adults more cautious, but there had been a reaction against casual sex before the medical dangers became publicized. The new medical reasons for sexual caution only added impetus to a social trend.

The 1960s counterculture looked down on both marriage and the nuclear family as dying institutions. Many feminist radicals felt that only easy access to divorce had allowed marriage to survive in contemporary America. They often argued that to continue its viability, marriage must be further reformed. Some feminists called for more open marriages; others called for strict marriage contracts. Some even advocated group marriages. Feminists also warned women not to marry too young. Women should, instead, imitate men and not marry until they were firmly established in their careers and independent. When young women complained that all the best men would be married if they waited, feminists suggested that they would have their pick of men who later divorced.

Throughout the 1970s, support for traditional approaches to marriage increased, and divorced women often remarried quickly. Statistics told the story in the 1980s. Roughly 65 percent of young women divorcees remarried within five years. Divorces were down and marriages and births were up. A record 2.5 million marriages in 1982 was the seventh consecutive annual rise and a 16 percent increase over 1975. The 1.2 million divorces in 1982 was the first decline since 1962. The birthrate for women over 30 was up almost 10 percent per year in the early 1980s and has continued to rise. Total births also set a record in 1982 and have continued to rise.[19]

Americans were turning from the fulfillment and self-actualization theories of such sixties gurus as social psychologist Abraham Maslow to the comfort of families. Maslow's ideas had been reinforced and popularized by such self-help 1970s best-sellers as Wayne Dyer's *Your Erroneous Zones* and Gail Sheehy's *Passages*. But the media move toward romance and marriage was quietly undercutting self-growth and self-actualization. The decided conservative trend in politics and among college students was part and parcel of a revolt against the 1960s. The Reagan revolution in the 1980s was prefaced by the romance-and-marriage revolution of the late 1970s. Reagan's political success partly resulted from appealing to and playing for traditional family values. In the 1980s, this not only got him the votes of the rich, whose lifestyle still allowed a stay-at-home mother, but also the new poor. These middle-class families were poor precisely because the wife stayed home to take care of children. They resented the DINC (double income no children) families on the block who enjoyed the good life, and these new have-nots were ready to celebrate family values with President Reagan. The new middle-class poor supported Reagan, even though Reaganomic economic policies hurt them. Reagan was able to attract the rich with his economic programs and the new poor with his profamily rhetoric. Housewives felt they had done the right thing: They had rejected abortion and not sentenced their children to day care. They were good traditional mothers, yet they were suffering because of it. They were obvious setups for Reagan's profamily line.

Even those women who were not romantic about traditional families often had second thoughts as their biological clock ran down. In her 1991 book *Prisoners of Men's Dreams*, Suzanne Gordon suggested that many career women suddenly became angry in their late thirties and early forties. These women were caught in the feminist "definition of success." They had allowed their lifestyle to become their life and suddenly that was not enough. When they began to think of romance now, they often found it hard to date, because their carefully cultivated persona of confidence and control often turned off men. Gordon thought that these women did not think enough about what a successful career might be like while they were building one.[20]

Although Gordon did not blame feminism directly for the emotionally empty lives careerism often led to, Sylvia Hewlett did. In her 1986 book *A Lesser Life: The Myth of Women's Liberation*, Hewlett argued that feminism shortchanged women by stressing rights instead of happiness. As a reformed feminist herself, Hewlett testified that women's liberation failed women because it had been consistently antifamily and ignored children's welfare. She accused feminists of largely promoting their own economic interests, while putting issues such as child care, maternity leave, and child support on the back burner. In so doing, feminists had deserted the ordinary woman to concentrate on the problems of white, well-educated women who were trying to move up the career ladder.[21] Because Hewlett and her banker husband were themselves wealthy and well-educated, their commentary was somewhat suspect. However, the warm reception both Hewlett and later Gordon received, showed how nostalgic and receptive America had become about traditional family values.

Whether the move back to romance and family represented a backlash against the sexual revolution or feminism or both is open to conjecture. However, the new stress on intimacy in the 1980s and the new relationship buzz words suggested a reaction against the cool "depersonalized" sex of the past two decades. Suddenly couples talked about caring, commitment, and communication the way activists used to talk about the environment and politics. The romantic backlash did not wipe out most elements of the sexual revolution, but only revolted against their unromantic effects. Previously controversial sexual techniques such as oral sex had become much more acceptable. Premarital sex and living with your lover, although unmarried, were also more acceptable. Soft pornography as evidenced in adult videos and magazines had been increasingly tolerated and, as such, became steadily more boring to most Americans. Even homosexuality had gained limited, though grudging, tolerance through more aggressive agitation by gay-rights groups and more sympathetic portrayal by the media. Americans seemed to draw the new line on rampant sexuality in hard core pornography and any child-related pornography.

Amazingly, though America accepted the specifics of the sexual revolution, it suddenly became critical of the social context of some sex. As physical sex became more common, on screen and off, and among steadily younger teenagers, Americans searched for more meaning. That search led away from group sex, open marriage, and sex for its own sake. It led back toward romance, family, and sex as a tool of intimacy.

Perhaps clothes, which cover the body, but often expose our thoughts and goals, reflected the new romanticism best. Not surprisingly in the 1980s Vassarette advertised its lingerie line as "the romantic lingerie" and teased that it was "not for everyone." The increasing vogue for lacy underwear fueled a sales explosion for the mail-order lingerie king, Frederick's of Hollywood. In the 1960s and 1970s, Frederick's had largely advertised its catalog in sleazy magazines. In the 1980s, it began to open stores in suburban shopping malls. Frederick's was soon competing with Victoria's Secret and other mall-based lingerie stores. High fashion had been trying to bury the miniskirt since the 1960s without success; however, in the 1980s and 1990s the miniskirt has made a decided comeback, along with plunging necklines, push-up bras, and generally sexy clothing.

As women had entered the business world, advisers both feminist and nonfeminist had advised women to wear more businesslike and less feminine clothes. Suzanne Gordon charged that businesswomen had been pressured to hide any femininity, because males sometimes interpreted feminine dress as an invitation to sex. This meant professional women should never dress in a sexy or flirtatious manner. The result, according to Gordon, was a drab, genderless dress code, which made women look like men. Gordon noted that counselors advised "women to conceal their femininity because any evidence of human vulnerability or gentleness" made "men patronize rather than respect female colleagues." One clothing counselor advised women: "Avoid wraparound skirts, casual shoes or hair-color changes. Dress like a lawyer in a conservative suit." Looking very feminine supposedly signaled men that you needed "to be taken care of." Even when dress codes relaxed in the 1980s, Gordon suggested that it still was not "acceptable to look too feminine—or too sexy or too cute—in corporate America."[22]

Although Gordon saw the defeminization of women's dress as a feminist plot, Susan Faludi in her 1991 book *Backlash: The Undeclared War on Women* saw the defeminization of dress as a plot by designers and apparel makers. In a chapter titled "Dressing the Dolls: The Fashion Backlash," Faludi claimed that fashion industry moguls used the conservative, dress-for-success look that feminists sometimes advised as a straw-man issue to sell women expensive frilly clothes. Her chief villain was French fashion designer Christian Lacroix, who sought to remake American women "as little girls." Faludi argued that even under fashion pressure, women refused to give up buying the comfortable suits and slacks to which they had become accustomed. Faludi thought that the real threat of the "dress for success" wardrobe that John Malloy's book pioneered was that it never went out of fashion. Faludi did make Lacroix seem foolish, but high-fashion campaigns have often fallen flat and Faludi failed to really explain the move toward sexier clothes. When Faludi suggested that the popularity of sexy lingerie was not really relevant because women buy more cotton panties at Victoria's Secret than lace teddies and also have accepted "Jockey for Her" underwear, she missed the special role of lace lingerie. Women may wear jockey underwear under work clothes, but the point is how do they see themselves at midnight with their man? Faludi also condemned the raunchy but successful Guess Jeans ads as hostile to feminism, because they tried to turn the fashion clock back to 1950s style femininity. Guess surely exploited and manipulated the desire for sexy clothing and the nostalgia for the 1950s, but they did not create that desire or nostalgia.[23]

Increasingly, the new romanticism merged with femininity. For example, in 1997 columnist Suzanne Fields wrote about "putting the femininity back into feminism." She noted that "a feminine woman enhances a man in a positive way not an accusatory one." For Fields, femininity was "about complementing and attracting men." She rhetorically asked why femininity was staging a comeback and answered: "Because it's fun. Because it feels good. Because it's natural. Because it works." How it worked was best answered by a nonfiction best-seller of 1996 and 1997: *The Rules; Time-Tested Secrets for Capturing the Heart of Mr. Right.* This book supposedly told women how to play "hard to get," so they could enjoy the chase. Fields also noted that decreasing numbers of women preferred the title Ms. after they marry and that more wanted to take their husbands name, because it boosted "his ego."[24] From *Fascinating Womanhood* and *The Total Woman* to *The Rules*, it seemed the new romanticism was seamless. It constantly confounded feminism with femininity and heterosexual bliss.

A good recent example of the continuing romantic turnaround was the 1998 film *City of Angels* starring Meg Ryan and Nicolas Cage. Ryan plays a pediatric surgeon who rejects the marriage proposal of her lover—a fellow surgeon—because he lacks romantic flair. Instead, in a romantic orgy, she opts to wed Cage who gives up his soft, ageless life as an angel to satisfy his compulsive romantic attachment to Ryan. As a human, stripped of his angelic powers, Cage is lovable, but seems extraordinarily ordinary, with no particular skills. Ryan dies before she can marry, but the message is clear. The most prestigious professions will fail to satisfy women. Neither will ordinary marriages lead to fulfillment. A woman has to find her romantic angel, whether real or imagined, even if the result is tragic. Although this romance was made in Hollywood and not in heaven, it reflected a steady, decade-long trend.

Powerful cultural trends have a life of their own. Feminists cannot simply pass the new romanticism off as the work of manipulative advertisers and free-market profiteers. The heart always has its reasons, and they are buried under layers of popular culture. To expose the cultural background is to explain the foreground, but this does not necessarily forecast the future. The countercultural test is always a generation removed. Thus, the new romanticism means one thing now and quite another thing later.

It is difficult to forecast generational effects. Media has its greatest effects on unformed minds. The new romanticism is created by the older generation as a conscious or unconscious response to their perception of current social conditions, and the cultural creators have little feel for the next generation. The new generation who will someday create songs and ads of their own are shaped by the media and culture of an older generation they do not understand. Media guru Marshall McLuhan put the problem best: "We shape our tools and then our tools shape us." Our media tools especially shape the young. Thus, the new romanticism is the creature of the present and the burden of the past. Whether the next generation can shake off that burden and create a relatively nonsexist future remains to be seen. However, the crucial battle for the future is clearly a cultural struggle and not a struggle against political backlash. Unfortunately, feminists have increasingly been ignoring cultural problems and centering on contemporary economic, political, and organizational problems.

7

From Counterculture to Networking: Winning the Battles and Losing the War

The last underground 1960s SDS Weatherpeople, such as Mark Rudd and Bernadine Dohrn, gave up their subterranean existence two decades ago, and long before his death in 1994, ex-Yippie Jerry Rubin, gave up counter-cultural agitation for Wall Street stock brokerage. A depressed co-Yippie leader, Abbie Hoffman, committed suicide in 1992, and Eldridge Cleaver, the sixties classic, black militant, earlier returned from Europe reborn, to sing the praises of white capitalist America, long before his recent death. Yet the depressed activist and sixties survivor may still exalt: FEMINISM LIVES! It is still, after all, the era of the woman. *Ms.* magazine still publishes monthly. Title VII complaints of hiring discrimination against women and equal pay suits still drive employers up the wall. And Title IX complaints of inequitable treatment of college women athletes still make the sports sections. Also, affirmative action hiring still drives gender equality. Although ERA and day care are no longer burning questions, abortion is still as fiery as an issue gets. But if feminism lives, where does it hang out?

You can easily tell where it does not abide. Women's liberation no longer dominates newspaper headlines or magazine covers. When feminism is mentioned in periodicals, it is usually in a piece on what happened to the woman's movement. Neither does nightly network news follow feminism. Similarly, the most popular campus speakers, such as Ralph Nader, Sam

Donaldson, Cokie Roberts, and William Bennett, are usually oblivious to feminist issues. Indeed, even "political correctness" has become a joking phrase and taken a place in the title of a popular television comedy show. Geraldine Ferraro has been defeated. Shirley Chisholm no longer runs for anything, let alone president. Barbara Bush (unlike Betty Ford) never disagreed with her husband, and although the present First Lady, Hillary Clinton, is the most active presidential wife since Eleanor Roosevelt, she does not argue with the president and polls showed she was a political liability by the 1996 election. Moreover, Mrs. Clinton passively accepts her husband's philandering and "stands by her man."

Thus, although feminism lives, it lives in a vacuum. We periodically hear about it, but do not really see it in action. We know that it is important, but increasingly most Americans do not know why. America has put women's liberation up on a pedestal and relegated it to history. With apologies to Betty Friedan, the woman's movement has a problem with no name.

Ironically, feminism has been undermined, in part, by its success. The problem reveals itself neatly in the Virginia Slim maxim, "You've come a long way baby." Many Americans now feel that the struggle for women's rights is largely over; others feel it has gone too far. All that remains is some mopping up by battle-hardened feminist veterans such as Gloria Steinem. Once the few remaining mossback chauvinists have been eliminated, the victory fires can be lit. Indeed, the only things keeping feminism indirectly newsworthy are the raging abortion struggle, the political gender gap, and sexual harassment of women in the armed services and in the workplace.

The real struggle has never been between chauvinists and feminists, but between feminists and traditional women who feel threatened by women's liberation. The proverbial woman on the street often says that although she's not a women's "libber [*sic*]," she is for equal pay and wants to come down hard on rapists and wife beaters. For her, feminism represents a status crisis, rather than an issue conflict. Traditional women often fear that if the aggressive feminist is the new model for womanhood, then they are the old model. They logically reason: better to be appreciated for what you are than to be damned for what you are not. Traditional women do not complain about oppression, they dwell on their selfless sacrifice. Such women can only be radicalized by convincing themselves that men do not really appreciate them as wives, mothers, and lovers. They feel that feminists do not respect them, whereas men constantly pay homage to their virtue, beauty, and usefulness in those roles. Also, for many traditionalists recent feminism smacks of political radicalism, homosexuality, sexual vulgarity, and atheism.

There has been no way to close the gap between the typical Kansas farm wife, for example, and *Ms.* magazine. Feminist sisterhood was tailor-made for urban women who craved careers, status, or relief from household drudgery. These women demanded equal economic opportunities and more equalitarian marriages, yet, because most of them were, at least, middle class, day care was never a crucial issue and abortion became their right. Increasingly, their struggle was an individual conflict with their husband or a group struggle with an employer. Even among these women, sisterly solidarity usually turned into networking. Divorced, separated, and single women used to constitute feminism's real base; however, now networking career women are the base.

But how about college women? Surely the young girls brought up in the age of the woman have soaked up a liberated spirit. They know that "women make policy, not coffee" and that "Adam was a rough draft." They understand sexism, chauvinism, and the tragedy of becoming "just a housewife." They believe in woman's rights and equality. However, like the Declaration of Independence and the Constitution, these things are too boring to talk about. Alas, the new generation of college women are not generally feminists: They have little reason to seek feminine support. Their parents encourage them to attend college in ever greater numbers; the university male/female ratio is still close to even; and coeds are treated equally by faculty and courted by males hungry for dates. Later, when these blissful coeds are saddled with children, or a selfish husband, or facing job discrimination, they might be recruited to feminism. But like their mothers they are more likely to network than agitate. Meanwhile, they are oblivious to calls for feminist sisterhood. They are even less interested in shaping young girls—those teenyboppers just starting to experiment with lipstick, bras, and boys. There is little hope that contemporary college women will become the vanguard of a revived feminism in the dawning new century.

Although Americans increasingly believe that feminism has recently declined, nobody knows when. Some books in the late 1980s and early 1990s, such as Susan Faludi's *Backlash* (1991), suggested general decline, but could not finger a watershed event.[1] It is eerily similar to the 1920s. Everyone knows that feminism died in the twenties, but nobody knows when it died, because when a movement dies from cultural causes, it dies very, very gradually as the next generation grows to maturity. We do know that in the 1960s and 1970s feminists had incredible energy, but it seemed as if sometime after 1976 there was some secret battle, which nobody reported, that resulted in a feminist defeat. The in-joke of 1992 was Washington journalist Sally Quinn's quip that she knew the feminist movement was dead when "Jane Fonda gave up her acting career to become a housewife."[2] Actually, Fonda's marriage to television mogul Ted Turner, at age fifty-four, was anticlimactic. Feminism might have died earlier when Fonda put out her first exercise video.

If feminist consciousness reached its low ebb in the 1950s, with triumphant suburban motherhood, it was ironically dipping down again in the early 1990s, when most mothers worked away from home. In a way, American women have come full circle on the problem of combining marriage and career. In 1966, as contemporary feminism caught the media's attention, *Newsweek* interviewed female college graduates and reported that they were much more confident that marriage and career could be merged successfully. Feminism had also reduced the "senior panic" that gripped girl's dorms as graduation approached. College women tended to marry at twenty-two, just two years over the national median. Feminism suddenly made it plausible, if not fashionable, to take more time finding a husband. In 1966, a Radcliffe college senior told *Newsweek*: "When girls marry by default, there is frustration at age thirty-five or forty, because they never see how realistic their dreams of glory were." A Hollins college senior added that "it would be tragic to go" from "parental control to college control to more control" through an early marriage. The new senior panic was not fear that you would not marry after college, but that you might not find a rewarding job. Another quite new worry was to find a man who would not be emasculated by the new stronger breed of educated women. One Vassar senior noted that "strong and independent women like us need men who are stronger."[3]

As the Vietnam War and campus revolt wound down, the print media spent more time on women's liberation. *Time* had roughly five times as many pieces on women's liberation in 1970 as it had in 1969. The increased attention also brought the first talk of backlash. For example, in March 1971 a *Look* senior editor wrote an article on backlash against feminism titled "They're a Bunch of Frustrated Hags." The criticism was from women who feared a loss of femininity or who charged that feminists undercut a biblical injunction that women should obey their husbands and fathers.[4] Sometimes, feminist critics formed femininity groups such as Women Who Want to Be Women, headquartered in Fort Worth, Texas. These women clearly did not want to be liberated. However, this type of antifeminism was not taken seriously by either the media or feminists. It was mostly played for laughs. And, after all, these antifeminist groups displayed a feminist style anger and organization. If anything, this kind of criticism helped women's liberation. With enemies like these, women's liberation did not need many friends.

Feminists were often their own worst enemy. Internal dissension had always plagued feminism, as it had most sixties radicalism. However, the rifts created by Betty Friedan in 1972 were far more damaging because she had more public credibility and access to the media. For example, in a *McCall's* article, "Beyond Women's Liberation," which appeared shortly after *Ms.* magazine began publishing, Friedan criticized feminism's new direction. *McCall's* billed Friedan as the "founder of the women's movement," and she attacked feminists "extremists." Friedan warned that "female chauvinist boors" were "inviting a backlash" from both women and men that jeopardized what feminists had recently accomplished. Friedan did not attack *Ms.* or Gloria Steinem directly, but she did criticize Steinem's *Ms.* article "Sisterhood." Friedan felt the essay was "female chauvinism" and that it was antimale. She noted that she had "always objected to rhetoric that" treated "the women's movement as class warfare against men" or argued that women were "oppressed as a class, by men." Friedan felt that sympathetic men were needed to protect feminist gains against the forces of reaction from "the Catholic hierarchy" to political, business, and union bosses, whose power rested "on women's passivity." It was now time for feminism to become a "two-sex movement for human liberation" from "obsolete sex roles of the feminine and masculine mystique." In closing, Friedan said: "It's time to leave behind as dinosaurs . . . male chauvinist pigs and female chauvinist boors alike."[5]

Friedan had done everything but call Gloria Steinem a chauvinistic female boor. Clearly Friedan's anger was partly about her own replacement as the national feminist leader by the more glamorous and younger Steinem. Yet, Friedan posed some real dangers for feminism. She not only invited backlash, she also described exactly the type that would be forthcoming in the next two decades. Friedan did not see that the backlash would be much more muted and stem much more from women than from men. Yet, slowly but surely, in the 1970s and 1980s increasing numbers of women came to see women's liberation as antifeminine, anticaring, antichild, antifamily, antiromantic, and antimale.

Disillusioned women began to attack selected feminist results and some disturbing social trends as products of women's liberation, and criticism from those who had grown up with feminism was much harder to handle. For example, in 1974 Anne Taylor Fleming, a freelance writer, wrote a *Newsweek* essay "Up from Slavery to What." She identified herself as a "feminist like any other halfway sane woman." She also declared: "I want it, and I want it all, and I want it now." However, she felt that achieving women were just turning out female versions of the junk that men had turned out for years. She felt that *Ms.* magazine was "so hard-edged, so tough, that it" made many men's magazines "look soft-headed and mushy by comparison." She found women politicians, such as Bella Abzug, harder than their male counterparts, and Barbara Walters tougher than her male television co-host. Fleming, however, refused to give up her "female ethnicity" and "specialness." She did not want "to carry a briefcase," wear a suit, "and anticipate clogged arteries at age 40." In short, she did not want "to make all the mistakes men" had made. She argued that the "much-mocked feminine intuition" would make women "better doctors, lawyers, and Indian chiefs."[6]

That same year Shana Alexander sounded a similar complaint in a piece titled "No Person's Land." Alexander felt that in the last decade, the war of the sexes had turned the gray area between what had been "recognizable male . . . and female turf into a rutted mine field." Alexander worried about hostility between women. She did not understand what the feminist slogan "If you can't stand the heat, stay in the kitchen" really meant. But she worried more that the "no person's land" she described as "a rutted mine field" would become a "void polluted by hatred, both the self-hatred of women and the self-defeating hatred that so many enraged feminists feel for men." Alexander felt in a battle of the sexes everybody lost, because men and women were so bound up with each other that when they struck "the other," they must "also cut the self."[7]

In the 1970s, women's liberation was caught between those who worried that feminist militancy was cutting feminists off from the wider society of men and those who felt the movement was retreating under the attack of its enemies. Ironically, those who criticized militancy most were often born-again moderates who were once influential cultural militants. For example, in 1974 Ti-Grace Atkinson, a founder of the radical group The Feminists in the late 1960s, had a decided change of heart. Atkinson now felt that feminists had turned inward and were now writing for each other instead of doing work in the community. She felt that "despite all the slogans, sisterhood" did not furnish individual identity, and this left feminists "empty inside." She now talked about "human needs" and solving "human problems." Atkinson admitted that change would take longer and would involve "a less hard line." She now asked women to think about what they got "from other persons that" was "necessary for existence."[8]

In late 1975, as the ERA Amendment began to flounder, even in big industrial states such as New York and New Jersey, N.O.W. showed the strain of doubt. Karen DeCrow narrowly won reelection as N.O.W. president over Mary Myers, a more conservative challenger. Myers argued that N.O.W. had strayed away from basic economic issues to crusade for controversial goals and issues, such as gay rights and abortion. DeCrow beat back the challenge, but some N.O.W. chapters around the country began centering on local economic issues. Feminism in general became less centralized as leaders such as Betty Friedan and Gloria Steinem adopted lower profiles. Steinem seemed relieved to get out of the limelight. In 1976, she noted: "After eight years of doing precisely what I feel least comfortable doing—speaking in public, organizing—I'd like to retreat into my solitary profession."[9]

In November 1976, *Harper's* front cover featured a woman in a black veil to illustrate Veronica Geng's lead article, "Requiem for the Women's Movement." The article spun out a more clever and comprehensive version of Atkinson's criticism of the woman's movement. Geng centered on the 1975 edition of the *New Woman's Survival Sourcebook*, which she described as "240 oversized pages . . . listing the far-flung activities and resources of organized feminism." Geng charged that the *Sourcebook* tried to make her believe that the feminist revolution was happening everywhere except where Geng was. She found it projected "the bullying perfect-woman propaganda that" had "spread from the women's colleges to "women's magazines." She argued that feminists had become specialized professionals, cut off from ordinary women. Geng found that the feminists "apparent vigor" only represented "self-perpetuating make-work . . . to provide . . . worldly experts with prestige, book contracts, and grants." She criticized the cult of sisterhood that forced lesbian and heterosexual women together, and apart from men. In general, Geng felt that feminism had allied itself with so many Left movements that it was no longer a women's liberation movement, but only an activist movement. The movement substituted "agendas" for "thoughts" and proclaimed: "I am invincible, and I'm going to get a piece of paper called the ERA that says so." Geng felt that men lied to women and as they tried to free women from those lies, feminists were now also "lying to women." They invoked a jargon about "social forces." More importantly feminists ignored "the sexual and emotional intimacy that most women" wanted from men. This created "a vacuum into which" *The Total Woman* rushed. Geng felt that feminism would continue to die until it turned its attention "back to where it" belonged—"to the truth about the daily relations between women and men."[10]

If women's liberation failed to unite women in universal sisterhood, it did often divide men. Some men continued their macho drive toward mastery and success. Although they usually had families, they were largely defined by their work. They continued to find feminism irrelevant and indeed often married a "total woman," who stayed at home if he could afford it, but did most of the housework and child rearing even if she worked. The men who were affected by feminism were usually first influenced by the 1960s attack on traditional career paths. The counterculture revolted against corporate success strategies in favor of individuality. Once on the organizational ladder, many ex-flower children succumbed to corporate uniformity, but expressed themselves in other ways. These men held different social standards than their fathers. They judged themselves and each other, not only as providers, but as family men and fathers. They often described their wives as their best friends and talked about relationships instead of marriages. These men were seldom workaholics or wife beaters, but they had their share of chauvinist vices. They seldom treated their wives the way they treated male roommates in college. Specifically, they failed to share household chores and child raising, and they expected the wife to sacrifice her career for theirs. They were also more uptight sexually. The new performance sexuality—a product of both the feminist demand for sexual satisfaction and the sexual revolution's stress on technique—put pressure on men to please their partners. Back when most women were not supposed to like sex much, if lovemaking turned out mediocre, it was nobody's fault. After the 1960s, when sex failed, it was somebody's fault—perhaps everybody's fault. Maybe the husband did not understand his wife's needs. Perhaps he failed to read the latest authoritative guide to lovemaking. As impotence among younger males rose, women's liberation, rather than the sexual revolution, usually got the blame. The point was that men now knew they were being graded on sex, and they both tried harder and felt more performance anxiety.

Feminism was also blamed for making men less protective and caring on average. In her 1978 book *Dominus*, Natalie Gittelson interviewed men who were married to, or living with, feminists. The males generally complained that their women were less caring than they expected, and this made them less caring in response. Gittelson found that these men were more uptight about pleasing women sexually and that psychological impotence was more common in this group. She also noted that the new equalitarian sex roles that feminism made possible, seemed to produce more female frigidity as well. Overall, she found that the strains of the new social equality followed couples into the bedroom. Studying feminism by its effect on men married to feminists was a fruitful approach. Gittelson put it well: "When femininity becomes a matter for conjecture, so too must masculinity."[11]

Men were not changing fast enough, relative to women, and that made feminist gains fleeting. Men did not attack women's liberation, they largely ignored it. They said, in effect, if women can become physicians and lawyers, fine, let them do it. It is not my problem. Most men believed that women who could compete on equal footing with men were the vast exception. Thus, many men had a quiet confidence that feminism was not really relevant. But if feminism did not revolutionize the workplace or marriage, it did change cultural styles and images although these changes affected women much more than men. For example, unisexual clothing freed women from restrictive dress codes, but had little effect on men. Women could now wear slacks and pantsuits, but men did not wear dresses. Women could now smoke Marlboro cigarettes, but men did not smoke Eve's or Virginia Slims. One big factor in feminist decline was that it changed women, without a corresponding cultural change in men. Some men were forced to react to feminism, especially when it touched the women in their lives, but most men did not have to change.

Every woman had a personal involvement with women's liberation whether she favored it or despised it. Throughout American history, traditional women had told career women that there was something wrong with them if they did not crave marriage and children. Now suddenly feminism seemed to turn the tables. Indirectly, housewives were told that if they did not want a career, there was something wrong with them. There was constant assurance that feminists favored vocational choice. They were not putting down women who chose to stay home. Feminists often testified about the sacrifices their own mothers had made to make a home for them. Yet, when feminists asked a woman what she did, housework and child rearing were not acceptable answers. Politically the women's liberation movement has been caught between right-wing conservatives, who use the family as a shield to protect the status quo and left-wing radicals, who want to liberate society and not just women. The Right attacked feminism by focusing on gender political issues that they could argue would destroy the nuclear family. These included day care, sexual education, divorce laws, gay rights, and abortion. Radicals usually really wanted to change family structure. They saw the nuclear family historically as an oppressive institution. Radicals criticized mainstream moderate feminists, such as Betty Friedan, Gloria Steinem, and Liz Carpenter, for trying to reform archaic institutions like the family, instead of restructuring them to serve new conditions. Moderate feminists could safely ignore the small number of radicals to their Left, and thus women's liberation spent most of the 1980s arguing that feminists were even more profamily than right-wing conservatives. It was feminists, they argued, who fought for adequate day care and head start programs, and who established shelters for battered women and championed single-parent families. Feminists argued that conservatives were only interested in conserving affluent nuclear families who had no social problems.

Being caught in the middle allowed moderate feminists to distance themselves from feminist radicals and provided a better image. No longer seen as a sloppily dressed bra burner, the moderate feminist was, by the 1970s, often a career woman on the make. Barbara Ehrenreich described the new organization feminist as "the Cosmo Girl with her shirt buttoned up and the heavy black eye-liner tastefully removed." As opposed to the Cosmo Girl, she did not "want to work for the boss, date the boss, or even marry the boss." She wanted "to be the boss." The new feminist, in short, was busy "making it in a man's world." As such she was a decent role model for educated middle-class women, but it cut her off from "millions of women" with handicaps such as "poverty, dead-end jobs, small children, or excess pounds."[12] The new flashy feminist image that Gloria Steinem made popular convinced many ordinary women that they were still losers.

Moreover, the successful businesswoman image suggested that women could make it on their own by copying men and networking with other women on the make. If this was possible, what need was there for a woman's movement? Moderate feminism did supply many educated women with good jobs, but it left the majority of American women in the lurch. It allowed an elite to forge ahead on the wings of networking and affirmative action. It was a large part of what Betty Friedan called "The Second Stage" of feminist activity. However, in this limited play, most women were offstage.

If female yuppies were now the vanguard of feminism, then new professional women's organizations would represent women. Indeed, in her book *The Second Stage*, Friedan asks whether feminist groups such as N.O.W., which had been important in the 1960s, would play as strong a future role. She suggested that new groups such as the Young Women's Christian Association (YWCA), Girl Scouts, League of Women Voters, church women organizations, Jewish women's groups, Catholic nuns, and the Junior League might be the power women's groups in the second stage.[13] By 1982, N.O.W.'s membership had fallen from a peak of two hundred twenty thousand to one hundred thirty thousand and it continued to fall through the 1980s. N.O.W. had become so identified with the struggle for ERA that its membership decline probably traced the decline in ERA fortunes. However, sexual demographics also might have hurt N.O.W. The 1980s offered increasingly bleak marriage possibilities for women aged over thirty-five. Also, N.O.W. membership fell as the leading edge of female baby boomers began to run out of child-bearing years. Women getting panicky about marriage or motherhood did not help swell the pool of card-carrying feminists.

When American feminists encouraged women to enter the job market on male terms and succeed by copying male strategies they lost touch with women who were trying to rediscover marriage and motherhood. These women were often trying to create the warmth of their own parent's marriage in an age of two-paycheck families, or trying to parent while in midcareer. Feminism had become preoccupied with success for single, childless, or at least older women. There were now many more women lawyers and doctors, but women were increasingly unable to balance professional work with motherhood. Women had freed themselves from the necessity of having children; however, they were increasingly not free to have them. Feminists did not offer much help. Very little feminist agitation dealt with issues that helped women with the daily problems of life. Feminism focused on legal equality, sexual equality, and controlling your own body. That agenda worked fine for women who chose not to have children, but not for working mothers.

European feminists always saw their job as equalizing the double burden that work and motherhood often dealt women. In America, feminists have said, by neglect, that women who choose to have it all must work it out themselves. Day care and maternity leave have been on the back burner of the feminist agenda for two decades. This is understandable, because many contemporary American feminist leaders, whether heterosexual or lesbian, choose not to have children. To be truly equal, a feminist had to completely exorcise any female weaknesses or disadvantages. Having children was to admit that women could not or would not compete with men across the board, except when they were not bearing children.

There has been very little feminist writing on motherhood, and less on maternity leave. One result is that today America is alone among the leading industrial countries in lacking a comprehensive national maternity program. Slowly, individual corporations are establishing maternity leave, but this has resulted more from community and union pressure than from feminist demands. Once a woman has a child, it tends to dominate her life emotionally, no less than physically or economically. It might have been difficult for feminists to be antimale and profamily at the same time. It should have been easy for them to be simultaneously prochildren, pro-mother and profamily. Feminists made a fatal mistake in concentrating more on upscale single women, who were inevitably feminist, than down-scale single mothers who had no natural affinity for feminism.

Among the silliest supposed threats to women's liberation was NOM (The National Organization for Men), founded in 1983 and headed by Sidney Siller, a fifty-seven year old New York divorce lawyer. NOM vowed to "take on the feminist cabal that" dominated "politics." Siller charged that men no longer had equal rights and that men under age forty in particular had "been wimpified . . . and emasculated" by feminist rhetoric. He charged that feminist leaders had "never said anything good about America or men." Just as national feminist groups were self-destructing, Siller imbued them with power. He claimed that N.O.W. was so strong it had "become a third political party," and that virtually "any woman could run for political office" and "win easily." He forecast that because women were taking over national politics, by 1992 they would "paint the Oval Office pink." Siller planned to spread out from New York City with chapters eventually across the nation, but NOM quickly fizzled.[14] Men organizing against women might have been the one thing that could have revitalized feminism, but clearly most men were satisfied with their social and gender positions. If they were not, there would have been a men's liberation movement long ago. Men would have complained about having to pay for all the dates, and not being able to cry, and not being able to wear silky, slinky, pastel clothes. Actually Warren Farrell had attempted such as movement in the late 1970s after his successful book *The Liberated Man*. It had collapsed almost as quickly as NOM.

If feminism had wounded men, they showed very little trauma,. But according to Barbara Ehrenreich, feminism was making casualties of vulnerable women. In her 1983 book *The Hearts of Men: American Dreams and the Flight from Commitment*, she argued that feminism gave many men an excuse to desert their families. Men anxious to relinquish their economic responsibilities to wives and children and tired of emotional tensions or loveless marriages used their interpretation of feminist rhetoric as an excuse to leave. They said, in effect, that women were now equal and thus could take care of themselves. The result was a vast increase in families headed by single women and what Ehrenreich helped label—the feminization of poverty.[15]

Feminism provided excuses for men, but offered little to single, deserted mothers. Ironically, feminism has made it easier for a middle-aged man to dump his wife for a new model. Meanwhile, the divorced wife had a lot more difficulty meeting a new man, especially if she had custody of children. In 1990, freelance writer Kay Ebeling seemed to have gotten Ehrenreich's message, seventeen years after she walked out of her marriage to make it on her own, while raising an infant. Ebeling complained: "Feminism freed men, not women. Now men are spared the nuisance of a wife and family to support. After childbirth, if his wife's waist doesn't return to twenty inches, the husband can go out and get a more petite woman." Ebeling felt that "feminism made women disposable," and it had contributed to the large number of forty-year-old single women "with a couple of kids to raise." For her, the "reality of feminism" was "a lot of frenzied and overworked women dropping off kids at day care centers." Eberling argued that women had no business in "12-hour-a-day executive" jobs, and she could not imagine what made women think they "would want to be there in the first place." She felt that the economy might even recover if more women came home. This would provide jobs for unemployed males "who could then support a wife and children." As a disillusioned ex-feminist, Eberling felt that she had bought the feminist myth that women can compete equally with men in the workplace. Ebeling stopped going club-hopping on Saturday nights because seeing so many women her age "dressed a little too young," using makeup to hide wrinkles, depressed her.[16]

Throughout the 1980s, women previously afraid to confront career women began to cast doubt on the idea that glowing fulfillment lay outside the home, marriage, and children, and drudgery lay within. Women were winning a place in politics, business, and the professions, but some female critics increasingly suspected that it was on men's terms and within a masculine society. Being "just a housewife" was somehow less embarrassing in the 1980s. Some housewives suggested that some professional women were "just . . . lawyer[s]." Indeed, when feminists added up how much the various family services of the average housewife would cost on the open market, housewives could argue that their family could never afford those services unless they stayed at home. The 1980s witnessed a subtle and largely uncovered war between women. The new front line was the home, not the workplace. The struggle pitted mothers who worked against mothers who stayed home. The two groups had usually made a choice to stay at home or not. And feminism was supposedly about choice, but it was also about solidarity.

What became known as the "mommy war" in 1990 had long separated women. Working mothers often found their children ostracized from play groups of cooperating housewives. The nonworking mothers thought they would become nonpaid baby-sitters if they involved themselves with working women's children. The war was fought with subtle verbal barbs and not-so-subtle social slights. The at-home mom often felt that the working mom did not really know her children; the working mom often felt that the housewife's children might know their mother, but would not respect her. The housewife mom craved the glamorous clothes and grooming that the career mom's job demanded and that her extra paycheck could buy; the working mom was jealous of the closeness between the at-home mom and her children. Husbands seemed rather peripheral to the mommy war, but they shared the guilt. The at-home mom felt she let the family down financially by not working. Her husband felt guilty about not making more. The working mom felt guilty of neglecting her children, and her husband felt guilty about not making enough to support his wife at home. As more mothers worked, the stay-home mom felt more isolated. She was the only one on her block her age who was home in the morning. The time of day she visited stores suggested her status to working women clerks. She was the block mother and den mother of the neighborhood, and for all her extra work, she got little credit or appreciation, because she had the time to do it.[17]

Not surprisingly, social relations between the two moms were icy at best. At parties, career women often ignored housewives and talked with each other and the men. In retaliation, housewife moms sometimes froze the children of working moms out of activities they had organized. Thus, children became social warfare victims. While standing in the supermarket checkout line, the house-mom checked out the career mom with her chic suit and silky nylons and the prepared fast food in her basket. She thought, I could look that good, too, if I had the time I spend cooking nutritious, inexpensive family meals and the money for fancy clothes. The career mom looked at the stay-home mom and thought, you would think she could take better care of herself with all the free time she has.

The mommy war even entered presidential politics in the 1990s. In May 1990, Wellesley College students protested the appearance of first lady, Barbara Bush, as their commencement speaker. As a stay-home wife, students felt that Mrs. Bush was not sending the right message. In March 1992, when Democratic frontrunner Bill Clinton was charged with favoring the law firm his wife worked for with public Arkansas funds, it was Clinton's wife, Hillary, who responded. She angrily retorted that she was practicing her chosen legal career instead of staying home and baking cookies. Although baking cookies clearly would not have brought conflict-of-interest charges, it did create a problem for Clinton's campaign. Although Hillary Clinton had a young child, she had insulted stay-at-home mothers by suggesting that their singular contribution was baking cookies. Mrs. Clinton tried to control the political damage by noting that she was emphasizing her choice as a woman and mother, but the incident will likely remain a famous historical battle of the mommy war. The chief legislative battles in this war concern full-day kindergartens, day care, and tax breaks for families. Working mothers clearly want kindergarten and day care; at-home moms desperately seek family tax relief. Clearly, government-provided child care would not be fair to stay-home mothers. However, working mothers are increasingly the norm.

Once the working mother left home, she encountered another struggle between women at the workplace. At almost the same time people used the term mommy war, they discovered the mommy track. This referred to a dichotomy between the more serious career women, who were completely dedicated to their jobs, and the combination career woman-mother, for whom family was as important or even more important than career. The family oriented woman would be tolerated on the job, as long as she understood that she would not receive the same opportunities and financial incentives that committed career women could expect. Grateful working mothers might accept the mommy track while their children were young, but would naturally be resentful once child rearing was finished. By that time, they might be so far behind straight career women and men, they might be on the sidetrack.

Supposedly the career sacrifices were all made for the children, but this became irrelevant in the war between the sexes and between women. Professional women responded to attacks on feminism in general, and career women in particular, by working even harder at networking. Thus, there emerged the vast increase in new local groups of women in communications, women in business, and women in law. At colleges and universities, women's studies programs often became secondary to the women caucuses within the program. The women's studies programs often grew weaker, but the academic networking grew stronger. Female networking usually worked more effectively than male bonding, because it created larger, more focused groups. Males generally bonded for profit and protection, with a small group of like-minded men. Only women bonded by gender alone. Women who started to network for protection in the 1970s, ended by networking for profit in the 1990s.

Networking was another example of feminist success in copying and sometimes improving male institutions, but networking seldom offered models for anything but business favoritism, and professional advancement. Networking told women it was dangerous not to be organized. It told men that organized women were, if not dangerous, something to carefully maneuver around. It told youth of either sex that America was divided by gender, and if they were not on one side, they were not helping their career. Networking, by definition, emphasized the differences between men and women, not their similarity.

Networking was the flagship symbol of how women's liberation was winning the battles and losing the war. Networking worked for well-educated career women. It secured the present for a few and ignored the future of the many—especially children. Networking was solidly in the American tradition of "Looking Out for Number One," as one best-selling book put it. It is thus unfair to hold networking women to a higher group standard than enterprising males. Yet networking was clearly related to feminism and feminism promised to liberate women. Moreover, women's liberation had accepted the challenge of stamping out sexism. In the 1960s and 1970s, almost all feminists agreed that the sexist frontier was the battle for children's minds and children's futures, but many feminists who earlier stressed the countercultural struggle to change youthful attitudes at a formative stage had become caught up in political struggles for the ERA, for equal pay, and other kinds of political and economic victories.

To be sure, political and economic change were important parts of the feminist agenda. However, by the end of the seventies these became the entire agenda. By the end of the eighties, networking had largely replaced political change. Just as feminists in the period 1900 to 1920 had given up their many diverse goals to center on suffrage, their great-granddaughters often devoted all their energies to making it in business and the professions. Women should, of course vote and enter the professions. However, just as letting women vote did not eliminate sexism, neither will making more women prosperous. Countercultural change aimed at the next generation was always the best hope.

However, countercultural change took too long and the results were too uncertain. The cultural approach involved images and models. It focused on boys as well as girls, because the image of women that needed to change most was that image in the minds of men. But men had to be influenced when young. By the time they were mature, they had seen too many sexist films, ads, and television shows. They had heard too many sexist songs. Once culturally formed, they could probably change only marginally, and even if some men and women did change, they would be surrounded by sexist institutions and people. As feminists in the 1960s were fond of saying: The nonsexist forest must be grown at the same time. The slogan today might well be "It takes a uniform forest," rather than "it takes a village."

In the 1970s, well-balanced and accomplished young men and women continued to grow up with ironic sexist images of the opposite sex. When male high school students were asked what they disliked about girls their age, they invariably replied that they were too feminine. They were always adjusting their clothes or brushing their hair. They were always complaining about the temperature or frightened about their safety. They were forever fixing their makeup. They did not like action, and their frail bodies prevented them from doing really physical things. In short, they were not like young men. Young males complained about girls in this vein constantly, but if pressed they would quickly admit that the girls who were not feminine, they cared for even less. Indeed, they would treat tougher girls like guys. They certainly would not ask them out.

High school girls had similarly sexist complaints about high school boys. The guys were too macho and not sensitive enough. They stamped around in their boots like they owned the world. They only wanted to talk about sports and cars. They acted crude and tough and thought that impressed girls. They constantly showed off and courted physical danger to show how really tough they were. In short, they were too macho-masculine. But similarly, when pressed, girls might admit that the guys who were not like that they did not care for either.

Betty Roszak put the problem best in 1970:

He is playing masculine. She is playing feminine. He is playing masculine because she is playing feminine. She is playing feminine because he is playing masculine.

He is playing the kind of man that she thinks the kind of woman she is playing ought to admire. She is playing the kind of woman that he thinks the kind of man he is playing ought to desire. . . .

So he plays harder. And she plays softer. . . . She is supposed to admire him for the masculinity in him that she fears in herself. He is supposed to desire her for the femininity in her that he despises in himself.[18]

These kinds of rigid cultural biases cannot be changed in adults. Mature people can recognize that they have these biases, but usually can do little about them. They are like sexual preference or color preferences. They are not logical. There is no logical reason why one prefers blue to red. Blue is equal to red logically, but not in the cultural mind of the beholder. Cultural bias must be erased early. Early feminists stressed this. This countercultural belief informed their stress on language images and images of women in media and textbooks. In moving away from countercultural approaches, feminism abandoned youth and any attempt to radically change the image and status of American women.

The results are quickly apparent. Although women continue to make some strides in areas such as college and graduate school enrollment and professional school admissions, a 1992 study commissioned by the AAUW (American Association of University Women) and titled "How Schools Shortchange Girls" concluded that American girls did not get an equal education because of bias they encountered from teachers, textbooks, tests, and classrooms. The study was done by Wellesley College's Center for Research on Women. It also found evidence that girls received much less teacher attention than boys, that sexual harassment of girls by boys was rapidly increasing, that the gender gap in science achievement was growing wider, and that curriculum was largely based on sexual stereotypes. Despite these handicaps, girls still have higher grades and a larger percentage go to college. What is even more shocking is that two thirds of America's teachers are women, yet they wittingly or unwittingly discriminate against girls. When surveys asked teachers who their favorite student types were, they found teachers liked assertive males best. Their least favorite student category was assertive females.[19] Two decades ago, the Wellesley report would have caused a storm of feminist protest. In 1992, it was all but ignored. Yet there is no way to know to what extent sexist attitudes resulted from school policies or to what extent the schools simply reflected sexist attitudes and images in the media.

Many of the cultural issues that 1960s feminists argued must be attacked in the schools have been ignored for twenty to twenty-five years. Thus, there is still a double-sexual standard that condemns promiscuity in women much more than in men. And although women know much more about birth control at a younger age, and have more reason to practice safe sex, they are still reluctant to use birth control to avoid pregnancies and/or AIDS. The double standard of aging is as strong as ever, and women must now work even harder to conform to appearance standards that make them appear young and feminine. Men's grooming has become simpler, while women's grooming has remained almost as time-consuming and uncomfortable as in the 1950s.

Young American women have largely bought the great American myth that they can have it all if they want it. This has been a myth for most American men, and those men who did become very successful usually had the help of a wife. How could a single woman do it when women earn 30 percent less than men? The 1970s and 1980s convinced many men and women that collective problems were insolvable and that personal conscience was irrelevant. The only thing that mattered was the individual quest. Anybody could make it, if they wanted to. There was no one to blame but yourself. It was not so much the "me generation" as the opportunity generation. This new consciousness hurt poor people most, because they had the least resources for personal initiative. However, it also hurt young women, who often found out too late that they started the race for the good life with several cultural disadvantages.

Only one issue still seems capable of mobilizing women, young and old—abortion. Since the 1973 Roe v. Wade decision that made abortion a right, women had grown up with the security of knowing they had a legal choice in bearing children. When the 1989 Hayne decision began limiting that right and antiabortion groups began making headway politically, younger and older women started to come together. However, young women are blind to almost every other cultural or economic issue. They believe most battles have been won, and they do not have any feel for sexual warfare. Young women know about Jane Fonda's exercises and Elizabeth Taylor's perfumes, but they do not recognize the names of feminist heroines such as Betty Friedan, Germaine Greer, and Gloria Steinem.

The first generation gap between feminists and young women appeared in the 1920s. Social feminists and suffragists had built a powerful, successful movement from 1900 to 1920 that culminated in women's right to vote. They continued to expand women's rights during the 1920s, and women made gains in the professions and general workplace as well. However, they had lost the younger Jazz Age generation of women, who found the older feminists as stodgy as their parents. The young women thought that the right to vote had largely settled the issue of equality. The only cultural issues they recognized were generational arguments over drinking, clothes, and sexual practice. These were not gender issues, and, indeed, most older feminists sided with traditionalists and against the young. The young women of the 1920s eventually experienced sexism, but by that time they had no allies. Feminism had declined through attrition, infighting, the general malaise, and the loss of new young supporters. Young women were left defenseless, and the feminist movement did not come back until the 1960s. Feminists had lost the hearts and minds of the young, while the suffragists celebrated voting. In short, they had won the battle and lost the war.

Mark Twain humorously noted that although history does not repeat itself, "it sometimes rhymes." In the 1990s, if history is not repeating itself, we can at least see it rhyming. Feminism is much stronger today than in the 1920s, and older women are much more conscious of economic and social issues, such as equal pay and abortion. Yet, although women are a much stronger political force, they are again losing the next generation of men and women. Compared with the powerful media socialization of the next generation, the struggle against sexist laws and institutions is a minor skirmish. And the semantic struggle between feminists and their conservative attackers is simply irrelevant. Conservatives constantly complain about "political correctness" and past sins, and feminists hiss "backlash" in response to every contemporary criticism.

Of course, women's studies scholars continue to write perceptive books about images of women in popular music, television, advertising, and film.[20] Also, women studies courses continue to enroll some interested students. Yet increasingly these books and courses and the scholars themselves have become separated from the woman's movement, and increasingly they write primarily for other academics. These important countercultural issues have become largely academic. That is, they matter only within the academy. They may well hibernate for decades, before some new women's movement picks up on them and makes them socially and politically relevant. Something similar happened in 1963, when Charlotte Gilman's turn-of-the-century cultural critiques found new relevance in Betty Friedan's book *The Feminine Mystique*. Indeed, Friedan's work opened the door to cultural feminists throughout American history. The women's liberation movement has steadily closed that door to both past and present counterculturists. Friedan was the first national leader of N.O.W., but, more importantly, she was a countercultural guerrilla. Contemporary leaders of N.O.W. are merely political strategists.

Thus, seventy years after the 1920s, contemporary feminists are again losing another generation of American women. The past decade has witnessed the steady fall of a feminist counterculture that was never firmly established, but always on the agenda and sometimes very effective.

Feminists have built an edifice called the Women's Liberation Movement, but it has no foundation. The feminist theory of countercultural change provided that base, with a focus on creating a continuous supply of young feminists. At the same time, countercultural feminism might also alter sexism by affecting young men. Perhaps another new feminist wave in the 21st century may profit from the fatal error of the last two 20th-century feminist movements. Perhaps the next women's movement will stay the countercultural course. In the future, there will surely be another feminist phoenix—rising out of its own ashes. Perhaps it will be both stronger and wiser.

Notes

For the period 1960 to 1980, I used primary materials wherever possible. Moreover, I consciously tried to use the older secondary works of feminist scholars and journalists to get a better feel for the countercultural climate during those years. Thus, these secondary sources are primary for my purpose. When I turned to events, ideas, and problems of the 1980s and 1990s, I of course used the more recent feminist studies.

CHAPTER 1

1. For good examples of these type of women, see Judith Nies, *Seven Women: Portraits from the American Radical Tradition* (New York: Viking Press, 1977); and Sheila Rowbotham, *Women, Resistance and Revolution* (New York: Pantheon Books, 1974).

2. Eleanor Flexner, *Century of Struggle* (New York: Harvard University Press 1959), pp. 9–12. Also see Laurel Thatcher Ulrich, *Good Wives: Images and Reality in the Lives of Women in Northern New England, 1650–1750* (New York: Oxford University Press, 1983).

3. Among the many books and articles on women and the western frontier, some of the most suggestive are Nancy Wilson Ross, *Westward the Women* (New York: Alfred A. Knopf, 1944); Elinore Pruitt Stewart, *Letters of a Woman Homesteader* (Lincoln: University of Nebraska Press, 1961); Johnny Mack Farragher, *Men and Women on the Overland Trail* (New Haven, Conn.: Yale University

Press, 1979); and Julie Roy Jeffrie, *Frontier Women: The Trans-Mississippi West, 1840–1880* (New York: Hill and Wang, 1979).

4. See Barbara Welter, "The Cult of True Womanhood," *American Quarterly* 18 (1966), 151–74; Barbara Welter, *Dimity Convictions: The American Woman in the Nineteenth Century* (Columbus: Ohio State University Press, 1975); Kathryn Kish Sklar, *Catherine Beecher: A Study in Domesticity* (New Haven, Conn.: Yale University Press, 1973); Ann Douglas, *The Feminization of American Culture* (New York: Alfred A. Knopf, 1977); and Judith Fryer, *The Faces of Eve: Women in the Nineteenth-Century American Novel* (New York: Oxford University Press, 1976).

5. See Gerda Lerner, *The Majority Finds Its Past: Placing Women in History* (New York: Oxford University Press, 1979); Frederick Rudolph, *The American College and University* (New York: Knopf, 1962); Barbara Cross, *The Educated Woman in America* (New York: Teachers College Press, 1965). Also see Barbara J. Harris, *Beyond Her Sphere: Women and the Professions in American History* (Westport, Conn.: Greenwood Press, 1978). Susan Anthony's comment on dress reform, quoted in Alice Felt Tyler, *Freedom's Ferment* (New York: Harper, 1962), 442.

6. On 19th-century feminists, see, Jean E. Friedman and William O. Shade, *Our American Sisters: Women in American Life and Thought* (Boston: Allyn and Bacon, 1976); Sklar, Kathryn Kish, *Catherine Beecher: A Study in Domesticity* (New Haven, Conn.: Yale University Press, 1973); Anne Firor Scott, *The Southern Lady: From Pedestal to Politics, 1830–1930* (Chicago: University of Chicago Press, 1970); Nancy Cott, *The Bonds of Womanhood* (New Haven, Conn.: Yale University Press, 1977); Deborah Gray White, *Ar'n't I a Woman: Female Slaves in the Plantation South* (New York: Norton, 1985); and Catherine Clinton, *The Plantation Mistress: Woman's World in the Old South* (New York: Pantheon, 1982).

7. See especially Ellen Dubois, *Feminism and Suffrage: The Emergence of an Independent Women's Movement in America, 1848–1869* (Ithaca, N.Y.: Cornell University Press, 1978); Carroll Smith-Rosenberg, "Beauty, the Beast, and the Militant Woman," *American Quarterly* 23 (1971), 562–87; William Leach, *True Love and Perfect Union: The Feminist Reform of Sex and Society* (New York: Basic Books, 1980); and Karen Lystra, *Searching the Heart: Women, Men and Romantic Love in Nineteenth-Century America* (New York: Oxford University Press, 1989).

8. Barbara Ehrenreich and Deirdre English, *Complaints and Disorders: The Sexual Politics of Sickness* (Westbury, N.Y.: Feminist Press, 1974); Barbara Welter, ed., *Dimity Convictions*; and Carroll Smith-Rosenberg, *Disorderly Conduct: Visions of Gender in Victorian America* (New York: Oxford University Press, 1985).

9. William L. O'Neill, *Everyone Was Brave: A History of Feminism in America* (New York: Quadrangle, 1971); Aileen S. Kraditor, *The Ideas of the Woman Suffrage Movement, 1890–1920* (New York: Atheneum, 1965); Lois W.

Banner, *Women in Modern America: A Brief History*, 2nd edition (New York: Harcourt Brace Jovanovich, 1984), 87–208; on Victoria Woodhull, see Irving Wallace, *The Nympho and Other Maniacs: Stories of Scandalous Women* (London: Cassell, 1971), 381–435.

10. On young 1920s women, especially see Paula Fass, *The Damned and the Beautiful: American Youth in the 1920s* (New York: Oxford University Press, 1977); also Estelle Friedman, "The New Woman: Changing Views of Women in the 1920s." *Journal of American History* 61 (September 1974), 372–93; and June Sochen, *The New Women: Feminism in Greenwich Village, 1910–1920* (New York: Quadrangle, 1972). On women in the 1930s, see Susan Ware, *Holding Their Own* (Boston: Twayne, 1982); and Jeanne Westin, *Making Do* (Chicago: Follett, 1976).

CHAPTER 2

1. Sara Evans, *Personal Politics. The Roots of Women's Liberation in the Civil Rights Movement and the New Left* (New York: Random House, 1979); Jo Freeman, *The Politics of Women's Liberation* (New York: David McKay, 1975). Both of these books have great feel for the mood of early women's liberation. Also see, Roberta Salper, ed., *Female Liberation: History and Current Politics* (New York: Alfred A. Knopf, 1972).

2. Betty Friedan, *The Feminine Mystique* (New York: Norton, 1963).

3. Kirkpatrick Sale, *SDS* (New York: Vintage Books, 1973) has the most details on SDS campus chapters around the country. Also see Priscilla Long, ed., *The New Left: A Collection of Essays* (Boston: Porter Sargent, 1969) for good diverse views of the New Left, along with Staughton Lynd and Michael Ferber, *The Resistance* (Boston: Beacon, 1971) for a more personal New Left view.

4. Sara Evans, *Personal Politics*, 108–11; Roberta Salper, "The Development of the American Women's Liberation Movement" in Roberta Salper, ed., *Female Liberation*, 169–83.

5. Robin Morgan, *Going too Far: The Personal Chronicle of a Feminist* (New York: Random House, 1977), 75–78; Judith Hole and Ellen Levine, *The Rebirth of Feminism* (Chicago: Quadrangle, 1971); J. Freeman, *The Politics of Women's Liberation*. For a good, later general study of sixties radicalism, including feminism, see James Miller, *Democracy Is in the Streets* (New York: Simon and Schuster, 1987).

6. Charles A. Reich, *The Greening of America* (New York: Random House, 1970); Sale, *SDS*; Jack Newfield, *A Prophetic Minority* (New York: New American Library, 1966); Abe Peck, *Uncovering the Sixties: The Life and Times of the Underground Press* (New York: Pantheon, 1985).

7. Robin Morgan, *Going too Far*, especially 71–81.

8. "Redstocking Manifesto," in Robin Morgan, ed., *Sisterhood Is Powerful: An Anthology of Writing from the Women's Liberation Movement* (New York: Vintage Books, 1970), 598–600.

9. Ibid.

10. Ti-Grace Atkinson, *Amazon Odyssey* (New York: Links Books, 1974), 91–92.

11. Shulamith Firestone, *The Dialectic of Sex: The Case for Feminist Revolution* (New York: William Morrow, 1970).

12. Ann Koedt, "The Myth of the Vaginal Orgasm," in *Notes from the First Year*, ed. New York Radical Feminists (New York: New York Radical Feminists, 1968), p. 11.

13. Sidney Abbott and Barbara Love, "Is Women's Liberation a Lesbian Plot," in *Woman in Sexist Society*, Vivian Gornick and Barbara K. Moran (New York: New American Library, 1971), 601–21, Robin Morgan, "Lesbianism and Feminism: Synonyms or Contradictions?" in *Going too Far*, 170–88.

14. Robin Morgan, *Sisterhood Is Powerful*, 3. Also see Robin Morgan, "Letters from a Marriage," in *Going too Far*, 21–56; Meredith Tax, "Woman and Her Mind: The Politics of Daily Life," in Roberta Salper, ed., *Female Liberation*, 228–32.

15. Erica Mann Jong, "Seventeen Warnings in Search of a Feminist Poem," *Nation* (April 5, 1972), 12.

16. Julie Lieblich, "Advice for the First Year," *Ms.* (September 1980), 58.

17. On FBI surveillance, see Letty Pogrebin, "The FBI Is Watching You," *Ms.* (June 1977), 42. The FBI claimed that it stopped its surveillance in 1973. Leah Fritz, *Dreamers and Dealers: An Intimate Appraisal of the Women's Movement* (Boston: Beacon, 1979), 136–37.

18. Robin Morgan, "Goodbye to All That," in *The Underground Reader*, ed. Mel Howard and Thomas King Forcade (New York: New American Library, 1972), 215–24. Also see Robin Morgan, Going too Far, 133–69.

19. For a good contemporary survey of university women's studies in the 1970s, see Betty Chmaj, ed., *American Women and Women's Studies* (Pittsburgh, Penn.: Know, 1971).

20. A good example of this confusion about national feminists is Alice Echols, *Daring to Be Bad: Radical Feminism in America, 1967–1975* (Minneapolis: University of Minnesota, 1989), 243–87. Echols does a marvelous job of recreating the history and mood of New Left feminism, largely from extensive interviews with feminist leaders and exhaustive general research. This book is still the starting point for any study of New Left feminism, although Echols is perhaps too close to her subjects to be very critical of New Left feminists.

21. Good examples of New Left countercultural tactics and mood are in David Horowitz, et al., ed., *Counterculture and Revolution* (New York: Random House, 1972); Mel Howard and Thomas King Forcade, eds., *The Underground Reader*.

22. Ms. (September 1972), cover.

23. San Francisco Media Women, "The Story of Sleeping Handsome," in *A Change Is Gonna Come* (January 1971), 2.

24. Bruno Bettleheim, "Growing Up Female," *Harpers* (October 1962), 120–21.

25. Susan Sontag, "The Double Standard of Aging," *The Saturday Review of Literature* (October 1972), 34–38.

26. Nancy Henley, "Facing Down the Man," leaflet printed by Know, a Feminist Network (Pittsburgh, Penn.: Know, 1972); Robin Morgan, *Going too Far*, 82–90, 131–40.

27. For example, see Jean Faust, "Words That Oppress," a Know printed leaflet (Pittsburgh, Penn.: Know, 1972). Also see Robin Lakoff, *Language and Women's Place* (New York: Harper and Row, 1975).

28. Abbie Hoffman, *Soon to Be a Motion Picture* (New York: Perigee, 1980), 207.

29. Herbert Marcuse, *One Dimensional Man* (Boston: Beacon, 1964), 84–123; and *Negations: Essays in Critical Theory* (Boston: Beacon, 1968), 3–42.

30. Christopher Lasch, *The New Radicalism in America, 1889–1963* (New York: Norton, 1965). Lasch also spotlights Mabel Luhan, Randolph Bourne, and Colonel House as new style radicals.

31. Jerry Farber, "The Student As Nigger," in *The Underground Reader*, ed. Mel Howard and Thomas King Forcade, 15.

CHAPTER 3

1. *Time* (June 1, 1962), 41; "Just Playin Folks," *Saturday Evening Post* (May 30, 1964), 25. Also see Jerome L. Rodnitzky, "The Evolution of the American Protest Song," *Journal of Popular Culture* 3 (June 1969), 35–45.

2. *Newsweek* (November 25, 1961), 84. On protest music's effect, see Jerome L. Rodnitzky, "The New Revivalism, American Protest Songs, 1945–1968," *South Atlantic Quarterly* 70 (winter 1971), 13–21.

3. All quoted in Jerome L. Rodnitzky, "The Decline of American Protest Music," *Popular Music and Society* 1 (1971), 44–50.

4. Joyce Cheney, et al., *All Our Lives: A Woman's Songbook* (Baltimore, Md.: Diana Press, 1976).

5. Record album, Elizabeth Knight, *Songs of the Suffragettes* (Folkways, no. 5281, 1972).

6. For other examples on record albums, see *Reviving a Dream: Songs for Women's Liberation* (Femme Records, no. 82671, 1971), and *Virgo Rising: The Once and Future Woman* (Thunderbird Records, no. 7037, 1973).

7. David Noebel, *Rhythm, Riots, and Revolution* (Tulsa, Okla.: Christian Crusade, 1966).

8. Betty Greiner-Shumick, "Get 'Cher Rocks Off Baby,' Cause It's a Man's Man's World!" *Paid My Dues* 1 (May 1974), 13.

9. Ibid., 14.

10. Record Reviews, *Sing Out!* (January-February 1974), 43.

11. Cheryl Helm, "No One Cries for the Losers," *Paid My Dues* 1 (January 1974), 12–13.

12. Jean Hunter, "Here Comes Kathy Gori!" *Paid My Dues* 1 (May 1974), 35.

13. Helen Reddy, quoted in "Helen's Hymn," *Newsweek* (December 18, 1972), 68–69.

14. *Paid My Dues* 1 (May 1974), 18.

15. Ellen Shumsky, "Womansong: Bringing It All Back Home," *Sing Out!* (January–February 1974), 9, 11.

16. Quoted in Mark Morris, "Olivia Records," *Win* (December 12, 1974), 5.

17. *Reviving a Dream: Songs for Women's Liberation* (Femme Records, 1972).

18. *Mountain Moving Day* (Rounder Records, 1972).

19. *Virgo Rising: The Once and Future Woman* (Thunderbird Records, 1973).

20. C. Hicks, "Reviews," *Paid My Dues* 1 (January 1974), 34.

21. *Hazel and Alice* (Rounder Records, 1973).

22. *I Hate the Capitalist System* (Paredon Records, 1973); *The Force of Life* (Paredon Records, 1974).

23. *Lavender Jane Loves Women* (Women's Wax Works, 1974).

24. *Hang in There* (Redwood Records, 1974); and *Holly Near: A Live Album* (Redwood Records, 1974).

25. Barbara Dane, Record Notes to *I Hate the Capitalist System*.

26. Joyce Cheney, *All Our Lives: A Women's Songbook*, 9–12.

27. Ibid., 8, 16–19.

28. Ibid., 60, 74, 79–80.

29. *Ladyslipper Catalog*, 1980, 1984, 1986, n.p.

30. Ibid.

31. *Ladyslipper 1984 Catalog*, 37.

32. Quoted in transcript of symposium of protest songs in Havana, Cuba, in *Sing Out* 17 (October 1967), 30.

33. John F. Kennedy quoted in *Sing Out* 10 (February 1966), 80.

34. Olivia Catalog, 1983, n.p.

35. *Ms.* (January 1985), 72–73.

36. For Reddy's comments and problems with NBC, see Aida Pavletich, *Sirens of Song* (New York: Da Capo Press, 1980), 164–65.

37. Pamela Brandt, "At the Top of the Charts, but Are They Playing Our Song?" *Ms.* (November 1979), 40–44.

38. Ibid.

39. Ibid.

40. *Ms.* (January 1985), 46–48.

41. "Madonna Rocks the Land," *Time* (May 27, 1945), 79.

42. Ibid.

43. For a good, perceptive survey of sexist songs and male and female images in songs, included in the wide spectrum of songs covered, see B. Lee Cooper, *Images of American Society in Popular Music* (Chicago: Nelson-Hall, 1982).

44. Quoted in Aida Pavletich, *Sirens of Song*, 243. Also, for a good survey of women in popular music, see Lucy O'Brien, *She Bop: The Definitive History of Women in Rock, Pop and Soul* (New York: Penguin, 1996). For a perceptive analysis of the relationship between the past and popular culture in general (in-

cluding chapters on popular music), see George Lipsitz, *Time Passages: Collective Memory and American Popular Culture* (Minneapolis: University of Minnesota Press, 1990).

CHAPTER 4

1. Marjorie Rosen, *Popcorn Venus: Women, Movies, and the American Dream* (New York: Avon, 1974).

2. Molly Haskell, *From Reverence to Rape: The Treatment of Women in the Movies* (New York: Penguin, 1974).

3. On the early history of film, see Alan Casty, *Development of the Film: An Interpretive History* (New York: Harcourt Brace Jovanovich, 1973); and Laurence Kardish, *Reel Plastic Magic* (Boston: Little, Brown, 1973).

4. Larry May, *Screening out the Past* (Chicago: University of Chicago Press, 1983), 200–236.

5. For the best insights on Mae West, see June Sochen, *Mae West: She Who Laughs Last* (Arlington Heights, Ill.: Harlan Davidson, 1992).

6. Judith Gustafson, "The Decline of Women among the Top Ten Box Office Stars," in *Image, Myth and Beyond*, ed. by Betty E. Chmaj, et al. (Pittsburgh, Penn.: Know, 1972), 286–89.

7. Joseph W. Baunoch and Betty E. Chmaj, "Film Stereotypes of American Women," in *Image, Myth and Beyond*, 275–84.

8. Brandon French, *On the Verge of Revolt: Women in American Films of the Fifties* (New York: Frederick Ungar, 1978).

9. Ibid.

10. Judith Gustafson, "The Decline of Women among the Top Ten Box Office Stars, in *Image, Myth and Beyond*, 286–89.

11. Julie Burchill, *Girls on Film* (New York: Pantheon, 1986).

12. Joseph W. Baunoch and Betty E. Chmaj, "Film Stereotypes of American Women," in *Image, Myth and Beyond*, 275–84.

13. Molly Haskell, "Lights . . . Camera . . . Daddy," *Nation* (May 28, 1983), 673–75.

14. Ibid.

15. Roger Rosenblatt, "Women Are Getting Out of Hand," *Time* (July 18, 1983), 72.

16. Julie Burchill, *Girls on film*, 180.

17. Russell B. Nye, *The Unembarrassed Muse: The Popular Arts in America* (New York: Dial Press, 1970), 35–37.

18. Ibid., p. 38.

19. Ella Taylor, *Prime Time Families* (Berkeley: University of California Press, 1989).

20. Judith Lemon, "Dominant or Dominated? in *Hearth and Home: Images of Women in the Mass Media*, ed. Gaye Tuchman, et al. (New York: Oxford University Press, 1978), 51–68; Susan Douglas, *Where the Girls Are* (New York: Times Books, 1995), 123–61.

21. Show titles from *T.V. Guide* magazine, 1965–1990.

22. Betty Friedan, "Television and the Feminine Mystique," *Time* (February 18, 1964), 32.

23. Ibid.

24. Harry F. Waters and Janet Huck, "Networking Women," *Newsweek* (March 13, 1989), pp. 49–52.

25. Ibid., 54.

26. Ibid.

27. Marya Mannes, "Should Women Only Be Seen and Not Heard?" in Barry Cole, eds., *Television* (New York: The Free Press, 1970), 276–80.

28. Ibid.

29. Betty Friedan, *The Feminist Mystique* (New York: Norton, 1963), 208.

30. Ibid., 208–12.

31. Ibid., 214–17.

32. Ibid., 216–19.

33. Ibid., 223–25.

34. Ibid., 230–31.

35. ABC News special, *Women's Liberation*, narrated by Marlene Saunders, September 5, 1970, has film clips of five minutes of the invasion of *Ladies Home Journal* editorial office.

36. Lucy Komisar, "The Image of Women in Advertising," in *Women in Sexist Society*, ed. Vivian Gornick and Barbara K. Moran (New York: New American Library, 1972), 305–6.

37. Ibid.

38. Commentary on advertisements from my extensive slide collection of published ads, portraying women in 1960s and 1970s.

39. Quoted in Evelyn Goldfield, et al., "A Woman Is a Sometime Thing," in *The New Left*, ed. Priscilla Long (Boston: Porter Sargent, 1970), 243.

40. Story about N.O.W. awards in UPI story, *Fort Worth Star-Telegram*, August 25, 1972, 5. N.O.W. protest against National Airlines described in *Women Today*, March 20, 1972, 5.

41. Muriel Akamatsu, "Liberating the Media: Advertising," *Freedom of Information Report, No. 290* (Columbia: University of Missouri at Columbia), September 1972.

42. Advertisement examples taken from my personal slide collection of published 1970s ads.

43. Lucy Komisar, "The Image of Women in Advertising," in *Women in Sexist Society*, 311–12.

44. Quoted in Muriel Akamatsu, "Liberating the Media: Advertising," *Freedom of Information Report*, no. 290, 3.

CHAPTER 5

1. On the nature of celebrities, see Daniel Boorstin, *The Image: Or What Happened to the American Dream* (New York: Atheneum, 1961), 45–76.

2. Speech by David Harris recorded on Joan Baez record album, *Carry It On* (Vanguard Records, 1971).

3. Christopher Lasch, *The New Radicalism in America, 1889–1963* (New York: Norton, 1965), especially see 286–349.

4. "Country Joe Unstrung," *Sing Out!* 18 (June 1968), 20–21.

5. For specific examples of the sexism of rock music, see Marion Meade, "The Degradation of Women," in *The Sounds of Social Change*, ed. by R. Serge Denisoff and Richard A. Peterson (Chicago: Rand McNally, 1972), 173–78. Also see "Cock Rock: Men Always Seem to End Up on Top," *Rat* (October-November 1970), 8–9.

6. The most reliable biographical information on Joplin is in Mrya Friedman, *Buried Alive: The Biography of Janis Joplin* (New York: William Morrow, 1973). Also see Robyn Archer and Diana Simmonds, *A Star Is Torn* (New York: E. P. Dutton, 1986), 180–93.

7. Interview with Joplin, taped in July 1970, printed in David Dalton, *Janis* (New York: Simon and Schuster, 1971), 54.

8. Joplin quoted in "Janis: 1943–1970," *Rolling Stone* (October 29, 1970), 2.

9. Seth Joplin quoted in David Dalton, *Janis*, 139.

10. Myra Friedman, *Buried Alive: The Biography of Janis Joplin*, 82.

11. Lillian Roxon, "A Moment too Soon," in *No One Waved Good-Bye*, ed. Robert Somma (New York: Outerbridge and Dienstfrey, 1971), 95.

12. Alfred G. Aronowitz, "Singer with a Bordello Voice," *Life* (September 20, 1968), 20.

13. Joplin quoted in Ellen Willis, "Rock, Etc.," *New Yorker* (March 15, 1969), 45.

14. "Interview with Country Joe McDonald," *Rolling Stone* (May 27, 1971), reprinted in David Dalton, *Janis*, 146.

15. Linda Gravenites quoted in Myra Friedman, *Buried Alive: The Biography of Janis Joplin*, 127.

16. Steve Katz quoted in "Rebirth of the Blues," *Newsweek* (May 26, 1969), 82.

17. John Poppy, "Janis Joplin: Big Brother's White Soul," *Look* (September 3, 1968), 60–61.

18. Joplin quoted in Hubert Saal, "Janis," *Newsweek* (February 24, 1969), 84.

19. 1970 interview with Joplin in David Dalton, *Janis*, 55.

20. Taped comments by Joplin in 1970 on record attached to David Dalton, *Janis*.

21. Florence Howe, "Feminism and Literature," in *Images of Women in Fiction*, ed. Susan K. Cornillon (Bowling Green, Ohio: Bowling Green University Popular Press, 1972), 259.

22. Myra Friedman, *Buried Alive: The Biography of Janis Joplin*, 138.

23. Mimi Farina's memorial ballad was titled "In the Quiet Morning." It was recorded by Joan Baez on her album *Come from the Shadows* (A & M Records, 1972).

24. For biographical data on Baez's early years, most writers relied on *Times*'s research staff. See their feature article on Joan, "Sibyl with Guitar," No-

vember 23, 1962, 54–56+. For much more detailed, though incomplete, information, see Joan Baez's semiautobiographical *Daybreak* (New York: Dial Press, 1968), especially, 1–66, and her autobiography *And a Voice to Sing With: A Memoir* (New York: Summit Books, 1987). Also see the most recent biographical information in Charley Fuss, *Joan Baez: A Bio-Bibliography* (Westport, Conn.: Greenwood Press, 1996), 1–28.

25. Interview with Joan Baez, Don Wakefield, "I'm Really a Square," *Redbook* (January 1967), 115. Joan Baez, *Daybreak*, 40, 42, 48–49. Joan added that since 1947, her father "never accepted a job that had anything to do with armaments, offense, defense, or whatever they prefer to call it."

26. Joan Baez, *Daybreak*, 40.

27. Joan Baez, *And a Voice to Sing With*, 72–86.

28. "To Prison with Love," *Time* (December 11, 1964), 60.

29. Joan Baez, "With God on Our Side," *Liberation* 10 (August 1965), 35.

30. Joan Baez, *And a Voice to Sing With*, photo section.

31. Robert Simple, "Vietnam Critics Stage Sit-Down at White House," *New York Times*, August 7, 1965, 1.

32. Peter Braestrup, "Joan Baez and the Interpreter, or What the Japanese Didn't Hear," *New York Times*, February 21, 1967, 16; editorial, *Sing Out* 17 (April 1967), 1.

33. Joan Baez, *Daybreak*, 31–35; "Caroling Joan Baez, Mother Arrested at War Protest," UPI dispatch in *Dallas Morning News*, December 20, 1967, 3.

34. For an account of David and Joan's antiwar activities before he entered prison, see Joan Baez, *Daybreak*, 149–57; and Nat Hentoff's excellent "Playboy Interview: Joan Baez," *Playboy* (July 1970), pp. 54–62+. Also, a documentary film, *Carry It On*, which covered their campus tours in 1968 and 1969, was released in 1970.

35. "The Dick Cavett Show," August 4, 1969. Howard K. Smith, quoted on *The ABC Evening News*, August 5, 1969. Baez's earlier appearances were *The Alan Burke Show*, October 28, 1967 and *The Les Crane Show*, August 30, 1968. She also was a guest on *The David Frost Show* with her son Gabriel, June 20, 1970. All comments are based on audiotapes of the television shows.

36. Quoted in *Newsweek* (September 14, 1970), 65.

37. News story, *Fort Worth Star-Telegram*, February 4, 1971, 2.

38. Jack O'Brian, column in *Fort Worth Star-Telegram*, February 23, 1971, 10. This had always been a problem when she toured with her husband. Crowds came to hear her sing, but were impatient with David's philosophical harangues.

39. Quoted on *The Dick Cavett Show*, February 9, 1971; and *The David Frost Show*, March 12, 1971.

40. Richard Farina, "Baez and Dylan: "A Generation Singing Out," in *The American Folk Scene*, ed. David A. DeTurk and A. Poulin Jr. (New York: Dell, 1967), 253. The article was originally printed in *Mademoiselle* in March 1964.

41. David Harris, *Goliath* (New York: Avon Books, 1970).

42. Joan Baez, *Daybreak*, 136.

43. Nat Hentoff, *"Playboy* Interview: Joan Baez," 54.

44. Joan Baez, *Daybreak*, 77.

45. Paul Nelson and Jon Panake, "Record Reviews," *Little Sandy Review* 18 (September 1961), 3–6.

46. Alan Weberman and Gordon Friesen, "Joan Baez and the Bob Dylan Songs," *Broadside*, 97 (March 1969), 1–2, 9–10.

47. Nat Hentoff, "Jazz and Pop '72," *Playboy* (February 1972), 211–12; Daniel Boorstin, *The Image*, 45–76.

48. Quoted in Don Wakefield, "I'm Really a Square," 120.

49. Joan Baez, *Daybreak*, 42–44.

50. For a typical attack on Baez's view of black power, see the editorial, *Broadside* 83 (August 1967), 8–9. For her older views on various activist groups (including women's liberation), see Nat Hentoff, "Playboy Interview: Joan Baez," 58.

51. David A. Noebel, *Rhythm, Riots, and Revolution* (Tulsa, Okla.: Christian Crusade Publications, 1966), 202–3.

52. Editorial, *Broadside* 79 (February 1967), 2.

53. "The Folk Girls," *Time* (June 1, 1962), 39.

54. "Hoots and Hollers on the Campus," *Newsweek* (November 27, 1961), 84.

55. Quoted in Tom O'Leary, "Joan Baez—A Lesser Flop," *World Campus* 2 (December 1967), 15.

56. Antioch Poll reproduced in *Parade*'s "Keeping Up with Youth" column, May 28, 1972, 4.

57. "To Prison with Love," 60.

58. Nat Hentoff, *"Playboy* Interview: Joan Baez," (December 1970), 61.

59. "Q and A, Joan Baez," *Los Angeles Times, West Magazine* (July 9, 1972), 18, 22, 23.

60. *Time* (March 13, 1973), 48.

61. Baez, *And a Voice to Sing With*, 432–39.

62. "Gloria Steinem," *Newsweek* (August 16, 1971), 51.

63. Ibid., pp. 52–55.

64. Ibid., pp. 53–54. For Gloria Steinem's moving essay on her complicated relationship with her mother, see the essay "Ruth's Song," in Gloria Steinem, *Outrageous Acts and Everyday Rebellions* (New York: Holt, Rinehart and Winston, 1983), 129–46. For her recent views on her past career as well as current philosophy, see Gloria Steinem, *Moving beyond Words* (New York: Simon & Schuster, 1994).

65. Gloria Steinem, "The Moral Disarmament of Betty Coed," *Esquire* (September 1962), 93, 153–57.

66. Gloria Steinem, "A Bunny's Tale," *Show* (May 1963), 90–93, 114–15; for her 1983 look back at her brief life as a bunny see, "I Was a Playboy Bunny," in Steinem, *Outrageous Acts*, 29–69; "Crazy Legs," *New York Times Magazine*, November 8, 1964, 6–8; "Julie Andrews," *Vogue* (March 15, 1965), 44–47.

67. "Gloria Steinem," *Newsweek* (August 16, 1971), 53–54.

200

68. "Thinking Man's Shrimpton," *Time* (January 3, 1969), 38. Steinem remarks on her looks, quoted in *Time* article. *Ms.* magazine reported on FBI surveillance and stereotyping of feminists in Letty Pogrebin, "The FBI Was Watching You," *Ms.* (June 1977), 42.

69. Gloria Steinem, "What It Would be Like If Women Win," *Time* (August 31, 1970), 22–23.

70. Gloria Steinem "Sisterhood," in *The First Ms. Reader*, ed. Francine Klagsbrun (New York: Warner, 1972), 4–10. On the founding of *Ms.* and Steinem's role, see Mary Thom, *Ms.: 25 Years of the Magazine and the Feminist Movement* (New York: Henry Holt, 1997), 1–64.

71. See Francine Klagsbrun, ed., *The First Ms. Reader*, for example of early *Ms.* articles.

72. See *Ms.* magazine, September, October, November, and December 1972, issues nos. 3–6.

73. Redstockings, ed., *Feminist Revolution* (New Paltz, N.Y.: Redstockings, 1975).

74. Friedan quoted in Alice Echols, *Daring to Be Bad* (Minneapolis: University of Minnesota Press, 1989), 155.

75. See "Tenth Anniversary Issue," *Ms.* (July 1982), for several examples of more socially-active articles in early 1980s.

76. Eileen Ogintz, "Feminist Still Fighting Cause," *Fort Worth Star-Telegram*, December 7, 1978, 2E.

77. Ibid.

CHAPTER 6

1. Marion Meade, "The Degradation of Women," in *The Sounds of Social Change*, ed. R. Serge Denisoff and Richard Peterson (Chicago: Rand McNally, 1972), 174.

2. Fran Taylor, "Oldies but Baddies," *Paid My Dues* 5 (October 1975), 32–34.

3. The female singers hit list is contained in the "Solo Female Vocalist Hit Sweep"—a list of sixty-three hits by female vocalists between 1940 and 1974. It was put together by the "Popular Music Research Project" at the University of Pennsylvania. It was available as an audiotape (1976).

4. Vivian Gornick, "The Next Great Moment in History Is Ours," in *Essays in Feminism*, ed. Vivian Gornick (New York: Harper and Row, 1978). Gornick's article appeared in *The Village Voice* in 1969.

5. See Bob Dylan's album, *Planet Waves* (Asylum Records, 1973) for his new prowoman songs.

6. See examples of these ads in "Calvin Meets the Marlboro Man," *Time* (October 21, 1985), 69.

7. Lucianne Goldberg and Jeannie Sakol, *Purr Baby Purr* (New York: Hawthorne Books, 1971).

8. Marabel Morgan, *The Total Woman* (Old Tappan, N.J.: Fleming H. Revell, 1973); Helen Andelin, *Fascinating Womanhood* (New York: Bantam, 1974);

Tracy Tanner, *How to Find a Man and Make Him Keep You* (New York: Pinnacle Books, 1976); J., *The Sensuous Woman* (New York: New American Library, 1972).

9. Described in Ellen Barker, "Queen of the House and Bringing Up Hubby: The Current Position of Women's Magazines on the Changing Roles of Women," *Journal of American Culture* 12 (winter 1988), 1–2.

10. Ibid., 3.

11. Nora Ephron, "So You're a Little Mouseburger," in *Wallflower at the Orgy* ed. Nora Ephron (New York: Ace Books, 1973); also see Helen Gurley Brown, ed., *The Cosmo Girl's Guide to the New Etiquette* (New York: Cosmopolitan Books, 1971).

12. Nora Ephron, "So You're a Little Mouseburger," in *Wallflower at the Orgy*.

13. Ibid.

14. Susan Brownmiller, *Femininity* (New York: Simon and Schuster, 1984).

15. Germaine Greer, *The Female Eunuch* (New York: McGraw-Hill, 1970); and *Sex and Destiny: The Politics of Fertility* (New York: Harper and Row, 1984).

16. Betty Friedan, *The Second Stage* (New York: Summit Books, 1981).

17. Erica Jong, "Ziplash: A Sexual Libertine Recants," *Ms.*, (May 1989), 49–50.

18. "The Revolution Is Over," *Time* (April 9, 1984), 74–75.

19. Ibid., 75–77. See also William H. Chafe, *The Road to Equality* (New York: Oxford University Press, 1994); Blanche Linden-Ward and Carol Hurd Green, *Changing the Future: American Women in the 1960s* (New York: Twayne, 1992).

20. Suzanne Gordon, *Prisoners of Men's Dreams: Striking Out for a New Feminine Future* (Boston: Little, Brown, 1991), 200–210.

21. Sylvia Ann Hewlett, *A Lesser Life: The Myth of Women's Liberation* (New York: Warner Books, 1986).

22. Suzanne Gordon, *Prisoners of Men's Dreams*, 72–75.

23. Susan Faludi, *Backlash: The Undeclared War against American Women* (New York: Crown, 1991), 169–97.

24. Suzanne Fields, "Putting the Femininity Back into Feminism," syndicated column, March 8, 1997, in *Fort Worth Star-Telegram*, 13.

CHAPTER 7

1. For example, Susan Faludi, *Backlash*; and Sylvia Ann Hewlett, *A Lesser Life: The Myth of Women's Liberation* (New York: Warner Books, 1986).

2. Quinn quoted in Patty Fisher, "Why Are Feminists, Whining?" *Fort Worth Star-Telegram*, February 16, 1992, 37.

3. "What Educated Women Want," *Newsweek* (June 13, 1966), 68–71.

4. Betty Rollin, "They're a Bunch of Frustrated Hags," *Look* (March 9, 1971), 15–19.

5. Betty Friedan, "Beyond Women's Liberation," *McCall's* (August 1972), 82–83, 133.

6. Anne Taylor Fleming, "Up from Slavery—To What," *Newsweek* (January 21, 1974), 14–15.

7. Shana Alexander, "No Person's Land," *Newsweek* (March 18, 1974), 43.

8. Atkinson quoted in Patricia McCormack, "Nothing Happened in Women's Movement," *Fort Worth Press*, September 30, 1974, 13.

9. Pam Proctor, "Has the Feminist Movement Reached a Turning Point?" *People Magazine* (February 15, 1976), 13–15.

10. Veronica Geng, "Requiem for the Women's Movement," *Harpers* (November 1976), 49–64.

11. Natalie Gittelson, *Dominus: A Woman Looks at Men's Lives* (New York: Farrar, Strauss and Giroux, 1978), 4, 113–43.

12. Barbara Ehrenreich, "Combat in the Media Zone," *Seven Days* (March 10, 1978), 13–14.

13. Betty Friedan, *The Second Stage* (New York: Summit Books, 1981), 201–342.

14. Cynthia Lollar, "Sidney Siller Interview," *Campus Voice* (October-November 1984), 81–82.

15. Barbara Ehrenreich, *The Hearts of Men: American Dreams and the Flight from Commitment* (Garden City, N.Y.: Anchor, 1983).

16. Kay Ebeling, "The Failure of Feminism," *Newsweek* (November 19, 1990), 9.

17. Nina Darnton, "Mommy vs. Mommy," *Newsweek* (June 4, 1990), 64–67.

18. Betty Roszak, "Foreword," in *Masculine/Feminine*, ed. Betty and Theodore Roszak (New York: Harper and Row, 1969), vii.

19. "Schools Shortchanging Girls?" *Texas State Teacher's Association Newsletter* (March 1992), 14–15; "Sexism in the Schoolhouse," *Newsweek* (February 24, 1992), 62.

20. Good examples of recent, perceptive studies of images of women in popular culture are Susan J. Douglas, *Where the Girls Are: Growing Up Female with the Mass Media* (New York: Times Books, 1995); Elayne Rapping, *Media-tions* (Boston: South End Press, 1994); Julie Burchill, *Girls on Film* (New York: Pantheon, 1986); and Mary Ann Watson, *Defining Visions: Television and the American Experience since 1945* (New York: Harcourt Brace, 1998).

Selected Bibliography

Andelin, Helen. *Fascinating Womanhood*. New York: Bantam, 1974.

Archer, Robin, and Diana Simmonds. *A Star Is Torn*. New York: E. P. Dutton, 1986.

Atkinson, Ti-Grace. *Amazon Odyssey*. New York: Links Books, 1974.

Baez, Joan. *And a Voice to Sing With: A Memoir*. New York: Summit Books, 1987.

Baez, Joan. *Daybreak*. New York: Dial Press, 1968.

Baez, Joan. "With God on Our Side." *Liberation* 10 (August 1965), 35.

Banner, Lois W. *Women in Modern America: A Brief History*. New York: Harcourt Brace, Jovanovich, 1974.

Belfrage, Sally. *Freedom Summer*. New York: Viking Press, 1965.

Bettleheim, Bruno. "Growing Up Female." *Harpers* (October 1962): 120–21.

Boorstin, Daniel. *The Image or What Happened to the American Dream*. New York: Atheneum, 1961.

Brown, Helen Gurley, editor. *The Cosmo Girl's Guide to the New Etiquette*. New York: Cosmopolitan Books, 1971.

Brownmiller, Susan. *Femininity*, New York: Simon and Schuster. 1984.

Burchill, Julie. *Girls on Film*. New York: Pantheon. 1986.

Burner, David. *Making Peace with the 60s*. Princeton, N.J.: Princeton University Press, 1996.

Carden, Maren Lockwood. *The New Feminist Movement*. New York: Russell Sage, 1974.

Castro, Ginette. *American Feminism: A Contemporary History.* New York: New York University Press, 1990.

Casty, Alan. *Development of the Film: An Interpretive History.* New York: Harcourt Brace Jovanovich, 1973.

Chafe, William H. *The Road to Equality.* New York: Oxford University Press, 1994.

Cheney, Joyce, et al. *All Our Lives: A Woman's Songbook.* Baltimore, Md.: Diana Press, 1976.

Chmaj, Betty, editor. *American Women and Women's Studies.* Pittsburgh, Penn.: Know, 1971.

Chmaj, Betty E., et al., editors. *Image, Myth and Beyond.* Pittsburgh, Penn.: Know, 1972.

Cole, Barry, editor. *Television.* New York: The Free Press, 1970.

Cooper, B. Lee, *Images of American Society in Popular Music.* Chicago: Nelson-Hall, 1982.

Cooper, B. Lee, and Wayne S. Haney. *Rock Music in American Popular Culture.* Binghamton, N.Y.: Haworth Press, 1985.

Cornillon, Susan K. *Images of Women in Fiction.* Bowling Green, Ohio: Bowling Green University Popular Press, 1972.

Cott, Nancy. *The Bonds of Womanhood.* New Haven, Conn.: Yale University Press, 1977.

Cott, Nancy. *The Grounding of Modern Feminism.* New Haven, Conn.: Yale University Press, 1987.

Cross, Barbara. *The Educated Woman in America.* New York: Teachers College Press, 1965.

Dalton, David. *Janis.* New York: Simon and Schuster, 1971.

Daniel, Robert L. *American Women in the 20th Century.* New York: Harcourt Brace Jovanovich, 1987.

Davis, Elizabeth Gould. *The First Sex.* New York: Penguin, 1973.

Davis, Ronald L. *Celluloid Mirrors: Hollywood and American Society since 1945.* New York: Harcourt Brace Jovanovich, 1997.

Denisoff, Serge R., and Richard A. Peterson, editors. *The Sounds of Social Change.* Chicago: Rand McNally, 1972.

DeTurk, David A., and A. Poulin, Jr., editors. *The American Folk Scene.* New York: Dell, 1967.

Douglas, Ann. *The Feminization of American Culture.* New York: Alfred A. Knopf, 1977.

Douglas, Susan J. *Where the Girls Are: Growing Up Female with the Mass Media.* New York: Times Books, 1995.

Dubois, Ellen. *Feminism and Suffrage: The Emergence of an Independent Women's Movement in America, 1848–1869.* Ithaca, N.Y.: Cornell University Press, 1978.

Echols, Alice. *Daring to Be Bad: Radical Feminism in America, 1967–1975.* Minneapolis: University of Minnesota Press, 1989.

Ehrenreich, Barbara. "Combat in the Media Zone." *Seven Days* (March 10, 1978): 13–14.

Ehrenreich, Barbara. *Fear of Falling: The Inner Life of the Middle Class.* New York: Pantheon, 1989.

Ehrenreich, Barbara. *Re-making Love: The Feminization of Sex.* Garden City, N.Y.: Doubleday, 1986.

Ehrenreich, Barbara. *The Hearts of Men: American Dreams and the Flight from Commitment.* Garden City, N.Y.: Anchor, 1983.

Ehrenreich, Barbara, and Deirdre English. *Complaints and Disorders: The Sexual Politics of Sickness.* Westbury, N.Y.: Feminist Press, 1974.

Eisenstein, Hester. *Contemporary Feminist Thought.* Boston: G. K. Hall, 1983.

Ephron, Nora. *Wallflower at the Orgy.* New York: Ace Books, 1973.

Evans, Sara. *Personal Politics: The Roots of Women's Liberation in the Civil Rights Movement and the New Left.* New York: Random House, 1979.

Ewen, Stuart, and Elizabeth Ewen. *Channels of Desire: Mass Images and the Shaping of American Consciousness.* New York: McGraw-Hill, 1982.

Faludi, Susan. *Backlash: The Undeclared War against American Women.* New York: Crown, 1991.

Farragher, Johnny Mack. *Men and Women on the Overland Trail.* New Haven, Conn.: Yale University Press, 1979.

Fass, Paula. *The Damned and the Beautiful: American Youth in the 1920s.* New York: Oxford University Press, 1977.

Filene, Peter Gabriel. *Him/Her Self: Sex Roles in Modern America.* New York: Harcourt Brace Jovanovich, 1974.

Firestone, Shulamith. *The Dialectic of Sex: The Case for Feminist Revolution.* New York: William Morrow, 1970.

Flexner, Eleanor. *Century of Struggle.* Cambridge, Mass.: Harvard University Press, 1959.

Forward, Susan. *Men Who Hate Women and the Women Who Love Them.* New York: Bantam, 1986.

Freeman, Jo. *The Politics of Women's Liberation.* New York: David McKay, 1975.

French, Brandon. *On the Verge of Revolt: Women in American Films of the Fifties.* New York: Frederick Ungar, 1978.

Friedan, Betty. "Beyond Women's Liberation," *McCall's* (August 1972): 82–83, 133.

Friedan, Betty. *It Changed My Life: Writings on the Women's Movement.* New York: Random House, 1976.

Friedan, Betty. "Television and the Feminine Mystique." *Time* (February 18, 1964): 32.

Friedan, Betty. *The Feminine Mystique.* New York: Norton, 1963.

Friedan, Betty. *The Second Stage.* New York: Summit Books, 1981.

Friedman, Jean E., and William O. Shade. *Our American Sisters: Women in American Life and Thought.* Boston: Allyn and Bacon, 1976.

Friedman, Myra. *Buried Alive: The Biography of Janis Joplin*. New York: William Morrow, 1973.

Fritz, Leah. *Dreamers and Dealers: An Intimate Appraisal of the Women's Movement*. Boston: Beacon, 1979.

Fryer, Judith. *The Faces of Eve: Women in the Nineteenth-Century American Novel*. New York: Oxford University Press, 1976.

Fuss, Charley. *Joan Baez: A Bio-Bibliography*. Westport, Conn.: Greenwood Press, 1996.

Gitlin, Todd. *Inside Prime Time*: New York, Pantheon, 1983.

Gitlin, Todd. *The Sixties: Years of Hope, Days of Rage*. New York: Bantam, 1987.

Gittelson, Natalie. *Dominus: A Woman Looks at Men's Lives*. New York: Farrar, Strauss and Giroux, 1978.

Goffman, Erving. *Gender Advertisements*. Cambridge, Mass.: Harvard University Press, 1979.

Goldberg, Lucianne, and Jeannie Sakol. *Purr Baby Purr*. New York: Hawthorne Books, 1971.

Gordon, Suzanne. *Prisoners of Men's Dreams: Striking Out for a New Feminine Future*. Boston: Little, Brown, 1991.

Gornick, Vivian. *Essays in Feminism*. New York: Harper and Row, 1978.

Gornick, Vivian, and Barbara K. Moran, editors. *Women in Sexist Society*. New York: New American Library, 1972.

Greer, Germaine. *Sex and Destiny: The Politics of Fertility*. New York: Harper and Row, 1984.

Greer, Germaine. *The Female Eunuch*. New York: McGraw-Hill, 1970.

Griffin, Susan. *Pornography and Silence*. New York: Harper and Row, 1981.

Harris, Barbara J. *Beyond Her Sphere: Women and the Professions in American History*. Westport, Conn.: Greenwood Press, 1978.

Harris, David. *Goliath*. New York: Avon Books, 1970.

Hartmann, Susan M. *The Home Front and Beyond*. Boston: Twayne, 1982.

Haskell, Molly. From *Reverence to Rape: The Treatment of Women in the Movies*. New York: Penguin, 1974.

Hentoff, Nat. "*Playboy* Interview: Joan Baez." *Playboy* (July 1970): 54–62.

Hewlett, Sylvia Ann. *A Lesser Life: The Myth of Women's Liberation*. New York: Warner Books, 1986.

Hoffman, Abbie. *Soon to Be a Motion Picture*. New York: Perigee, 1980.

Hoffman, Abbie. *Steal This Book*. New York: Grove Press, 1971.

Hole, Judith, and Ellen Levine. *The Rebirth of Feminism*. New York. Quadrangle, 1971.

Horowitz, David, et al., editors. *Counterculture and Revolution*. New York: Random House, 1972.

Howard, Mel, and Thomas King Forcade, editors. *The Underground Reader*. New York: New American Library, 1972.

J. *The Sensuous Woman*. New York: New American Library, 1972.

Jeffrie, Julie Roy. *Frontier Women: The Trans-Mississippi West, 1840–1880.* New York: Hill and Wang, 1979.

Jong, Erica. "Ziplash: A Sexual Libertine Recants." *Ms.* (May 1989): 49–50.

Jong, Erica Mann. "Seventeen Warnings in Search of a Feminist Poem." *Nation* (April 5, 1972): 12.

Kardish, Lawrence. *Reel Plastic Magic.* Boston: Little, Brown, 1973.

Klagsbrun, Francine, editor. *The First Ms. Reader.* New York: Warner, 1972.

Kraditor, Aileen S. *The Ideas of the Woman Suffrage Movement, 1890–1920.* New York: Atheneum, 1965.

Lakoff, Robin. *Language and Women's Place.* New York: Harper and Row, 1975.

Lasch, Christopher. *The New Radicalism in America, 1889–1963.* New York: Norton, 1965.

Leach, William. *True Love and Perfect Union: The Feminist Reform of Sex and Society.* New York: Basic Books, 1980.

Lerner, Gerda. *The Majority Finds Its Past: Placing Women in History.* New York: Oxford University Press, 1979.

Linden-Ward, Blanche, and Carol Green Hurd. *Changing the Future: American Women in the 1960s.* New York: Twayne, 1992.

Lipsitz, George. *Time Passages: Collective Memory and American Popular Culture.* Minneapolis: University of Minnesota Press, 1990.

Long, Priscilla, editor. *The New Left: A Collection of Essays.* Boston: Porter Sargent, 1969.

Lynd, Staughton, and Michael Ferber. *The Resistance.* Boston: Beacon, 1971.

Lystra, Karen. *Searching the Heart: Women, Men and Romantic Love in Nineteenth-Century America.* New York: Oxford University Press, 1989.

Marc, David. *Demographic Vistas: Television in American Culture.* Philadelphia: University of Pennsylvania Press, 1984.

Marcuse, Herbert. *One Dimensional Man.* Boston: Beacon, 1964.

Marcuse, Herbert. *Negations: Essays in Critical Theories.* Boston: Beacon, 1968.

May, Larry. *Screening Out the Past.* Chicago: University of Chicago Press, 1983.

McLary, Susan. *Feminine Endings: Music, Gender and Sexuality.* Minneapolis: University of Minnesota Press, 1991.

Miller, James. *Democracy Is in the Streets.* New York: Simon & Shuster, 1987.

Millet, Kate. *Sexual Politics.* Garden City, N.Y.: Doubleday, 1970.

Moody, Anne. *Coming of Age in Mississippi.* New York: Dell, 1968.

Morgan, Marabel. *The Total Woman.* Old Tappan, N.J.: Fleming H. Revell, 1973.

Morgan, Robin. *Going too Far: The Personal Chronicle of a Feminist.* New York: Random House, 1977.

Morgan, Robin, editor. *Sisterhood Is Powerful: An Anthology of Writing from the Women's Liberation Movement.* New York: Vintage Books, 1970.

Nies, Judith. *Seven Women: Portraits from the American Radical Tradition.* New York: Viking Press, 1977.

Noebel, David A. *Rhythm, Riots, and Revolution*. Tulsa, Okla.: Christian Crusade Publications, 1966.

Notes from the First Year. New York: Radical Feminists, 1968.

Nye, Russell B. *The Unembarrassed Muse: The Popular Arts in America*. New York: Dial Press, 1970.

O'Brien, Geoffrey. *The Phantom Empire: Movies in the Mind of the 20th Century*. New York: Norton, 1993.

O'Brien, Lucy. *She Bop: The Definitive History of Women in Rock, Pop and Soul*. New York: Penguin, 1996.

O'Neill, William L. *Everyone Was Brave: A History of Feminism in America*. New York: Quadrangle, 1971.

Patai, Daphne, and Noretta Koertge. *Professing Feminism*. New York: Basic Books, 1994.

Pavletich, Aida. *Sirens of Song*. New York: DaCapo Press, 1980.

Peck, Abe. *Uncovering the Sixties: The Life and Times of the Underground Press*. New York: Pantheon, 1985.

Postman, Neil. *Amusing Ourselves to Death*. New York: Viking Penguin, 1985.

Rapping, Elayne. *Media-tions*. Boston: South End Press, 1994.

Redstockings, editor. *Feminist Revolution*. New Paltz, N.Y.: Redstockings, 1975.

Reich, Charles A. *The Greening of America*. New York: Random House, 1970.

Rich, Adrienne. *Of Woman Born: Motherhood as Experience and Institution*. New York: Norton, 1976.

Rodnitzky, Jerome L. "The Decline of American Protest Music." *Popular Music and Society* 1 (Spring 1971): 44–50.

Rodnitzky, Jerome L. "The Evolution of the American Protest Song." *Journal of Popular Culture* 3 (June 1969): 35–45.

Rodnitzky, Jerome L. "The New Revivalism: American Protest Songs, 1945–1968." *South Atlantic Quarterly* 70 (winter 1971): 13–21.

Rosen, Marjorie. *Popcorn Venus: Women, Movies, and the American Dream*. New York: Avon, 1974.

Rosenberg, Rosalind. *Divided Lives: American Women in the Twentieth Century*. New York: Hill and Wang, 1992.

Ross, Nancy Wilson. *Westward the Women*. New York: Alfred A. Knopf, 1944.

Roszak, Betty, and Theodore Roszak, editors. *Masculine/Feminine: Readings in Sexual Mythology and the Liberation of Women*. New York: Harper and Row, 1969.

Rowbotham, Sheila. *Women, Resistance and Revolution*. New York: Pantheon Books, 1974.

Rudolph, Frederick. *The American College and University*. New York: Knopf, 1962.

Sale, Kirkpatrick. *SDS*. New York: Vintage Books, 1973.

Salper, Roberta, editor. *Female Liberation: History and Current Politics*. New York: Alfred A. Knopf, 1972.

Scott, Ann Firor. *The Southern Lady: From Pedestal to Politics, 1830–1930*. Chicago: University of Chicago Press, 1970.

Sklar, Kathryn Kish. *Catherine Beecher: A Study in Domesticity*. New Haven, Conn.: Yale University Press, 1973.

Sklar, Robert. *Movie-Made America*. New York: Random House, 1975.

Skolnick, Arlene. *Embattled Paradise: The American Family in an Age of Uncertainty*. New York: HarperCollins Publishers, 1991.

Smith-Rosenberg, Carroll. *Disorderly Conduct: Visions of Gender in Victorian America*. New York: Oxford University Press, 1985.

Sochen, June. *Mae West: She Who Laughs Last*. Arlington Heights, Ill.: Harlan Davidson, 1992.

Sochen, June. *The New Women: Feminism in Greenwich Village, 1910–1920*. New York: Quadrangle, 1972.

Somma, Robert, editor. *No One Waved Good-Bye*. New York: Outerbridge and Dienstfrey, 1971.

Sontag, Susan. "The Double Standard of Aging." *Saturday Review of Literature* (October 1972): 34–38.

Steinem, Gloria. "A Bunny's Tale." *Show* (May 1963): 90–93, 114–15.

Steinem, Gloria. *Moving beyond Words*. New York: Simon & Schuster, 1994.

Steinem, Gloria. *Outrageous Acts and Everyday Rebellions*. New York: Holt, Rinehart and Winston, 1983.

Steinem, Gloria. "The Moral Disarmament of Betty Coed." *Esquire* (September 1962): 93, 153–57.

Steinem, Gloria. "What It Would Be Like If Women Win." *Time* (August 31, 1970): 22–23.

Stewart, Elinor Pruitt. *Letters of a Woman Homesteader*. Lincoln: University of Nebraska Press, 1961.

Tanner, Leslie, editor. *Voices of Women's Liberation*. New York: New American Library, 1970.

Taylor, Ella. *Prime Time Families*. Berkeley: University of California Press, 1989.

Thom, Mary. *Inside Ms.: 25 Years of the Magazine and the Feminist Movement*. New York: Henry Holt, 1997.

Tuchman, Gaye, et al., editors. *Hearth and Home: Images of Women in the Mass Media*. New York: Oxford University Press, 1978.

Tyler, Alice Felt. *Freedom's Ferment*. New York: Harper, 1962.

Ulrich, Laurel Thatcher. *Good Wives: Images and Reality in the Lives of Women in Northern New England, 1650–1750*. New York: Oxford University Press, 1983.

Wallace, Irving. *The Nympho and Other Maniacs: Stories of Scandalous Women*. London: Cassell, 1971.

Ware, Celestine. *Woman Power: The Movement for Women's Liberation*. New York: Tower Publications, 1970.

Ware, Susan. *Holding Their Own*. Boston: Twayne, 1982.

Watson, Mary Ann. *Defining Visions: Television and the American Experience since 1945*. New York: Harcourt Brace & Company, 1998.

Weibel, Kathryn. *Mirror Mirror: Images of Women Reflected in Popular Culture*. Garden City, N.Y.: Anchor Books, 1977.

Welter, Barbara. *Dimity Convictions: The American Woman in the Nineteenth Century*. Columbus: Ohio State University Press, 1975.

Welter, Barbara. "The Cult of True Womanhood." *American Quarterly* 18 (1966): 151–74.

Westin, Jeanne. *Making Do*. Chicago: Follett, 1976.

White, Deborah Gray. *Ar'n't I a Woman?: Female Slaves in the Plantation South*, New York: W. W. Norton, 1987.

Index

About the Author

JERRY L. RODNITZKY is a Professor of History at the University of
Texas at Arlington.

ISBN 0-275-96575-9